CW00520533

*"In taking us straight to the h[...]
served us magnificently. We so r[...]
let the Scriptures get into us. The[...]
and with such submission to Bib[...]
genuinely helped to be sh[...]*

– Terry Virgo

"Fresh. Solid. Simple. Really good stuff."
– R. T. Kendall

*"Phil makes the deep truths of Scripture alive and accessible. If
you want to grow in your understanding of each book of the Bible,
then buy these books and let them change your life!"*

– PJ Smyth *– GodFirst Church, Johannesburg, South Africa*

*"Most commentaries are dull. These are alive.
Most commentaries are for scholars. These are for **you**!"*

– Canon Michael Green

*"These notes are amazingly good. Lots of content and depth of
research, yet packed in a **Big Breakfast** that leaves the reader
well fed and full. Bible notes often say too little, yet larger
commentaries can be dull – missing the wood for the trees. Phil's
insights are striking, original, and fresh, going straight to the
heart of the text and the reader! Substantial yet succinct, they
bristle with amazing insights and life applications, compelling us
to read more. Bible reading will become enriched and informed
with such a scintillating guide. Teachers and preachers
will find nuggets of pure gold here!"*

– Greg Haslam *– Westminster Chapel, London, UK*

*"The Bible is living and dangerous. The ones who teach it best
are those who bear that in mind – and let the author do the
talking. Phil has written these studies with a sharp mind and a
combination of creative application and reverence."*

– Joel Virgo *– Leader of Newday Youth Festival*

"Phil Moore's new commentaries are outstanding: biblical and passionate, clear and well-illustrated, simple and profound. God's Word comes to life as you read them, and the wonder of God shines through every page."

– Andrew Wilson – *Author of* Incomparable *and* If God, Then What?

"Want to understand the Bible better? Don't have the time or energy to read complicated commentaries? The book you have in your hand could be the answer. Allow Phil Moore to explain and then apply God's message to your life. Think of this book as the Bible's message distilled for everyone."

– Adrian Warnock, *Christian blogger*

"Phil Moore presents Scripture in a dynamic, accessible and relevant way. The bite-size chunks – set in context and grounded in contemporary life – really make the Word become flesh and dwell among us."

– Dr David Landrum, *The Bible Society*

"Through a relevant, very readable, up to date storying approach, Phil Moore sets the big picture, relates God's Word to today and gives us fresh insights to increase our vision, deepen our worship, know our identity and fire our imagination. Highly recommended!"

– Geoff Knott, *former CEO of Wycliffe Bible Translators UK*

"What an exciting project Phil has embarked upon! These accessible and insightful books will ignite the hearts of believers, inspire the minds of preachers and help shape a new generation of men and women who are seeking to learn from God's Word."

– David Stroud, *Newfrontiers and ChristChurch London*

For more information about the Straight to the Heart series, please go to **www.philmoorebooks.com**.

John

60 BITE-SIZED INSIGHTS

Phil Moore

MONARCH
BOOKS

Oxford, UK & Grand Rapids, Michigan, USA

First published in the UK in 2012 by Monarch Books
(a publishing imprint of Lion Hudson plc)
Wilkinson House, Jordan Hill Road, Oxford OX2 8DR, England
Tel: +44 (0)1865 302750 Fax: +44 (0)1865 302757
Email: monarch@lionhudson.com
www.lionhudson.com

ISBN 978 0 85721 253 5 (print)
ISBN 978 0 85721 316 7 (Kindle)
ISBN 978 0 85721 317 4 (epub)
ISBN 978 0 85721 318 1 (PDF)

Distributed by:
UK: Marston Book Services, PO Box 269, Abingdon, Oxon, OX14 4YN
USA: Kregel Publications, PO Box 2607, Grand Rapids, Michigan 49501

British Library Cataloguing Data
A catalogue record for this book is available from the British Library.

Printed and bound in the UK by Clays Ltd, St Ives plc.

This book is for my youngest son Ethan.
May it teach you to know Jesus as well as John did.
May it teach you to look and see the Living God.

CONTENTS

PART THREE: LOOK AT WHAT JESUS HAS GIVEN YOU

PART FOUR: LOOK AT JESUS AND WIN

About the *Straight to the Heart* Series

On his eightieth birthday, Sir Winston Churchill dismissed the compliment that he was the "lion" who had defeated Nazi Germany in World War Two. He told the Houses of Parliament that *"It was a nation and race dwelling all around the globe that had the lion's heart. I had the luck to be called upon to give the roar."*

I hope that God speaks to you very powerfully through the "roar" of the books in the *Straight to the Heart* series. I hope they help you to understand the books of the Bible and the message which the Holy Spirit inspired their authors to write. I hope that they help you to hear God's voice challenging you, and that they provide you with a springboard for further journeys into each book of Scripture for yourself.

But when you hear my "roar", I want you to know that it comes from the heart of a much bigger "lion" than me. I have been shaped by a whole host of great Christian thinkers and preachers from around the world, and I want to give due credit to at least some of them here:

Terry Virgo, David Stroud, John Hosier, Adrian Holloway, Greg Haslam, Lex Loizides and all those who lead the Newfrontiers family of churches. Friends and encouragers, such as Stef Liston, Joel Virgo, Stuart Gibbs, Scott Taylor, Nick Sharp, Nick Derbridge, Phil Whittall, and Kevin and Sarah Aires. Tony Collins, Jenny Ward and Simon Cox at Monarch Books. Malcolm Kayes and all the elders of The Coign Church, Woking. My fellow elders and church members here at Queens Road Church, Wimbledon.

My great friend Andrew Wilson – without your friendship, encouragement and example, this series would never have happened.

I would like to thank my parents, my brother Jonathan, and my in-laws, Clive and Sue Jackson. Dad – your example birthed in my heart the passion which brought this series into being. I didn't listen to all you said when I was a child, but I couldn't ignore the way you got up at five o'clock every morning to pray, read the Bible and worship, because of your radical love for God and for his Word. I'd like to thank my children – Isaac, Noah, Esther and Ethan – for keeping me sane when publishing deadlines were looming. But most of all, I'm grateful to my incredible wife, Ruth – my friend, encourager, corrector and helper.

You all have the lion's heart, and you have all developed the lion's heart in me. I count it an enormous privilege to be the one who was chosen to sound the lion's roar.

So welcome to the *Straight to the Heart* series. My prayer is that you will let this roar grip your own heart too – for the glory of the great Lion of the Tribe of Judah, the Lord Jesus Christ!

Introduction: Look and See the Living God

These are written that you may believe that Jesus is the Messiah, the Son of God, and that by believing you may have life in his name.

(John 20:31)

John may have been the only one of Jesus' twelve disciples not to die a violent death, but don't let that fool you that his lot in life was easy. As the last surviving disciple by far, he was burdened by a barrage of unwanted attention.

The enemies of Christianity, particularly the Romans, had marked him out as a dangerous eyewitness to the life of Jesus. He had been there when Jesus healed the blind and fed the hungry, there when he was nailed to a Roman cross and there when he left behind an empty tomb. John hadn't stopped preaching about what he had seen for sixty years, and he knew that if old age didn't claim his life soon then his increasingly agitated enemies surely would.[1] In around 90 AD, just before the Emperor Domitian exiled him to the Greek island of Patmos, John decided it was time to preserve his memories in a gospel.[2] Irenaeus, who was taught by John's young helper Polycarp, informs us that *"John the Lord's disciple, the one who leaned*

---

[1] John had recounted these events so often over sixty years that, in conjunction with what he describes in 14:26, they were still as fresh in his memory as the events of the day before.

[2] See Revelation 1:9. Despite John's use of a present tense to describe Jerusalem in 5:2, his language and perspective backs up the united view of the Early Church leaders Irenaeus, Tertullian, Origen and Clement that John wrote this gospel at the end of the first century.

back on his chest, published a gospel whilst living at Ephesus in Asia... John made his permanent home in Ephesus until the time of Trajan."[3] When John saw that his time witnessing on earth was nearly over, he wrote his gospel as a witness to generations yet to come.

John was also being watched by the many false teachers who had latched themselves onto the growing Christian faith like limpets to the hull of a mighty warship. Some of them played down Jesus' divinity while others played down his humanity, but both groups found common ground in their resentment towards the aged apostle who refuted their theories with facts about the Jesus that he knew. Note the way John fills his gospel with vivid eyewitness descriptions,[4] and with words like *seeing* and *knowing* and *bearing testimony* and *the truth*.[5] John wants his readers to appreciate that he knew the real Jesus – fully God and fully man – and that his gospel exposes the speculations of people who try to reshape the Messiah in a mould of their own making.

Most concerning of all, John was troubled by the star-struck gaze of the many well-meaning Christians who hailed him as their hero. Note the way he writes his gospel in a manner that prevents us from placing him on a pedestal as a saint. Matthew, Mark and Luke mention John and his brother James a total of thirty-nine times in their gospels, but John never mentions himself or his brother by name at all![6] He might mention less famous disciples such as Philip, Thomas and Nathanael, but he

---

[3] Trajan became emperor in 98 AD, and Irenaeus wrote in c.180 AD in *Against Heresies* (3.1.1 and 3.3.4). Linked to John 21:20 and 24, this quote tells us that the anonymous disciple in the gospel is John.

[4] John describes scenes in particular detail in 6:10, 12:3, 13:23–25 and 18:10.

[5] John uses five different Greek words for *seeing*, and also stresses he is an eyewitness in 1 John 1:1–3.

[6] The closest he comes is when he refers to *"the sons of Zebedee"* in 21:2. No one but John himself could make such a glaring omission, which supports the unanimous Early Church view that John wrote this gospel.

purposely redirects his readers' attention away from himself by making anonymous references to *"the disciple Jesus loved"*.[7] As for the rumour among his fans that he might not die until Jesus returned in glory, he quashes their misguided hero worship in 21:23. In a world where too many people looked at John instead of Jesus, he wrote this gospel to plead with each of his readers to *Look and see the Living God!*

All of this makes John's gospel essential reading for anyone who wants to know the real Jesus today. Like us, John had copies of the gospels that Matthew, Mark and Luke had written earlier, but he believed that we needed something more. They are known as the "synoptic" gospels because they all "share a common perspective" on the life and ministry of Jesus, whereas the second-century church leader Clement of Alexandria explains that John's gospel takes a different view: *"John, perceiving that the outward facts had been set forth in those gospels, urged on by his friends and inspired by the Spirit, composed a spiritual gospel."*[8] John doesn't tell us that Jesus told parables, drove out demons, healed lepers, was transfigured or prayed agonized prayers in the Garden of Gethsemane. Instead, he duplicates as little material as possible in order to tell unrecorded stories which open our eyes to see the real Jesus in his untold glory.

In chapters 1–4, John uses fresh incidents from Jesus' early ministry to encourage us to *look at Jesus alone*. In chapters 5–12, he uses more new stories to teach us to *look at who Jesus really is*. In chapters 13–17, he records Jesus' handover teaching to his disciples and encourages us to *look at what Jesus has given you*. This leads into his conclusion in chapters 18–21, where he gives final reasons to *look at Jesus and win*. All along the way, he punctuates his gospel with frequent exhortations to *"Look!"* and *"Come and see!"* and *"Open your eyes!"* to see the Living God.

15

---

[7] John 13:23; 19:26; 20:2; 21:7, 20, 24.

[8] Quoted by Eusebius of Caesarea just after 300 AD in his *Church History* (6.14.7). Since Luke 1:1–4 suggests that Luke had copies of the first two gospels, it is also fair to assume that John had copies of all three.

If you are unsure what you believe about Jesus of Nazareth, this should all strike you as very good news. John wrote this gospel to give you a ringside seat from which to watch the Galilean carpenter whose message changed the world. Mark writes to tell us *what* Jesus did, and Matthew and Luke write to explain *why* Jesus did it, but John's main concern is to help us discover *who* Jesus is and what it means for us to follow him today. He tells us in 20:31 that he wrote this gospel for you and me, so that *"you may believe that Jesus is the Messiah, the Son of God, and that by believing you may have life in his name"*.

If you already believe in Jesus but want to know him more, this should also strike you as very good news. The most accurate Greek manuscripts of 20:31 use a present tense which can be literally translated *"so that you may **go on believing** that Jesus is the Messiah, the Son of God, and that by **going on believing** you may **go on having** life in his name"*. Read that way, John is telling us that he wrote his gospel to turn our head knowledge about Jesus into genuine experience of new life through him.

So sit back and enjoy the life-changing message of John's gospel. It was the message which the early Christians needed to hear in the face of Roman persecution, false teaching and hero worship, and it's still the message we need to hear amidst the pressures of today.

John therefore hands us his gospel, still as fresh as when he wrote it, and tells us to do the same as his first-century readers. He invites us to fix our eyes on the Jesus that he knew. He tells us to look and see the Living God.

Part One:

Look at Jesus Alone

(Chapters 1–4)

First Word (1:1–18)

In the beginning was the Word...

(John 1:1)

If you aren't shocked by John's opening verses, it probably means you haven't understood them. John writes them very carefully to capture your attention, regardless of how well or little you know the Bible.

Mark had connected with his Roman readers by starting his gospel in the thick of the action with the coming of John the Baptist. Matthew had connected with his Jewish readers by beginning with Jesus' family tree back to Abraham and with King Herod's shock discovery from a group of foreigners that the true King of Israel had just been born in his backyard. Luke had connected with his Gentile readers by beginning with a Roman census, with Simeon's prophecy that Jesus would save many non-Jews and with a family tree that traced his ancestry back to Adam. John didn't think there was anything wrong with those beginnings. He just didn't think that any of them went back far enough in Jesus' story.

That's why he starts his gospel with the words *"in the beginning"*. He knew that anyone familiar with the Greek Old Testament would instantly recognize them as the opening words of the Jewish Scriptures. They would know the Genesis account of God creating the universe from nothing – solely by the power of his spoken Word and of his Spirit.[1] John tries to shock us by telling us that Jesus' story started long before an angel appeared

---

[1] Psalms 33:6 and 107:20 also talk about God's Word being both our Creator and our Saviour.

to Mary or she laid her baby in a manger. It started before the dawn of time because the baby born in Bethlehem's filthy stable was the eternal Word of God.[2] Jesus is the one who revealed himself to the Israelites as Yahweh, and there never was a time when he was not.

Not everybody knew the Greek Old Testament, of course. John lived in Ephesus, the vibrant capital city of Asia, where his mainly Gentile readers were more familiar with the thoughts of the pagan Greek philosophers.[3] Accordingly, he chooses a word which he knows will shock them too. Heraclitus, the great Ephesian philosopher, had used the Greek word *Logos*, or *Word*, in around 500 BC to describe the divine force of Reason which governs the universe.[4] His teaching was so influential that we still refer today to bio*logy*, geo*logy*, cosmo*logy* and astro*logy*, so John chooses this word to grab the full attention of the Greeks as he did the Jews. He tells them that the divine Reason which Heraclitus groped for in the darkness was not just a principle but a person. Long before Jesus became a baby in a stable, the best Greek minds had sensed his presence as the ruler of the universe.[5]

We can see how shocking the Jews found this message by flicking forward a few pages to John 10:33. When the Jews grasped that Jesus was claiming to be Yahweh, they picked up stones and tried to lynch him for blasphemy. That's why John

---

[2] Don't be confused by the word *monogenēs*, or *only begotten*, in verses 14 and 18, or by the fact that John uses the word more than the rest of the New Testament writers put together. Hebrews 11:17 uses it to describe Isaac, who was not Abraham's only son, so it speaks about Jesus' unique *status*, not about his *birth*.

[3] We can tell that John wrote mainly for Gentiles from the way he translates Hebrew and Aramaic words for his readers in 1:38, 41, 42, 6:1, 9:7, 19:13, 17 and 20:16.

[4] John deliberately echoes Heraclitus' teaching that *"all things come to be in accordance with the Logos"* (fragment DK 22B1).

[5] Paul argues this when he preaches the Gospel in Athens in Acts 17:23, saying that Jesus is their *"unknown God"*.

tells them in verse 17 that Jesus is greater than their great leader and lawgiver Moses because he fulfils the Law with grace and truth. It's why he tells them in verse 18 that what Moses saw on Mount Sinai was nothing compared to the way that Jesus has made God fully known.[6] It's why he takes the word for Moses' Tabernacle in the Greek Old Testament (*skēnē*) and uses it as a verb in verse 14 to tell them that God truly tabernacled (*skēnoō*) on the earth in the flesh and blood of Jesus' body. Remember, the Jews didn't kill Jesus for healing people and telling pithy parables. They killed him because they knew he was telling them to look at him and see the Living God.

We can also see how shocking the Gentiles found this message by flicking forward a little further to Acts 14. The Lystrans liked Paul and Barnabas when they thought they were preaching that the gods were just like them. Things turned nasty when the Lystrans grasped that they were challenging their Greek idols and urging them to *"turn from these worthless things to the Living God"*. Epictetus, another great philosopher from the vicinity of Ephesus, summed up the Greek view that the spirit is good and the body is bad when he wrote that *"You are a little soul, burdened with a corpse"*,[7] so the idea that the Living God had taken a human body was so offensive to the Greeks that they stoned them. They were happy with the inoffensive message peddled by the Gnostic false teachers that Jesus had merely *seemed* to be a human,[8] but they angrily refused to surrender to a message about God's incarnate Son.

LOOK AT JESUS ALONE

20

---

[6] The Greek word *exēgeomai* at the end of verse 18 means *to declare* or *unfold fully*, and is the root of the English word *exegesis*. Jesus repeats this claim later in 14:9.

[7] Epictetus was a Stoic and a contemporary of John. This quotation comes from "Fragment 26" of his work.

[8] Since the Greek word for *to seem* is *dokeō*, the late first-century Gnostics who denied the full humanity of Jesus are commonly called Docetists. John insists repeatedly that the Word always *was* (*ēn*), but that at a certain moment in verse 14 he suddenly *became* (*egeneto*) a real human being.

We can be like the first-century Jews and Greeks if we let our own cultural baggage divert our gaze away from who Jesus really was. The villains in John's nativity story aren't Matthew's jealous King Herod or Luke's overworked innkeepers. They are the entire human race which wants to force-fit Jesus into the domesticated role of a mere prophet or good teacher.[9] That's why the Greek word *katalambanō* in verse 5 has a deliberate double-meaning – either *to grasp* in the sense of *understanding* a mystery, or *to grasp* in the sense of *overcoming* an enemy. John tells us that few people understand who Jesus is, but that none of those who oppose him can succeed in domesticating the Living God. He calls us to surrender to the fact that God has come to earth to save all those who will receive him as he really is.[10]

If you are prepared to look where John is pointing; if you are prepared to humble yourself and step out of the darkness into God's light; if you are prepared to respond with faith to the crucified carpenter who called John to follow him on the shore of Lake Galilee – then John promises to guide your footsteps through his gospel. He promises to help you to look and see the Living God.

---

[9] Ironically, Jehovah's Witnesses twist this very passage to repeat the ancient heresy of Arius that *"There was a time when the Son was not"* (Socrates of Constantinople in *Church History*, 1.5.2). John uses something called an "incomplete predication" in the Greek of verse 1 by dropping the definite article to clarify that he means *"the Word was God"* (one person of the Trinity) and not that *"God was the Word"* (in his entirety). Jehovah's Witnesses fail to understand this and mistranslate his words to mean merely that *"the Word was a god"*.

[10] John tells us that the Gospel is for *everyone* in verses 7 and 9, but he qualifies this by saying that many will reject the salvation which could have been theirs.

Good Man Isn't God-Man
(1:19–34)

Among you stands one you do not know. He is
the one who comes after me, the straps of whose
sandals I am not worthy to untie.

(John 1:26–27)

John wasn't the only one who drew a lot of unwanted attention from the celebrity chasers at Ephesus. They still held John the Baptist in such high regard that when Paul's church-planting team arrived there in 53 AD, they found the foremost Christian preacher in the city telling the Ephesians to be baptized into John the Baptist instead of into Jesus.[1] The desert preacher who revived backslidden Israel in 27–28 AD was still held in such high regard by the early Christians that an Arabian merchant named Muhammad would even list him as a prophet alongside Jesus over five centuries later in the Qur'an.

John had more reason than Matthew, Mark or Luke to give in to his readers' desire to place John the Baptist on a pedestal. He is the unnamed disciple in verses 35–40, so he and his fishing partner Andrew had been some of John the Baptist's earliest disciples. It comes as no surprise, therefore, that he spends much of chapters 1 and 3 clarifying what his former teacher's message was. He, more than anyone, knew that John the Baptist was a good man, but he is alive to the danger that our admiration for a good man may actually distract us from obeying his call to look and see the God-Man.

---

[1] Acts 18:19–19:7.

John has already told us in verses 6–8 that John the Baptist was simply a witness sent from God to prepare the Jewish nation for its Messiah.[2] He called them to be baptized, which was not new in itself because Gentile converts to Judaism were baptized at the same time as they were circumcised as part of their entry into the People of God. What made John's baptism new was that it was a baptism for Jews as an outward sign of their inner repentance and their confession that Jewishness was not enough to save anyone. When some Jews refused to be baptized, he warned that being descended from Abraham didn't change the fact that they were the *"offspring of vipers"* until they surrendered to the Lord.[3]

Now, in verses 19–28, John clarifies his former teacher's message further. He tells us that John the Baptist freely confessed that he was not the Messiah predicted by Moses when he talked about the coming of "the Prophet" in Deuteronomy 18:15–19.[4] Even though the three synoptic gospel writers rightly link him to the prophecy in Malachi 4:5–6 that a man like Elijah would lead Israel in revival before the Messiah came, he insists in verse 21 that he is not Elijah in the sense that most Israelites assumed. The prophet who had ascended to heaven in a chariot of fire without dying nine centuries earlier in 2 Kings 2 had not returned.[5] John the Baptist was merely *like* Elijah in his calling to turn Israel away from false objects of worship in order to

---

[2] He tells us John the Baptist is not the *Light* in 1:8, not the *Messiah* or *Christ* in 3:28, not the *greatest witness* in 5:36 and not a *miracle-worker* in 10:41.

[3] John expects us to know this already from Luke 3:7–9.

[4] Although John wrote his gospel in Greek, we can tell that he still thought like a Jew from the way he uses a Hebrew "synthetic parallelism" to tell us in verse 20 that *"he did not fail to confess, but confessed freely"*. We can also tell from 3:29 where he says *"he rejoices with joy"*, instead of using a Greek adverb.

[5] The rumour that he might actually *be* Elijah stemmed from their similar clothing (2 Kings 1:8 and Matthew 3:4) and the fact that he ministered on the east side of the Jordan near the place where Elijah had ascended to heaven.

see the Living God.[6] Those who truly honour John the Baptist as a good man are those who gaze beyond him to the God-Man whose shoelaces he was too unworthy to untie. *"Look!"* he directs our gaze in verse 29, *"the Lamb of God, who takes away the sin of the world!"*[7]

John knew that many of his readers were so in love with their human hero that their admiration stopped them from doing the very things he said. Therefore he does not tell the story of Jesus' baptism like Matthew, Mark and Luke, but tells us in verses 30–34 what John the Baptist finally realized when Jesus came up out of the water. They were close relatives and had known one another from early childhood,[8] but he hadn't guessed that Jesus was the Son of God until he saw the Holy Spirit descend on him at his baptism and remain on him for ministry.[9] At once, he recognized his own frail limitations and beat a hasty retreat out of the limelight so that Jesus could take centre-stage. The Bridegroom gets noticed and the groomsman gets forgotten, he insists in 3:29–30. *"He must become greater; I must become less."* He refused to let a good man take the focus off the God-Man.

To help us, John tells us in verses 35–39 that he has already had to walk the road he is telling us to travel. He had once fixed

---

[6] Luke 1:16–17; Mark 9:11–13; Matthew 11:7–14; 17:10–13. The quotation in verse 23 comes from Isaiah 40:3, which goes alongside those in Malachi 3:1 and 4:5–6 to teach that John the Baptist would *straighten the path* or *clear the way* for Jesus (the same phrase is used in 1 Thessalonians 3:11). John the Baptist was simply the warm-up act. Jesus was the headline superstar.

[7] John deliberately uses an unusual Greek word for *lamb* in verses 29 and 36, because Isaiah 53:7 used this same word to prophesy that the Messiah would be God's sacrificial *lamb* for sin.

[8] Since their mothers were related, Luke 1:35–45 tells us they had a dramatic first encounter while both of them were still inside their mothers' wombs.

[9] John the Baptist confesses in 1:33 that, even though his mother recognized that Mary was *"the mother of my Lord"* as early as in Luke 1:43, he himself did not grasp this until much later.

his eyes on John the Baptist with all the eager devotion of a young disciple, but he had learned to honour his teacher by doing what he taught and shifting his gaze from the messenger and onto the Messiah. *"Look, the Lamb of God!"* John the Baptist had told him, and John had started following a new rabbi instead. Unlike the star-struck Ephesians, he had let nothing distract him from the one who could forgive him and change his life from the inside out by baptizing him with the Holy Spirit.[10]

I recently spent time with a group of young church leaders who were concerned about what will happen when the ageing leader of their denomination retires. It brought home to me how easy it still is for us to let respect for a good man dilute our faith in the God-Man who has worked through that great leader and will continue to work through many fresh leaders when he has gone. That's one of the reasons why the Lord has only granted each one of us a brief lifespan, because Church history only has room for one hero and it isn't one of us. Retirements and deaths are God's way of shifting his People's gaze away from the unhealthy human hero worship which infected the church at Ephesus. As John prepared the believers for the day that he would die, as the last of Jesus' twelve disciples, he warned them not to fix their eyes on any good man who might distract their focus from the God-Man.

Charles Wesley was inspired many centuries later to write a hymn from John the Baptist's words, when he and his brother were at the height of their fame:

> *His only righteousness I show, His saving grace*
>   *proclaim;*

---

[10] Matthew 3:11–12; Mark 1:8; Luke 3:16; John 1:29. Focusing too much on John the Baptist stopped the Ephesian believers from receiving the Holy Spirit in Acts 19, so John tells us to fix our eyes on the one on whom the Spirit both descended and remained. He is the one who will baptize us with that same Spirit.

'Tis all my business here below to cry "Behold the
    Lamb!"
*Happy if with my latest breath I may but gasp His
    Name,*
*Preach Him to all and cry in death, "Behold, behold the
    Lamb!"*[11]

[11] From the hymn "Jesus! the Name high over all", written by Charles Wesley in about 1750.

What Jacob Saw (1:35–51)

When Jesus saw Nathanael approaching, he said
of him, "Here truly is an Israelite in whom there is
no deceit."

(John 1:47)

Genesis tells us that as the patriarch Jacob got older he started to go blind.[1] It also tells us that as his eyesight failed he finally learned to see. The troubles in his life shifted his focus away from himself and onto God.

John expects us to know about Jacob as he introduces some of Jesus' twelve disciples, starting their story several months earlier than Matthew, Mark and Luke.[2] Jacob's twelve sons had founded twelve Old Testament tribes, and Jesus' twelve disciples were called to become twelve New Testament patriarchs.[3] Therefore the first thing Jesus did with them was to teach them to see the same things that Jacob saw.

Jacob had looked at *his own inadequacies*. He knew his father loved his older brother Esau more than him, and he disguised himself as Esau in order to fool his father into blessing him as the son he truly loved. John therefore begins with Andrew, a man who also lived in the shadow of his louder and more confident brother. When he and his fishing partner

[1] Genesis 48:8, 10.

[2] The events of John 1:35–42 took place in the autumn of 27 AD, and the calling of the fishermen in Matthew 4:18–22, Mark 1:16–20 and Luke 5:1–11 took place in the summer of 28 AD, after the events described in John 4.

[3] Unlike the other gospel writers, John never lists the twelve disciples by name since that would mean having to name himself. However, he makes it clear in Revelation 21:12–14 that the twelve disciples were New Covenant counterparts to Jacob's twelve sons.

responded to John the Baptist's call in verse 36 – *"Look, the Lamb of God!"* – they followed Jesus home and were surprised when he turned and asked them abruptly, *"What do you want?"* Would the two smelly fishermen look at themselves and retreat from Jesus' company because of who they were, or would they pass the test by pushing further in and hailing Jesus as their *rabbi*? The word meant *my great one* and was the Hebrew title which a disciple used for his master, so Jesus was delighted when they used it and proved that they were looking at him instead of at themselves. He cleared his diary and invited them to spend the rest of the day with him in his home.[4]

Just a few hours in Jesus' company taught Andrew the lesson that Jacob had taken many years to learn. When he saw there was no need to struggle to impress Jesus or to behave like someone else, he ran to fetch his brother Simon, unafraid that his more gifted brother might eclipse the Messiah's love towards him. Jesus had started to teach his disciples to see what Jacob saw.

Paradoxically, Jacob had also been too focused on *his own abilities*. He lived up to his name, which could mean *Deceiver* in Hebrew, by devising schemes to climb the ladder of success and compensate for his father's rejection. In Genesis 25:27, he meditated in his tent on the promises God had made to his grandfather Abraham and plotted how he might grab them. When Esau came home hungry from a hunt, he persuaded him to sell his birthright for a bowl of soup. When their father tried to pass his blessing onto Esau anyway, Jacob tricked him into blessing him instead.[5]

[4] The Jewish clock would make *the tenth hour* 4 p.m., but this doesn't fit with John's statement that *"they spent that day with him"*, or with John's use of the clock in 19:14. Since Pliny the Elder tells us that the official Roman day ran from midnight to midnight (*Natural History* 2.79.188), John may actually mean 10 a.m. here.

[5] Genesis does not explicitly condemn Jacob for this, but it tells us that having deceived his father with a dead goat in 27:16 he was also deceived by his own sons with a dead goat in 37:31–33.

That's why John moves the spotlight in verse 42 onto Andrew's brother Simon, another man who thought too much of his own abilities and who lived up to his name. *Simon* is the Greek way of writing *Simeon*, the reckless and impulsive son of Jacob, who was cursed by his father for losing his temper and slaughtering a city.[6] Simon was the most impulsive and self-confident of the Twelve – trying to persuade Jesus he was wrong, boasting that he would never deny him and cutting a person's ear off with his sword during Jesus' arrest in the garden.[7] Jacob had needed the Lord to rename him *Israel*, declaring that the Deceiver was now *One Who Prevails With God*. In the same way, Jesus greets Simon by renaming him *Cephas* in Aramaic and *Peter* in Greek, both of which are the equivalent of the English name *Rocky*.[8] Jesus pledged from the outset that he would strip him of his impulsive nature and fashion him into a rock-solid leader in his Kingdom. Several months later, Peter would leave his nets to follow Jesus because he had learned to see what Jacob saw.

Jacob had relied on *his own capacity to see what God was doing*. God had needed to ambush him while he was on the run from Esau by showing him a ladder stretching up to heaven from the deserted wasteland where he slept under the stars in fear. When Jacob saw God at work in the unlikeliest of places, he declared that it was the gate of heaven and the place must be named Bethel, meaning *House Of God*. Amazed, he exclaimed in Genesis 28:16: *"Surely the Lord is in this place, and I was not aware of it!"* The spotlight therefore moves onto Philip who also invites a friend, like Andrew, to come and discover Jesus.[9] The other gospel writers call the friend Bartholomew, but John uses

---

[6] Genesis 34:30–31; 49:5–7.

[7] Matthew 16:22–23; Luke 22:31–34; John 18:10–11.

[8] Jesus reminded Simon of this new name two years later in Matthew 16:18, telling him that his rock-solid strength came from fixing his eyes on *"the Messiah, the Son of the living God"*.

[9] You may never preach a sermon like Peter, but you can easily issue an invitation like Andrew or Philip. Anyone can say with Philip in verse 46, *"Come and see!"*

his other name Nathanael, which means *Gift of God*, because he was about to be surprised by God's grace like Jacob.[10]

Jesus greets Nathanael by telling him that he is just like Jacob. He had cynically assumed that God could not be at work in lowly Nazareth, but he did so as an honest straight-talker like Jacob when he finally learned his lesson and was renamed Israel. Jesus tells him that he saw him meditating under the fig tree like Jacob among the tents, and Nathanael suddenly grasps that God is at work in very unexpected places. He exclaims that Rabbi Jesus must be the Son of God, the long-awaited heir to David's throne. Jesus responds by explaining that the heavenly ladder Jacob saw in Genesis 28 was actually a picture of God's Messiah. Nathanael may have been reading that passage under the fig tree, since Jesus uses it to call him to be part of an adventure far more exciting than the book of Genesis. He is looking at God's bridge between heaven and earth and has been chosen as one of the twelve New Testament patriarchs. Nathanael bows in worship. He has seen what Jacob saw.[11]

We can also be too focused on our own inadequacies, our own abilities or our own capacity to see what God is doing. John wants these early experiences of the disciples to teach us to lift our eyes off ourselves and onto Jesus so our gaze can be filled with the Living God. Fixing our eyes on ourselves is just as destructive as fixing them on any human hero. John tells us to lift up our eyes off ourselves so we can see what Jacob saw.

---

[10] Since Mark 3:17 tells us that Jesus renamed James and John in the same way as Simon Peter, Jesus may well have given Bartholomew the new name Nathanael.

[11] Jesus addresses Nathanael as *you singular* throughout, but switches to *you plural* in verse 51 to include us in the promise that we can see what Jacob saw.

Nations Have Eyes Too
(1:49, 51)

*Very truly I tell you, you will see "heaven open, and
the angels of God ascending and descending on" the
Son of Man.*

(John 1:51)

If John had simply wanted to call individuals to look at Jesus and
see the Living God, then he could have ended chapter 1 right
there. But he didn't, and he didn't for a reason.

John knew that nations, cultures and sectors in society can
look together in one direction through the sheer force of peer
pressure and deep-seated tradition. That's why he ends chapter
1 with two verses that set out to challenge and win over the
misdirected focus of whole nations.

First, John sets out to win over *Jewish* readers. He needs
to be sensitive because shortly after Matthew, Mark and Luke
wrote their gospels Jerusalem had been destroyed. Rome had
responded to the Jewish Revolt with a tidal wave of destruction
which swept away the city of Jerusalem and the entire province
of Judea. Still reeling, the Jews began to live more than ever
with their eyes turned backwards to a golden age in the past or
forwards to a better future. John needed to convince them that,
in Jesus, God had brought their past promises and future hopes
together in a much more glorious present.

With this in mind, read Nathanael's words in verse 49 a bit
more slowly. He hails Jesus as a *rabbi*, one of the great teachers
of the Law, despite the fact he is a carpenter from Galilee and
has had no formal religious training. He recognizes Jesus as an

altogether different type of rabbi, like John the Baptist,[1] whose authority is not derived from certificates or diplomas, but from his anointing with the Holy Spirit.

Nathanael doesn't stop at calling him rabbi, but also hails him as *"the Son of God"*. Later, that title would be used to describe Jesus' divinity, but it meant something else in the mouth of a Jew in 27 AD.[2] Nathanael unpacks what he means when he says, *"You are the Son of God; you are the King of Israel."* He is recognizing Jesus as *"the Son of God"* whom the Lord had promised would be born to David's royal dynasty in 2 Samuel 7:12–16.[3] He is telling John's Jewish readers that they must reshape their national culture because he has just discovered their Messiah.

Next, John sets out to win over *Roman* readers. He already has their attention since each Roman emperor claimed to be *"the son of a god"*. The emperor at the time John wrote his gospel was Domitian, and he had just begun to force his subjects to address him as *"My Lord and my God"*.[4] John is therefore challenging his Roman readers to confess that Jesus is far greater than their Caesars, but he also goes a step further in verse 51.

"Son of Man" is not simply a Hebrew way of saying Jesus was a human.[5] The Romans knew enough about the Jews whose rebellion they had just crushed to recognize that this

---

[1] John 3:26.

[2] The angel taught this in Luke 1:35, but people only grasped it later in Matthew 27:54 and John 19:7. Because John reaches the autumn of 29 AD by the end of chapter 6 in order to focus most of his account on the weeks leading up to Jesus' crucifixion, and Matthew only reaches that point at the end of chapter 18, John makes the disciples' journey of discovery appear much quicker than the synoptic gospels.

[3] See also 1 Chronicles 28:6; Psalm 2:7; 89:26. John the Baptist calls God's anointed Messiah *"the Son of God"* in 1:34, and Martha speaks of *"the Messiah, the Son of God, who is to come into the world"* in 11:27.

[4] Suetonius in his *Life of Domitian* (chapter 13). Compare this boast with the words of Thomas in John 20:28.

[5] It meant this in Numbers 23:19, Job 25:6, Psalm 8:4 and 93 times in Ezekiel, but Daniel redefined it to refer to the Messiah as the ultimate Human Being.

was the name of the one Daniel had prophesied about in 553 BC who would rise during the reign of the Caesars to overthrow the Roman Empire. Daniel 7:13–14 prophesied that

> *I looked, and there before me was one like a son of man, coming with the clouds of heaven. He approached the Ancient of Days and was led into his presence. He was given authority, glory and sovereign power; all nations and peoples of every language worshipped him. His dominion is an everlasting dominion that will not pass away, and his kingdom is one that will never be destroyed.*

The Roman general Titus had destroyed Jerusalem in 70 AD, but John declares that Israel's King is about to eclipse, overtake and outlast the Roman Empire. It was time for the Romans to stop looking at the self-made god Domitian and for their nation to shift its gaze onto Jesus, the Living God.

Finally, John sets out to win over *pagan* readers. First-century culture had countless gods and even more countless ways in which they could reach them. It treated all religious viewpoints as equally valid, like Pilate when he glibly asks in 18:38, *"What is truth?"* John therefore uses one of Jesus' key phrases for the first time in verse 51, and it is a phrase which he will use twenty-six times in his gospel: *"Amen, Amen"*, which many English translators render *"Very truly I tell you"*. Don't be so over-familiar with the phrase that you miss what Jesus is controversially saying. To a pagan world which had given up on the discovery of objective spiritual truth, he is declaring that *"I am the way and the truth and the life. No one comes to the Father except through me."*[6] This is what Jesus means when he tells Nathanael that he alone is Jacob's ladder, because only he can

---

Jesus upgrades the accusation that he is *"the Son of God"* in Matthew 26:63–65 by adding that he is also *"the Son of Man"*.

[6] John 14:6. See also 1 Timothy 2:5.

bridge the gulf between humankind and God. He alone is God and able to forgive sin, human and able to atone for sin, and the God-Man who can raise us up to sit with him at the Father's side in heaven. It was time for the pagans to shake off their culture's lies and renew their culture by looking at Jesus, the Living God.

As we end this chapter, let's not fool ourselves that our own nations do not need to hear John's words too. Some are like the Jews who looked back to a golden age or longed for a better future. Others are like the Romans who surfed on a wave of success and imagined that the world would always be their playground. Others are like the pagans who so lost sight of spiritual truth that in the end they assumed it didn't matter what a person believed so long as they were sincere and didn't harm anybody. Whichever one of those cultures you belong to, John tells you to look at Jesus – the Jewish Messiah, the King of all the earth, and the only Saviour of the world.

He commands us to renounce the deep-seated lies which control the culture of our nations. He calls whole communities to look at Jesus, both as individuals and as nations. He tells us that our culture must surrender to Christ, because nations have eyes too.

Signs (2:1–11)

What Jesus did here in Cana of Galilee was the first
of the signs through which he revealed his glory, and
his disciples believed in him.

(John 2:11)

Chapter 1 should make you worship, but it should also make you ask an obvious question: If God has become a human being and called the world to look at him, then why do so few people believe in him? Why doesn't he perform such great miracles that the world has no choice but to snap to attention and surrender? That's the question John sets out to answer at the start of chapter 2.

The answer begins with a whispered conversation between Jesus and his mother at a wedding reception in Cana. Mary urges Jesus to perform a miracle because their host has run out of wine, and Jesus replies, *"My hour has not yet come."* Although some people assume Jesus must be saying that his ministry has not yet started, that can't be the case since Jesus has already been baptized in the River Jordan, tempted for forty days in the desert and *"returned to Galilee in the power of the Spirit"*.[1] He has already started gathering disciples, and 5:19 makes it clear that he would not have been persuaded by his mother if his Father hadn't told him that his public ministry had begun.

We need to take Jesus' statement that *"my hour has not yet come"* in the context of the rest of John's gospel. Jesus refuses to go up to Jerusalem in 7:6 and 7:8 because *"my time is not yet*

---

[1] Luke 4:14. It is now late 27 AD, so this took place after Matthew 4:11 and Luke 4:13.

here", meaning it would prematurely provoke his execution. John tells us he escaped execution in 7:30 and 8:20 because *"his hour had not yet come"*, and Jesus teaches in 12:23 and 13:1 at the start of the week when he was crucified that at last *"the hour has come for the Son of Man to be glorified."* John therefore answers our question by telling us that people refuse to believe in Jesus, not because of lack of *information*, but because of lack of moral *inclination*. If Jesus had performed an even greater miracle at Cana 27 AD, he would not have converted more people but simply have been crucified two and a half years early. John tells us in verses 24–25 that *"Jesus would not entrust himself to them, for he knew all people... he knew what was in each person"*, so instead he opted for a subtler, far cleverer strategy. He performed miracles which served as signposts for anyone humble enough to lift their eyes from themselves and from their culture's lies in order to recognize him as the Living God.

There is another part of the answer to this question in Jesus' response to his mother's request. He is not being rude to Mary when he calls her *"Woman"*, since he does the same when speaking to her tenderly from the cross in 19:26. The phrase *"What do you and I have in common"* is a Greek rendering of the Hebrew phrase that King David often used to rebuke the foolish sons of Zeruiah who tried to extend his kingdom rule by force. It is also the phrase that the demons use in the gospels when they recognize the difference between Jesus' Kingdom purposes and their own.[2] Jesus is telling his mother that he will no more force people to be saved against their will than David was willing to force the Israelites to receive him as their king. He will only set up signposts which guide the humble home.

In the movie *Bruce Almighty*, Jim Carrey vents his fury against God for not being more visible on a day when he gets fired. *"Fine, the gloves are off, pal!"* he shouts at the sky. *"You're*

---

[2] The issue in 2 Samuel 16:10 and 19:22 is whether or not David will force himself as king on those who are unwilling to receive his rule, like the demons in Matthew 8:29, Mark 1:24 and 5:7, and Luke 4:34 and 8:28.

the one who should be fired. The only one around here not doing his job is you!" In a calmer moment, he asks God, *"What should I do? Give me a signal,"* as he drives full throttle down the road. A neon sign lights up in the darkness – *"Caution ahead"* – but he accelerates even more. *"I need your guidance, Lord. Please send me a sign,"* he prays as a truck pulls out in front him filled with road signs which read "wrong way", "dead end" and "stop". He ignores the signs and crashes his car, yet he then blames God for not answering his prayers. It is only at the end of the film, when he has been humbled by many trials, that he suddenly notices God's signs and cries out, *"You win! I'm done!... Please. I don't want to do this any more. I don't want to be God. I want you to choose what's right for me. I surrender to your will."*[3] God gives us enough signposts to see him if we are humble enough to go looking, but he will not force himself on those who arrogantly want to reject his rule.

John loved watching Jesus perform miracles. He even tried to pressure him into performing a killer miracle which would force the world to sit up and listen.[4] He is therefore remarkably self-restrained in his gospel in not mentioning any of the amazing miracles in the synoptic gospels except for two. No lepers healed; no demons cast out; no paralysed man lowered through the roof; no man with a shrivelled hand in the synagogue; not even Jairus' daughter or the widow of Nain's son being brought back to life. Instead, he restricts himself to seven miracles which serve as signposts towards who Jesus really is.[5] He records the feeding of the five thousand, then teaches that Jesus is the true Bread of Life. He records the healing of a blind man, then explains that Jesus is the true Light of the World. He records Lazarus being raised from the dead, then teaches that Jesus is the Resurrection and the Life. There is enough revelation

[3] *Bruce Almighty* (Universal Pictures, 2003).

[4] Luke 9:51–56.

[5] The seven signs are in 2:1–11; 4:46–54; 5:1–9; 6:5–13, 19–21; 9:1–7; 11:1–44. Two are also mentioned in the synoptic gospels, but five are new to John.

in each miracle for those who are humble, but not enough to force the hand of those who hate God's Son.[6]

So let's read the first half of chapter 2 with that perspective. First, Mary tells the wedding waiters to look at Jesus and *"Do whatever he tells you."* That's what each of us must do in response to any of his signs. Next, Jesus looks for the perfect object which can serve as a signpost for guests at an all-Jewish wedding reception,[7] and his eyes alight on six stone water jars, *"the kind used by the Jews for ceremonial washing"*. We can read in 3:25 that many Jews rejected baptism because they believed that the ceremonial washing commanded in Moses' Law was enough to purify them. Jesus could have simply filled the empty jars with wine, but he involves the waiters by telling them to fill the jars with water so that their simple act of faith can form part of the sign. When the unsuspecting master of the feast declares that the bridegroom has served the cheap wine first and *"saved the best till now"*, it shows what simple faith in Jesus' word will do.

Suddenly a whisper goes round the wedding guests that the carpenter from Nazareth is in the wine business as well.[8] The sign is not so brash that it provokes violence from the proud, but it is clear enough to stir any humble-hearted guests to faith.[9] Jesus is the Messiah whose Gospel is better than the

---

[6] Whereas the synoptic gospels emphasize that Jesus performed miracles out of compassion, John emphasizes in 2:11, 9:3 and 11:4 that Jesus performed them as signposts which revealed God's glory.

[7] 18:28 and Acts 10:28 and 11:1–3 tell us that no Jew would invite a Gentile to his wedding feast.

[8] Mark 6:3. Since none of the gospel writers mentions Joseph after Jesus' childhood and Jesus treats Mary as a widow in John 19:25–27, it appears that Joseph died and Jesus inherited the family trade as the eldest son.

[9] In fact, since verse 10 implies some wedding guests *were drunk*, Jesus' provision of the equivalent of 800 more bottles of wine enabled hard-hearted guests to drink even more and ignore the sign. Wishing God would force people to believe makes us as guilty of "turning wine into water" as those who teach that Christians must be teetotal.

best of Moses' Law.[10] John was one of the wedding guests and still remembers that this first signpost *"revealed his glory; and his disciples believed in him"*. He adds in verse 23 that during the months that followed *"many people saw the signs he was performing and believed in his name."*

If you are still driving full throttle through life like Jim Carrey at the start of *Bruce Almighty*, then pull up on the hard shoulder and read the signs. Jesus will not force you to take your eyes off yourself, but he invites you through his miracles to look at him and see the Living God.

---

[10] See 2 Corinthians 3:6–11, or Jeremiah 31:31–34 as explained in Hebrews 8:6–13.

God in a Box (2:12–25)

Jesus answered them, "Destroy this temple, and I will raise it again in three days." They replied, "It has taken forty-six years to build this temple."

(John 2:19–20)

John thinks you might not believe him when he tells you that people refuse to look at Jesus because they don't want to be saved. He suspects you may protest that there are far too many lovely, God-fearing unbelievers to class them all as wilful rebels. That's why he fast-forwards his account of Jesus' ministry to six months on from the miracle at Cana,[1] and introduces us to a group of deeply religious people who thought they had God in a box.

The Pharisees controlled the synagogues, but it was the Sadducees who ruled the Temple. Unlike Matthew, Mark and Luke, John doesn't name their group in these verses because they ceased to exist after the destruction of Jerusalem in 70 AD. Led by Annas and Caiaphas, the Sadducees were chilling proof that the deeply religious can hate Christ's rule as much as out-and-out unbelievers.

Frankly, the Sadducees should have known better. When the Lord told Moses to build a Tabernacle in the desert fifteen centuries earlier, he had never meant them to think its box-shaped inner room was large enough to contain his glory. He promised that the cloud of his presence would dwell between the cherubim on the lid of the Ark of the Covenant in the inner

---

[1] Verse 13 is very important for dating Jesus' ministry. Since John mentions two more Passovers before Jesus' crucifixion in 6:4 and 12:1, this must have occurred in April 28 AD.

room,[2] but then filled the entire Tabernacle with such glory on the day of its dedication that Moses could not enter and was forced to stand and listen to God's voice from outside.[3]

King Solomon had found the same thing when he upgraded Moses' Tabernacle to a magnificent gold Temple in 958 BC. Even though its inner room was bigger, Solomon had laughed on dedication day at the idea that God might fit inside a box of any size. *"Will God really dwell on earth?"* he asked in 1 Kings 8:27. *"The heavens, even the highest heaven, cannot contain you. How much less this temple I have built!"* Sure enough, God's glory filled the Temple in 2 Chronicles 7:2 and the priests were left outside, as Moses had been many years before. When the Jews forgot this and thought they had God in a box, he abandoned the Temple in 592 BC, although none of them even noticed except for the prophet Ezekiel.[4] When they built a new Temple after their return from exile in Babylon, they ignored the fact that the Ark had been lost and there was no cloud of glory on dedication day. The Temple rulers assumed that God was pleased with their worship of a box-sized God, and John uses them to demonstrate that even religious and respectable non-Christians are wilful rebels too.

This is Jesus' first recorded visit to the Temple as an adult, but we must assume that he had been there many times since the incident as a twelve-year-old which is recorded in Luke 2.[5] Herod's Temple was magnificent, a real wonder of its day, but on this visit Jesus was angered by the Sadducees and their

---

[2] Exodus 25:22; Numbers 7:89.

[3] The cloud of God's glory filled the Tabernacle in Exodus 40:34–35, forcing Moses to listen to God's voice from the outside until he was finally admitted in Leviticus 9:23.

[4] Ezekiel 9:3; 10:3–5, 18–19; 11:22–23. Ezekiel saw God's presence refilling the New Temple in 43:1–12, but his description of that spiritual temple was very different from the one ruled by the Sadducees.

[5] Luke 4:23 tells us that Jesus performed many miracles when he stayed at Capernaum in verse 12, but he still took time to leave the town on the shore of Lake Galilee to go up to the Temple in Jerusalem.

box-sized God. They had taken God's grand Temple and used it to obscure God's true grandeur. They had taken God's great mission to call the nations of the earth to worship at the Temple and used it as an excuse to profiteer from pilgrims by selling sacrificial animals at inflated prices in the Temple courtyards.[6]

Jesus was furious but he didn't lose his cool, governed by godly zeal instead of human anger as he carefully made a whip of cords. As he drove out the market traders, his disciples remembered Psalm 69:9 and its promise that the Messiah would be zealous for God's Temple.[7] Faced with a Temple which presented the world with a scaled-down, money-grubbing false version of Yahweh, he worshipped his Father by tearing some of it down.

The Sadducees refused to listen to what he was saying.[8] They were so concerned with preserving the fabric of the Temple that they had forgotten to preserve its meaning. Far from signposting the world to Yahweh, they had turned it into an ugly idol which obscured his glory from the world. When Jesus purged the Temple courtyards, they rushed to reinstate the market stalls just as they were before.[9] When he threatened to break their box, they complained that it had taken them forty-six years to build it.[10] When he told them that their Temple

---

[6] The Sadducees forced worshippers to buy their animals from the expensive market stalls in the Temple courtyards, and it seems they charged them a commission first to change their money into Temple tokens.

[7] David wrote this Psalm during his exile from his Tabernacle in Jerusalem during Absalom's rebellion. The disciples grasped that this was a shadow of Jesus' far greater passion for the Temple. Note that Jesus calls the Temple *"my Father's house"*, not just *"our Father's house"*. Calling God "Father" at all was radical enough. Calling him "my Father" was sufficient to get a person killed.

[8] They demand a sign to prove his authority, despite the fact that verse 23 tells us he was performing many signs all around them.

[9] We read in Matthew 21:12–13, Mark 11:15–19 and Luke 19:45–48 that Jesus was forced to cleanse the Temple courtyards again in a very similar fashion two years later at the Passover of 30 AD.

[10] The first-century Jewish historian Josephus tells us that Herod began building his Temple in 20 BC, 46 years before 28 AD. It was not fully completed

had become an idol in their hearts which must be destroyed, they started plotting to destroy him instead.[11] They hated the message of 1:14 that Jesus *was* the true and living Temple and the message of chapters 14–16 that he wants to make his followers into living, breathing temples of the Holy Spirit too. They revealed the ugly rebellion which lies beneath the surface of man-made religion and the bitter hatred of God which hides behind a mask of respectability. When people think they have God in a box, they hate the news that Jesus lets him out.

That's why John ends chapter 2 by making his challenge personal. He tells us that Jesus knows what is in each person's heart, and that many who pretend to accept his signposts actually do not.[12] He challenges us to throw off the suffocating blanket of respectability so that we can see the Lord.

These Sadducees would lead the way in Jesus' crucifixion later, so don't let the religious devotion which puts God in a box trick you and obscure your own view of Jesus too. He is calling people to look willingly at him to be saved. He warns that we can all be like the Sadducees, and that even those who look very respectable can be wilful rebels too.

---

until 66 AD, only four years before its destruction.

[11] John 11:48 tells us that the Sadducees feared that Jesus would make the Romans take away *"our place"*, in other words the Temple. Because they refused to let go of their idol, God took it away forcibly in 70 AD.

[12] John uses the same verb *pisteuō* twice here as a play on words which tells us that many in the crowd *put their trust* in Jesus but that he refused to *entrust* himself to the crowd.

The Good, the Bad and the Ugly (3:1–8)

Now there was a Pharisee, a man named Nicodemus who was a member of the Jewish ruling council. He came to Jesus at night.

(John 3:1–2)

A little local knowledge can go a long way. Once, when I was working for a big American company in Britain, our product was savaged viciously by the BBC consumer programme *Watchdog*. Our senior director at the global head office in Ohio commanded us to threaten to pull all our advertising with the BBC. I left it to one of my colleagues to break the news to him that the BBC is publicly funded and doesn't run any commercials. If we want to understand the message of John 3 and 4, then we need to do a bit more local homework than a quick-tempered manager in Ohio.

What we find is that first-century Israel was divided into three different regions: the good, the bad and the ugly. Judea – the good – was in the south and was the Bible belt of Israel. When the ten northern tribes broke away from God's anointed rulers in 930 BC and started to worship idols, any northerner who remained loyal to Yahweh migrated south so they could worship at his Temple in Jerusalem.[1] The kings of Judah were generally godlier than those of the northern kingdom, and even when they sinned and God sent Judah into exile in 586 BC, he preserved a remnant of faithful southern worshippers and

---

[1] 2 Chronicles 11:13–17; 15:9.

brought them back to repopulate Judea in 516 BC. Judea was very proud of its spiritual history with God.

In the middle of the country was Samaria – the bad – which had a far less glorious spiritual history. It was home to the mixed-race descendants of the Israelites who had been left behind after the exile of the northern kingdom in 722 BC and who had married the foreigners the Assyrians had settled in the land in order to undermine the Jewish nation. Not content with betraying their race, these Samaritans had gone further by mixing the religion of Yahweh with the idols of their foreign wives. At around the same time as Jesus burst onto the scene, some of them led pack animals into one of Israel's holy shrines and encouraged them to defecate on all that the faithful Jews held dear.[2] We need to understand that "good Samaritan" was thought to be a complete contradiction in terms if we are to grasp what John is trying to teach us as he takes us on Jesus' tour of these three regions in 3:1–36, 4:1–42 and 4:43–54.

In the north of the country was Galilee – the ugly – which was a region so ravaged by foreign raids and annexation that Isaiah 9:1 dubbed it *"Galilee of the Gentiles"*. John was himself a fisherman from Galilee, but even he admits that his region was despised by southerners as ethnically suspect and spiritually second-rate.[3] It was the third of Israel's three regions: the good, the bad and the ugly.

These first eight verses focus on Jesus' ministry among "the good" in Judea. Having clashed with the temple-ruling Sadducees in chapter 2, he seems to find a better audience when he receives a night-time visit from one of the synagogue-ruling Pharisees. The Pharisees – their name means literally *separatists* – were the deeply religious Jewish sect which tried to revive backslidden Israel with a call to resist the sinful practices of their foreign

---

[2] 2 Kings 17:24–41, Ezra 4:1–10 and also Douglas Adams's *The Prostitute in the Family Tree* (1997).

[3] See John 7:41, 52. 1:46 tells us that even the Galileans themselves despised Jesus' home town of Nazareth.

masters. Although most Christian readers tend to look down on the Pharisees (rather like the Pharisee in Luke 18:11–12!), these were spiritual heroes in their own day, and they planted synagogues across the country which won the hearts of the common people. If religion could save anyone then it would have saved Nicodemus and his Pharisee friends. In fact, he looks as though he pays attention to God's signposts, hailing Jesus as *rabbi* and confessing that he and the rest of the Sanhedrin can tell from Jesus' miracles that he has been sent by God.[4]

Nicodemus sounds very plausible – religious people normally do – but Jesus doesn't shrink from confronting his false humility.[5] While the Sadducees tried to keep God in a box, the Pharisees tried to keep him in a book. They pored over Moses' Law and categorized it into 248 commands, 365 prohibitions and 1,521 amendments. They hoped to gain eternal life by following them to the letter.[6] Jesus therefore tells him that he can't have truly seen God's signposts because *"Very truly I tell you, no one can see the kingdom of God unless they are born again."* The very fact that he visited Jesus at night because he was afraid of what his Pharisee friends might think of him betrayed the fact that they were spiritually in the dark and hated the light like any godless unbeliever. He might be the best of "the good", one of the most devout religious leaders in Israel, but he hadn't even got his foot through the doorway of salvation through his obedience to the Law. Being a good person just isn't enough. We need to be *"born again"*.

Jews, Muslims and respectable churchgoers are usually keen to stress the common ground they share with Jesus Christ.

---

[4] The Sanhedrin was the Jewish ruling council of seventy-one religious leaders, which Rome allowed to govern Israel's internal spiritual affairs.

[5] Nicodemus' profession of faith merely proves that people reject the Gospel for moral reasons, not intellectual ones. The Pharisees knew that Jesus had come from God, yet they refused to surrender to him.

[6] Unlike the other gospel writers who use the word "kingdom" 118 times between them, John only uses it in 3:3 and 5 and 18:36. He refers to "the Kingdom of God" as "eternal life", since it meant more to his Gentile readers.

John records this encounter which is missing from the other gospels in order to show that Jesus says they do not share true common ground with him at all. Unless God raises their dead souls to life, they cannot even see the Living God, much less work their way into his Kingdom. They might as well try to catch the wind as to categorize salvation,[7] because human effort yields a human child but only the Holy Spirit can give birth to a child of God. Only if we die to our fleshly attempts to save ourselves through religion can we be "born of water" through Christian baptism as a sign that we place all our trust in Jesus' death and resurrection.[8] Only if we are "born of the Spirit" through baptism in the Holy Spirit can our lives truly be changed, for *"it is God who works in you to will and to act in order to fulfil his good purpose"*, and God who promises that *"I will put my Spirit in you and move you to follow my decrees and be careful to keep my laws."*[9] John wants us to grasp from one of the very best men in Judea that being good can actually prevent us from looking at Jesus and seeing the Living God.

Later in his gospel, John will give us a happy ending to this story. He will tell us in 7:50–53 and 19:38–39 that Nicodemus listened to Jesus' challenge, responded with humble faith and was indeed born again. He shifted his eyes from his religious rule book to look at Jesus and grasp that our religious devotion can never be good enough to satisfy the perfectly holy God.

If you are a good person, then this should cause you to ask along with Nicodemus in verse 4: *How can we be born again?* That's the question which John was hoping you would ask. It's the question he now answers in the verses which follow.

---

[7] Jesus is using a play on words since *pneuma* (Greek) and *rūach* (Hebrew) both mean either *wind* or *spirit*.

[8] Romans 6:1–5 explains that this is the meaning of Christian water baptism.

[9] Philippians 2:13; Ezekiel 36:27. In the context of John the Baptist's ministry in Matthew 3:11, Nicodemus would have instantly understood "water" and "Spirit" to refer to baptism in both.

Faith Has Feet (3:9–21)

*For God so loved the world that he gave his one
and only Son, that whoever believes in him shall not
perish but have eternal life.*

(John 3:16)

John didn't have any trouble writing Greek. He came from
"Galilee of the Gentiles", where Greek was spoken in the streets
as much as native Aramaic, and he had settled in the Greek-
speaking city of Ephesus. He might not write with a classical
flourish like Luke, but he wrote well enough not to make a basic
error unless he meant to. Since he makes the same grammatical
mistake thirty-six times in his gospel, we should recognize that
he is deliberately trying to teach us something. He wants us to
understand that Christian faith has feet.

Ancient Greek, like English, talked about believing in a
concept or a person. The pagan writers and translators of the
Old Testament always used the little word *en* to describe people
placing faith *in* what they saw. John, on the other hand, breaks
the rules of grammar by using the little word *eis* to express that
Christian faith means believing *into* a person.[1] It may be terrible
Greek, or terrible English for that matter, but it is also a very
clever way of contrasting the faith that saves with the faith that
doesn't. Greek expert Marvin Vincent explains that it means

> *more than mere acceptance of a statement. It is so to
> accept a statement or a person as to rest upon them,*

---

[1] Luke, Paul and Peter also talk occasionally about believing *into* the Lord, but
John does so five times as often as all of the other New Testament writers put
together.

to trust them practically... Hence to believe on the Lord Jesus Christ is not merely to believe the facts of His historic life or of His saving energy as facts, but to accept Him as Saviour, Teacher, Sympathiser, Judge; to rest the soul upon Him for present and future salvation, and to accept and adopt His precepts and example as binding upon the life.[2]

John himself shows the difference in 6:29–30, when the crowd ask Jesus for proof why they should believe in him and he replies that God will only save them if they go a step further and believe *into* him.

Got that? Then note a second linguistic quirk of John's gospel. He loves to talk about the importance of believing, using the verb *pisteuō* or *to believe* a record ninety-eight times, which is three times as often as the other gospel writers put together, but he never once uses the noun *pistis* or *belief* because a noun is far too static to convey the faith he has in mind. Another Greek expert, Gerald Hawthorne, adds that *"Faith to John was not static or passive, but was dynamic and active, reaching out to appropriate and make the object of faith one's own. There was in it, too, an element of dependency, a recognition of the absolute need for the object, with a consequent willingness to come to that object."*[3]

To illustrate this to Nicodemus, Jesus reminds him of a strange incident which happened during Israel's journey through the desert in Numbers 21. When they sinned and were judged by a plague of venomous snakes, God commanded Moses to erect a bronze statue of a snake in the camp so that those who had been bitten could be saved.

Jesus wants to teach Nicodemus that *saving faith means facing up to sin.* Any Israelite who ignored the fang marks in his skin was absolutely doomed to die. Medicine was no substitute

---

[2] Marvin Vincent in *Word Studies in the New Testament,* Vol. 2 (1904).

[3] Gerald Hawthorne, professor of Greek at Wheaton College, Illinois, in the journal *Ex Auditu,* Vol. 5, (1989).

for a miracle, just as reform is no substitute for rebirth. Unless he left the darkness of his tent and ran into the light towards the bronze snake, his failure to use his feet showed he hadn't any faith at all. *"Whoever does not believe stands condemned already,"* Jesus warns.[4] Saving faith begins by frank confession that we are snake-bitten sinners in desperate need of God's Gospel serum.[5]

Jesus wants to teach Nicodemus that *saving faith is seen by what we do*. Good works can save no one, but nor can protestations of faith which do not result in good works. *"Even the demons believe,"* we read in James 2:19–20, but *"faith without deeds is useless"*. If an Israelite said he believed that Moses' bronze snake could save him but failed to go and look at it, then he died alongside those who claimed no faith at all.

Jesus wants to teach Nicodemus that *saving faith is faith in Jesus Christ alone*. Three times in these verses he says he is the "Son of God", Israel's Messiah. Twice more he claims he is Daniel's "Son of Man", and he adds in verse 13 that no other Saviour has come down from heaven. An Israelite who put his faith in Moses or in the Tabernacle or in the Ark of the Covenant might be very sincere, but his faith in those objects wouldn't stop him from dying. The same is true today when sincere people put their faith in Moses the Lawgiver, in Muhammad the prophet, or in any of the false saviours peddled by our pluralist culture.[6] It is only by looking towards Jesus, lifted up at Calvary, that anyone can find a cure for sin's deadly venom.

---

[4] Verse 36 repeats that rejecting Christ means God's wrath *remains* on us, because we have been bitten by sin's venom and Jesus' blood is the only cure. Verses 16–21 may be John's own commentary on Jesus' words.

[5] Jesus loves Nicodemus enough to rebuke him forcefully in verses 10–12 for his self-delusion in verse 2. True love always dares to tell sinners they are as good as dead.

[6] This includes the lie that God will not send anyone to hell. Comparing verse 16 with 17:12 and Matthew 26:24 shows that the word *apollumi* or *to perish* must refer to hell here. The most famous verse in the Bible is therefore about God's eternal justice as well as about his love.

Jesus wants to teach Nicodemus that *saving faith doesn't mean no doubt*. This should encourage you if sin's venom has been so long in your bloodstream that you struggle with the idea that Jesus is the only Saviour of the world. An Israelite who claimed strong faith in the bronze snake but failed to look at it died, while a neighbour who confessed his faltering faith but used what faith he had was cured. Jesus wants to reassure us that it is not the strength of our faith which saves us but the strength of the one in whom we place our faith. Paul explains in 1 Corinthians 1:18 that *"the message of the cross is foolishness to those who are perishing, but to us who are being saved it is the power of God."* The power isn't in the size of our faith in the message of Jesus' cross, but in the power of the cross itself.

Finally, Jesus wants to teach Nicodemus that *saving faith always perseveres*. Those who looked at the bronze snake and were cured still went on to die, but Jesus says that their faith in the one who was lifted up for their salvation meant that they had eternal life. He promises that we can also experience the life of the eternal age right now, but he adds in chapter 15 that the proof we have this saving faith is that we remain in Jesus. Looking at Jesus and seeing the Living God is not an add-on to our existing lives, but complete spiritual rebirth.

So let's search our hearts like Nicodemus and ask ourselves if we are truly born again. Do you possess the kind of faith which has feet and runs to Jesus, or are you nursing your snakebite and trying to staunch its poison through protestations of passive faith? Have you believed *into* God's one and only Son, so that you may not perish but have eternal life?

Above and Below (3:22–36)

The one who comes from above is above all; the one who is from the earth belongs to the earth, and speaks as one from the earth. The one who comes from heaven is above all.

(John 3:31)

Socrates cleared his throat and told a story. His young Greek philosophy student edged closer to listen carefully. *Imagine a group of people who have spent their whole lives imprisoned in a cave. They have never seen the sunlight because they are chained to a wall and can only see the shadows projected onto the opposite wall by a light somewhere behind them. Would they not start to believe that those shadows were reality?* His student nodded, as did the citizens of Ephesus when they read the story later in Plato's classic book, *The Republic*. John's readers were all familiar with the famous Allegory of the Cave.[1]

Socrates continued. Suppose somebody told the prisoners that these things were nothing but mere shadows. Would they believe what he said? If he freed them and forced them to gaze into the light, would they not be angry and run back into the shadows? Only a few would embrace the light and learn to look upon the sun and then go back to preach reality to those who were satisfied with shadows.

If you want to understand the message of John 3, don't be fooled by the fact that John is a Jew writing about the Jewish Messiah in conversation with a Jewish rabbi. If you have any

---

[1] Plato tells this story in *The Republic* (book VII), which he wrote in about 380 BC to preserve the teachings of his teacher, the great Greek philosopher Socrates.

doubt that John was trying to reach the Greek culture of his city, compare his style and structure with the very different Jewish style of Matthew's gospel. John knew that his readers were familiar with Socrates and Plato's story about the cave, so he fills his gospel with references to *light* and *darkness*, and to *things above* as opposed to *things below*.

Nicodemus came to Jesus at the start of chapter 3 and started boasting about all the things that he and the other Jewish teachers knew and saw. Jesus rebuked him in verse 3 by telling him he hadn't seen the Kingdom of God at all. He needed to be born *anōthen* – Greek for *from above* – which can mean *born again* in the sense of returning to the top of the page or *born from above* in the sense of deriving from heaven.[2] John wants his Ephesian readers to grasp that the Jewish rabbis had only seen shadows on the wall of Plato's cave. Swapping sinful shadows for religious ones had no power to save anyone; they needed someone to come and break their chains and lead them out of the cave and into the world of sunlight. Flesh gives birth to flesh; shadows give birth to shadows; things from this world give birth to things from this world. But the man from heaven gives birth to heavenly children – through the death and resurrection of water baptism and through the power of the Holy Spirit.[3]

Like the prisoners in the cave, Nicodemus runs back to the shadows. The light hurts his eyes and he cries out in pain, so Jesus rebukes him again in verses 10–21. I'm still talking in shadow-language yet you don't understand, he warns. What use is there in talking to you in light-language, even though you style yourself as Israel's teacher?! *"No one has ever gone into heaven except the one who came from heaven – the Son of Man."* Jesus

[2] *"Born again"* fits in with the way Paul uses the word in Acts 26:5 to refer to the Jews knowing him *from the beginning*. *"Born from above"* fits in better with the teaching of John 3:22–36.

[3] *"Plenty of water"* in verse 23 indicates that when John says "baptism" he means enacting burial and resurrection through immersing people in water, rather than simply sprinkling them like the Pharisees.

is the liberator in Plato's story who helps the captive world to see. *"This is the verdict: light has come into the world, but people loved darkness instead of light because their deeds were evil. Everyone who does evil hates the light, and will not come into the light for fear that their deeds will be exposed. But whoever lives by the truth comes into the light."*

Socrates cleared his throat again and told an epilogue to his story. Suppose that one of the released prisoners were to step back into the cave. Would he be able to return to the blinkered chatter of his former friends? When they talked in shadow-language and made plans with shadow-wisdom, would he run after their prizes as before? Yet when he refused and started preaching about a world of light, would they not hate him and try to kill him?

Now we're beginning to understand why what happens to John the Baptist in verses 22–36 is very much the epilogue to Jesus' conversation with Nicodemus in verses 1–21. Without this, we will get confused when great Gospel heights turn to petty squabbling and arguments about ceremonial washing. It all makes sense when we remember Plato's story about the cave.

Some Jewish students of Nicodemus and his fellow Pharisees are trying to provoke John the Baptist to be jealous because Jesus is now baptizing more people than he is. They hail John as a rabbi, despite flatly ignoring his message, and try to stop him from telling people to fix their eyes on Jesus. But John has seen the light and isn't interested in fighting for fame any more in their shadowland. *"The one who comes from above is above all,"* he insists, and *"the one who is from the earth belongs to the earth."* Jesus is the great Saviour who has come into the cave to enlighten a world blinded by sin. The Jews resent his intrusion into their dark world because they think they are "the good", but if they believe his message they will receive *zōē aiōnion*, which is Greek for either *eternal life* or *the life of the eternal age.*[4] John tells the Jews to stop their chattering about ceremonial washing in the shadows. The one who used ceremonial washing jars to turn water into wine is here! *"He must become greater; I must become less,"* he says.[5] It's time to open our eyes and look beyond our shadow world.

John has almost finished talking about "the good", so he takes a moment at the end of chapter 3 to set a choice before his readers.[6] If they ignore Jesus' words, they prove they are under God's wrath and are heading for eternity in hell.[7] Their refusal to see life and their rejection of God's rescue plan demonstrate that they are destined for the place which 2 Peter 2:4 calls *"gloomy dungeons"* or *"chains of darkness"*.

But if they accept the words of Jesus and receive his forgiveness by admitting that they aren't "the good" but are in dire need of salvation,[8] then they can receive in verse 27 what can only come from heaven and experience in verse 34 the God who gives his Holy Spirit without limit.[9]

They can be "born again" or "born from above" – it doesn't really matter what we call it. What matters is letting Jesus lead us out of the cave so that we can see God's sun.

---

[4] John uses this phrase sixteen times in his gospel and six times in his first letter as his Greek equivalent of "the Kingdom of God". We can see from 17:3 that it is not just about our getting up from earth to heaven when we die, but also about our getting heaven down to earth while we still live!

[5] Don't take verse 30 out of context. John needed to slip away so that Jesus might be seen, whereas we often need to speak up and be noticed so that Jesus can be seen (see Galatians 1:16, 24). In fact, Jesus went south in verse 22 so that John could be seen in the north, only returning in 4:1–3.

[6] Like 3:16–21, it is not clear whether 3:31–36 is reported speech or the apostle John's own commentary.

[7] John insists in verse 36 that rejecting Jesus doesn't *incur* God's wrath; it simply leaves us under it.

[8] John tells us literally in verse 33 that whoever believes Jesus *sets his seal* that God is truthful. 2 Corinthians 1:22 and Ephesians 1:13 add that God then *sets his seal* on us as true believers by filling us with his Spirit.

[9] The Greek of verse 34 simply says *he* rather than *God*, and it could therefore mean either that God gives the Spirit without limit to Jesus, or that Jesus gives the Spirit without limit to us. Jesus clarifies in 4:14 and 7:37–38.

God Keeps on Digging
(4:1–30)

*Are you greater than our father Jacob, who gave us
the well and drank from it himself, as did also his
sons and his livestock?*

(John 4:12)

Jacob hadn't found it easy when he finally decided to settle
down in Canaan. Not only did he have to pay 100 silver coins for
the hilly field near Shechem, but he also had to take up arms to
drive a group of Amorite squatters off his land. Having done so,
he knew he needed to dig a well fast. He wasn't going to repeat
his father's mistake and let lack of water supply force him to
relinquish his new field.[1]

Digging wells is hard work, and Jacob's was no exception.
The well at Sychar (probably a Greek variant of the Hebrew
name *Shechem*) was dug through rocky earth and limestone.
Jacob's well still stands today and is almost 50 metres deep. As
he dug through the unpromising soil, it's a wonder he had the
faith to keep on digging.

Perhaps that's why John decides to take us to Jacob's well
in chapter 4 as he moves the story on from "the good" to "the
bad". John tells us that Jesus *"had to go through Samaria"* to
get from Judea to Galilee, but we know that many Jews chose
to cross the River Jordan to bypass the polluted pathways of
Samaria altogether. He only "had to" go to Sychar because he
knew that, like Jacob, God keeps digging deep below the surface.

---

[1] Genesis 33:19; 48:22; Joshua 24:32. See also Genesis 26:12–22.

When Jesus arrived at the well, exhausted from his journey,[2] God had come in human flesh to carry on Jacob's hard labour. He was determined that his tiredness would not prevent him from digging.

No one but Jesus would have bothered digging very deep into the heart of the woman who appeared at the well with her water jar. Jews hated the Samaritans in general, but they particularly taught that *"the daughters of Samaritans are as [dirty as] menstruating women from the cradle"*.[3] John doesn't have to name the woman to make it clear that she was "the bad", but instead of writing her off as beyond saving, Jesus simply dug a little deeper. He asked her for a drink – it's always easier to share the Gospel with someone when we start with questions instead of acting like spiritual know-it-alls – and he used her response to share God's promises in language she could understand. Why did she keep coming to the well for water every day, when Jesus could turn her into a well full of God's living water?[4] The woman is interested and asks him *are you greater than our father Jacob, the well-digger?* Jesus notices that she has just confessed that Jacob is her father. He smiles at the first sign of fruit from his faithful digging.

Then Jesus hits more hard rock. She is more interested in cutting down her daily chores than she is in his gift of eternal life. Undeterred, he keeps on digging with some prophetic

---

[2] Some readers assume that *the sixth hour* means midday and that Jesus was tired from the heat, but if we agree that *the tenth hour* in 1:39 means 10 a.m. and *the sixth hour* in 19:14 means 6 a.m., then it was in fact 6 p.m. and he was tired from having walked all day. His disciples went into town for dinner, not for lunch.

[3] Niddah 4:1, which is part of the Mishnah in the Jewish Talmud. She is surprised that Jesus mixes with a Samaritan in verse 9, but the disciples are particularly surprised that he mixes with a female one in verse 27.

[4] The Hebrews called running water "living water", as opposed to stagnant water. This phrase is used in Genesis 26:19 and Jesus uses it to contrast Isaac and Jacob's wells with God's true Water of Life. He also wants to link back to Jeremiah 2:13 and 17:13, where the Lord is called *the spring of living water*.

knowledge from his Father.[5] He asks her to call her husband and reveals that he knows all about her five divorces and her current sexual sin. Surprised, she acknowledges that he is a prophet, which is more than Nicodemus even grasped in 3:2. Jesus' digging is finally getting somewhere.

Suddenly he hits more hard rock. She changes the subject to avoid God's prophetic challenge. Sychar was on the slope of Mount Gerizim, which the Lord had blessed in Deuteronomy 11:29 and which the Samaritans had therefore chosen as their site for a rival temple to the one in Jerusalem. The furious Jews had destroyed it in 128 BC, but the Samaritans continued to worship there defiantly. Jesus simply does a bit more digging. He teaches more about worship to this woman than he ever does to any of the Jews who harass him in the gospels. He tells her that what matters is not the location of a worshipper's feet but the orientation of a worshipper's heart. *"Salvation is from the Jews,"* since he is the Jewish Messiah, but God accepts the good, bad or ugly if they worship him in spirit and in truth.[6] This final thrust of the spade finally breaks her limestone heart. She admits she is waiting for the Messiah, and when she grasps that she has found him she leaves her water jar behind because she now cares only for his living water.

Do you see what John is trying to teach us by adding this fresh story to the synoptic gospels? Having shown us that devout Jews are not good enough to be accepted, he now adds that wicked Samaritans are not bad enough to be rejected. Like Jacob who dug faithfully to find water in his field at Shechem, Jesus just keeps digging until he hits upon the humility and spiritual

---

[5] Jesus explains in 14:10–11 that he knew about this and about Nathanael in 1:47–48 because the Father revealed it to him by the Holy Spirit. Paul calls this the spiritual gift of prophecy in 1 Corinthians 14:1, but warns in 13:2 that we must use the gift with the same loving sensitivity as Jesus.

[6] This phrase links back to the Allegory of the Cave. True worshippers have been freed by the Spirit to see true spiritual realities, and they therefore worship the Father with enlightened hearts.

thirst which form fertile soil for God's forgiveness. Before we know it, a whole town full of Samaritans is proclaiming in verse 42, in stark contrast to the Jews in chapter 3, *"We know that this man really is the Saviour of the world."*

If you know that you are a sinful person, John wants you to confess this with the Samaritans too. He wants you to note how little Jesus chides the woman for her sin and how much he promises that God keeps digging to find a humble heart which admits the truth and cries out to him through his Spirit.

If you are a Christian but feel inadequate, John wants you to look at Jacob's well. It didn't matter how plain the well was but how good the water was inside. The well at Sychar went deep but it was fed by an underground spring which ensured that it kept providing water when all the other local wells ran dry. John wants you to believe the promise of 3:34 that *"God gives the Spirit without limit."* He wants you to stop looking at your own limitations and to start looking at God's faithfulness.[7] If you do, then he will turn you into a spiritual spring which brings eternal life to others.

Finally, if you are a Christian, John wants you to roll your sleeves up and start digging too. Last week I attended an event for Christians at London's most prestigious palace, and I felt quite annoyed when a young girl turned up late in outrageous clothes and sat at my table, texting throughout the mealtime. When the after-dinner speaker showed a DVD, I suddenly recognized her as one of the recently converted prostitutes from the Christian ministry we had gathered to celebrate. I felt deeply ashamed because I had just glimpsed the little Pharisee that lurks inside me and which John says can lurk inside you too. How dare we write anyone off for salvation, when Jesus has shown us that he writes them in?

Because when God sees "the bad", he doesn't give up and move on to others. He rolls his sleeves up and keeps on digging to let his Holy Spirit flow.

---

[7] Jesus calls being filled with the Holy Spirit a *gift* in verse 10. He doesn't just let us drink from the well of the Spirit – he actually turns us into one! Jesus will expand on this theme in 7:37–39.

God's Goal-Hangers
(4:31–42)

*I sent you to reap what you have not worked for.
Others have done the hard work, and you have
reaped the benefits of their labour.*

(John 4:38)

When I first started to play schoolboy soccer, I wanted none of the hard graft and all of the glory. I used to wait around by the other team's goal and expect my team mates to do the tackling and then pass the ball for me to score. *"Nobody likes a goal-hanger,"* one of my team mates told me firmly. That may be true in schoolboy soccer, but it isn't true when it comes to God. John teaches us how to share the Gospel with "the bad" by telling us that God wants to use us as his goal-hangers.

The disciples were very surprised when they returned from buying dinner. They found Jesus about to lead a Samaritan woman to salvation. They were the ones who had gone into town yet Jesus had borne more fruit than they had as he rested in the shade. How could he have led this woman so rapidly to salvation? Because he is God? 5:19 says no. Because he possessed spiritual gifts which are unavailable to us? 14:12 says no again. John wants to show us that Jesus bore rapid fruit because he expected his Father to cross the ball into the box for him to score.

First, *Jesus expected God to be at work all around him.* When John and his fellow disciples were "on duty" in Samaria in Luke 9:51–56, they were furious that the townspeople refused to listen to the Gospel.[1] On this occasion, however, they felt "off duty", so they didn't bother to share at all. Jesus was just as exhausted as they were, but he didn't take dinner breaks from his mission. *"My Father is always at his work,"* he explains in 5:17, so *"My food is to do the will of him who sent me."* He found ministry refreshing, not exhausting, because he had learned to let his Father do the hard graft and then let him score the goal.

Second, *Jesus expected God to have been at work already.* The disciples saw little point in a hasty Gospel chat with the Samaritans. How could they win over such stubborn heretics in just one hearing? Jesus, on the other hand, knew that God uses each conversation in a long chain towards salvation. Some conversations get uninterested people hungry to hear more. Other conversations help hungry people to process the Gospel message. Still other conversations reap the fruit of the ones which have gone before. *"Do not say, 'Four months more and then the harvest'!"* he commands, because God planted Gospel seed in Sychar long before he and his disciples got there.[2] *"I tell you, open your eyes and look at the fields! They are ripe for harvest."*

Let's reconsider this chapter in the light of Jesus' explanation. He knows when the woman arrives at the well that she isn't an easy candidate for salvation. He asks her a question to dig and see what God is already doing in her life and is pleased to find that she owns Jacob as her ancestor and believes she still has a place in his story. God has kicked the ball from defence to midfield, so Jesus gently prods her conscience with her sexual sin to find out more.[3] He is thrilled when she doesn't deny her

---

[1] John had actually wanted Jesus to obliterate the village with fire. By the time he wrote this chapter, God had completely turned around his thinking and had used him to bring holy fire to Samaria in Acts 8:14–25.

[2] I prefer Young's Literal Translation, which treats Jesus' words as a command (*"Do not say"*) rather than as a question (*"Do you not say?"*). Satan does not mind you sharing the Gospel, so long as it is tomorrow.

[3] We may need to use the direct assault of 3:3 to shock "the good" who think they are saved, but a gentler approach is usually far more effective with those who know they are "the bad".

sin and hails him as a prophet, and he even takes her slight red herring about the right mountain on which to worship as a sign that she has a hunger deep down to connect with God. The ball has been crossed into the box, so Jesus corrects her wrong thinking by reminding her that *"salvation is from the Jews"*, and he calls her to repent by offering God the kind of worship he is looking for. *"I know that Messiah is coming,"* she replies. *"When he comes, he will explain everything to us."*

Jesus immediately recognizes that this means the ball is on the goal line. People are forgiven by coming to the Messiah for salvation. She is looking for the Messiah. He is the Messiah. All he has to do, therefore, is simply tap the ball into the back of the net. It's Kingdom of God *one* and kingdom of Satan *nil*. It's an away win at Sychar even though the rest of Jesus' team are still in the dressing room.

If you grasp this principle, it will mark a revolution in your personal evangelism. It will stop you despising those snatched Gospel conversations which never seem to go very far. It will help you understand that *"The saying 'One sows and another reaps' is true"*, and that sometimes we get to do the build-up while at other times we get to score the goal. A two-minute conversation which turns a God-hater into a God-listener or a brief chat which gets a person thinking in preparation for the next one are both parts of God's great plan that *"the sower and the reaper may be glad together"*. If God is always working, it doesn't matter which of the two roles we get to play.

You will also find that it transforms your expectations when you share. If we see evangelism as our job from start to finish, we will only share occasionally. If we see it as God's job in which we get to share, we will share every day with anyone who will listen.[4] One of my friends recently confessed to me that she never tries to share her faith with Muslims because she finds

---

[4] Jesus tells us in 15:26–27 that evangelism is the Father's job, then the Son's job, then the Spirit's job, then only fourthly our job.

them too entrenched in their views, so I asked her to explain to me what some of those views were. They included belief in one God, that Jesus is his Messiah, and that all have sinned and face judgment in hell unless they turn to God for forgiveness before Jesus returns to end world history. I've talked with enough Muslims not to be naïve about their many problems with the Gospel, but doesn't this at least mean that they believe more of the Bible than some bishops?! We will never meet a Muslim in whose life God has not already been kicking his Gospel ball.

Third, *Jesus expected God to have planned a massive victory.* He wasn't satisfied with a 1–0 result at Sychar because he knew that his Father had been working throughout the whole town. *"Go, call your husband and come back,"* he says as a hint to the woman that he wants to save her neighbours too, and she instinctively runs back and preaches in the town that she thinks she has found the Messiah that they are all looking for. Jesus clears out his diary and agrees to stay two more days, with the result that many more Samaritans become believers too.[5] By the time the whistle blows at Sychar, it's a treble-digit scoreline. God is always working like that in the people around us too; the question is whether we are willing to be his goal-hangers and receive the ball.[6]

John is about to move on from "the bad" to the "the ugly", so he ends with a statement which should ring in our ears and cause us to start goal-hanging too: *"This man really is the Saviour of the world."* Let's believe it and let's start seeing the same kind of scoreline in our cities too.

---

[5] William Booth used this strategy in his Salvation Army missions. He told his officers to seek out the worst sinner in a new town, confident that their salvation would make the rest of the town sit up and listen.

[6] Jesus reminds us of this in Matthew 9:37–38 and Luke 10:2. Most Christians underestimate the size of the harvest God has for them because they see sowing conversations as unfruitful.

Galilee Is Not Judea
(4:43–54)

*Now Jesus himself had pointed out that a prophet
has no honour in his own country.*

(John 4:44)

Imagine being cast as the third leading actor in *The Good, the
Bad and the Ugly*. It was fun for Clint Eastwood to play "the good"
and for Lee Van Cleef to play "the bad", but it was a dubious
honour for Eli Wallach to go down in movie history as "the ugly".
John doesn't seem to mind the stigma as he moves the action
north from Samaria to Galilee. He is happy to cast himself and
his Galilean friends as "the ugly", as he completes his account of
the three different groups to whom Jesus ministered.

The key to understanding the end of chapter 4 lies in John's
seemingly throwaway comment in verse 44. Since we know that
Jesus worked as one of the local carpenters in Nazareth, some
readers assume that John is saying that he found no honour
when he returned to his home region of Galilee, but this can't
be the case in light of the verses which follow. We need to
remember that John emphasized in 4:22 that Jesus is the Jewish
Messiah, and that he told us in 2:16 that Jesus' family home
was in Jerusalem. He had been born in Bethlehem in Judah,
only five miles south of Jerusalem, and he had only grown up
in Nazareth because his parents had been forced to flee there
to save the life of their son. John is telling us that Jerusalem was
Jesus' hometown and Judea his home country, and that this trip

to Galilee was a return to the land of his exile where he had once been forced to seek refuge among "the ugly".[1]

John was a Galilean fisherman, but he was under no illusions about the north. Unlike Matthew or Mark who set well over half of their gospels in Galilee, John sets less than a fifth of his gospel in Galilee, and he tells us almost as much in 4:43 to 7:9 about Jesus' brief holiday in Jerusalem as he does about his sixteen months of ministry in the north![2] Perhaps he felt that the synoptic gospel writers had already extensively reported Jesus' ministry in Galilee, or perhaps he knew that both Jews and Greeks were more interested in what happened in the bright lights of Jerusalem than in what happened in fishing villages. The Jews despised Galilee for being far too Greek, and the Greeks despised it for being too barbarian. It wasn't "good" like Judea or "bad" like Samaria. It was simply an ugly mishmash of Israel and Greece and Rome.

It therefore comes as a bit of a surprise that the Galileans believed in Jesus far more readily than the Jews of Judea.[3] In fact, John tells us in verse 45 that they welcomed him precisely because of the way he had clashed with "the good" in Judea. Other than miracles, there is nothing more attractive to the irreligious than God's messengers being willing to take on the stuck-up and self-righteous religious establishment. The common Galileans flocked to this new kind of whip-wielding rabbi, who seemed to hate the moralistic finger-wagging of the Pharisees as much as they did.

Rome's puppet ruler in Galilee was King Herod, who embodied the spiritual ugliness of the north. Yet it is his royal

---

[1] Matthew 2 tells us that Joseph and Mary stayed in Judea long after the census and would have settled there after Egypt had they not feared that the Jews might still try to kill Jesus.

[2] John 4:43–7:9 covers the time period between May 28 AD and September 29 AD.

[3] It is vital we understand that when John says *Jews* he tends to mean *southern Judeans*. Some readers misunderstand this and accuse him of anti-Semitism, but he is contrasting southern Jews with northern ones.

official who comes and persuades Jesus to perform the second of his seven miraculous signs. Unlike the Jews in Jerusalem, who were more interested in their Temple than their Messiah, this Galilean courtier comes from Capernaum to Cana in order to beg Jesus to heal his son before he dies. *You Galileans are just like the southern Jews,* Jesus retorts, *rejecting my message unless I prove it by performing signs and wonders on demand.*[4] He is testing the northerner to dig deep into his heart, and he is delighted to find that he carries on his begging. The man has a faith in Jesus which was largely missing in the south, having heard about the miracle at Cana and the healings in Capernaum.[5] He believes Jesus when he says his son is healed and proves his faith has feet by setting off back home. When the boy is cured, John ends part one of his gospel with this whole Galilean family looking at Jesus and believing in the Living God.

Let's stop and consider what John has taught us in this section before we start part two. He has told us repeatedly that we can only be saved if we fix our eyes on Jesus alone. Not on the aged apostle John and not on the prophet John the Baptist. Not on ourselves and on our own strength or weakness, and not on any of the cherished icons of our culture. Not on our good works or on the conviction that we have God in our religious box, because good religious people are often the blindest of them all. Instead, John has encouraged us to confess our sin like a Samaritan and to run to Jesus like a Galilean. He alone is Jacob's ladder, Moses' bronze snake and the man from heaven who steps into our cave to smash our chains and lead us into the light.

John has introduced us to some of Jesus' Galilean disciples in this section: Andrew, Peter, Philip, Nathanael and himself. In part two he will introduce us to the only southerner among the

[4] Jesus uses the "you plural" form of the two Greek verbs in verse 48. He is challenging the Galileans in general rather than just this one Galilean in particular.

[5] Luke 4:23 tells us that Jesus had performed many miracles when he stayed at the royal official's hometown of Capernaum in John 2:12.

Twelve, a man from the Judean town of Kerioth by the name of Judas Iscariot.[6] Judas will be so full of natural gifting that he gets chosen even over the former tax collector Matthew to manage the disciples' money. He will be so full of natural character that when he slips out of the Last Supper to betray Jesus his friends will assume he is going to perform one of his trademark errands of mercy. When Jesus warns that one of the Twelve is about to betray him, nobody will think that it is Judas.[7] He is "the good" and they are "the ugly", but he will also prove to be *the one doomed to destruction"* because he refuses to fix his eyes on Jesus alone.

John does not expect your fate to be like that. The fact that you have finished his first section shows that you are thirsty for Jesus like the Samaritan woman and eager to find him like the Galilean royal official. John expects you to be like Nicodemus in 7:50–53, when he withdraws from the company of the self-righteous Pharisees and bears their angry accusation that he was born a southerner but has become like a common Galilean. He expects you to be like Nicodemus in 19:36–42, where John tells us he believed in Jesus when he saw him raised up like the bronze snake and moved his feet to risk everything in order to identify with Jesus in his death.

Because in the end, it doesn't matter whether we start out as the good, the bad or the ugly. What matters is how we respond to John's command to look at Jesus and see the Living God.

---

[6] The Greek name *Iskariōtēs* is a transliteration of the Hebrew *Ish-Kerioth*, and simply means *Man-from-Kerioth*.

[7] John 6:70–71; 12:4–6; 13:21–30.

Part Two:

Look at Who Jesus Really Is

(Chapters 5–12)

I Am (5:1–12:50)

"Very truly I tell you," Jesus answered, *"before Abraham was born, I am!"*

(John 8:58)

In the movie *Indiana Jones and the Last Crusade*, the archaeologist adventurer needs to spell out the name of God to reach the treasure. The plot is a bit silly – he is looking for an ancient cup of Jesus' blood which he believes will grant him eternal life – but the idea of needing to spell out God's name is not. It's what John tries to do in the second section of his gospel.

Indiana Jones is faced with a wide floor made up of individual stepping stones which each bear a single letter. If he gets one of the letters in God's name wrong, the stepping stone will give way and he will tumble to his death far below. Fortunately, he remembers that the Lord told Moses at the burning bush in Exodus 3 that his name is the *"I AM"*. Since the Hebrew for *"I AM"* is transliterated into English as *Yahweh* or *Jehovah*, Indiana safely leaps across the seven stepping stones which bear the letters which spell his name. At one point he almost lands on the wrong letter and the stones beneath him start to give way, but he knows enough about what God told Moses at the burning bush to reach the cup of eternal life, which is the object of his quest.

Part one of John's gospel told us to look at Jesus alone in order to see the Living God. In part two, John is concerned that we will misunderstand who Jesus really is, so he makes this the longest section of his gospel and spells it out very clearly. It isn't enough to look at Jesus as a mighty human teacher or prophet, as some of the false teachers at Ephesus were doing. It isn't enough to look at him, like some of the other false teachers, as one who might be fully God but who only pretended to be a man. Nor is it enough for us to domesticate and modify him until he looks like the toothless Jesus who is preached in many of our churches today. Make no mistake, we misspell his name at our peril. We need to read these chapters slowly and look at who Jesus really is.

The key verse in part two is 8:58. Jesus is back in hard-hearted Jerusalem and the Pharisees accuse him of being demonized or a heretic Samaritan. In response to their claim that they are the true children of Abraham, he announces that *"Abraham rejoiced at the thought of seeing my day; he saw it and was glad... Before Abraham was born, I AM."* Instead of picking Jesus up on his grammar, they pick up stones to execute him for blasphemy. They are in no doubt that *"I AM"* is a claim that he is Yahweh, and John wants to make sure that we are in no doubt either.

We noted in part one that John gives us seven miraculous signs which prove that Jesus came from God. The two in part one and the five in part two are deliberate reminders that he is Yahweh Jireh (*The Lord Who Provides* in Genesis 22:14), Yahweh Rophek (*The Lord Who Heals You* in Exodus 15:26) and Yahweh Shalom (*The Lord is Peace* in Judges 6:24). Now he adds to these seven signs seven *"I AM"* sayings in which Jesus spells out who he is to the watching world.

In chapter 6 he is the true manna from heaven, the only one who really satisfies. In chapter 8 he is the true light of the world, the one who leads us out of our darkened cave so we can gaze into his glory. In chapter 10 he is the good shepherd and the gate, the only way for us to enter God's Kingdom and the one who protects us from the enemy once we have entered. In chapter 11 he is the resurrection and the life, which he proves by performing the last of his seven signs. Each time he spells out who he is, using the name of God: *"I AM"*. Each time he encourages us to look at him and see the Living God.[1]

It therefore shouldn't surprise us that in part two things start to turn nasty. The southern Pharisees who were happy to acclaim him as a good teacher and miracle worker in 3:2 are so offended that they convene a special meeting and decree that he must die. The common people who marvelled at his miracles are forced to face up to the meaning of the names which John gave him in section one: the Lamb of God, the Son of God, the Son of Man, the Messiah, the Rabbi, Jacob's Ladder, Moses' bronze snake and the Saviour of the world. When they hear his *"I AM"* sayings, the crowds are divided. Some drift away, while others hail him as a great human teacher or prophet, but they all struggle to confess that they are looking at the Living God. Part two will end with division, as the crowds worship Jesus as their Messiah while clearing their throats to call for Caesar's troops to crucify him. Part two will even result in one of the twelve disciples being so offended by who Jesus really is that he starts plotting how he can betray him to his enemies.

There is a Judas figure named Walter Donovan in *Indiana Jones and the Last Crusade*, an American who is secretly in league with the Nazis. He stands with Indiana as he prepares to spell out the name of God, and he illustrates why we need to read this section very slowly.

Walter Donovan: As you can now see, Dr. Jones, we are about to complete a great quest that began almost two thousand years ago. We're only one step away.

Indiana Jones: That's usually when the ground falls out from underneath your feet.[2]

---

[1] The first five *"I AM"* sayings are in part two, John's longest section (6:35; 8:12; 10:7, 11, 14; 11:25). The final two *"I AM"* sayings are in part three (14:6; 15:1).

[2] *Indiana Jones and the Last Crusade* (Paramount Pictures, 1989).

John is about to use these chapters to show us who Jesus really is, so don't tread carelessly like Walter Donovan. Make sure you study his words carefully as Jesus spells out his true name.

Not everyone we read about in this section will make it safely to the other side, and nor will everyone who reads about them either. We will only taste the salvation which John describes for us if we humble ourselves and take Jesus on his own terms. We will only make it safely to the other side if we let Jesus guide our steps and help us recognize that he is the Living God.

It's Time for a Showdown
(5:1–15)

> *When Jesus saw him lying there and learned that he had been in this condition for a long time, he asked him, "Do you want to get well?"*
>
> (John 5:6)

Church history was always meant to be like the final fight scene in an action movie. Whenever it hasn't been so, things have always started to go wrong. When we miss the message of John 5 and start majoring on minors, the action of Church history very quickly turns into tragedy.

The early Christians understood that Jesus used miracles as signposts to point the world to the truth of his being the Living God. How else could he break through the Jewish resistance to the idea that Yahweh would ever become a man? More to the point, how could they themselves convince the pagan world that Jesus wasn't just another deity for them to cram into what was already a crowded pantheon? They understood that it would take a showdown with sickness to convince the world that Jesus was the Living God.

Ramsay MacMullen, history professor at Yale University, explains that

> *Driving all competition from the field head-on was crucial. The world, after all, held many dozens and hundreds of gods. Choice was open to everybody. It could thus be only a most exceptional force that would actually displace alternatives and compel allegiance; it could be only the most probative*

demonstrations that would work. We should therefore assign as much weight to this, the chief instrument of conversion, as the best, earliest reporters do.[1]

This was, after all, what Jesus had always taught them to do. On a brief trip south to celebrate a festival in Jerusalem,[2] he had made a beeline for the Pool of Bethesda where the city's invalids spent their days in hope of healing.[3] He knew that the only way to make the Jewish capital take him seriously was to perform a miracle like one of the ones performed by Yahweh in the pages of the Old Testament.

N.T. Wright adds:

Jesus was not primarily a "teacher" in the sense that we usually give that word. Jesus did things and then commented on them, explained them, challenged people to figure out what they meant. He acted practically and symbolically, not least through his remarkable works of healing – works that today all but the most extreme sceptics are forced to regard as in principle historical... Jesus soon became better known for healing than baptizing. And it was his remarkable healings, almost certainly, that won him a hearing. He was not a teacher who also healed; he was a prophet of the kingdom, first enacting and then explaining that kingdom.[4]

---

[1] Ramsay MacMullen in *Christianizing the Roman Empire, AD 100–400* (1984).

[2] This trip was not made during the Passover since John calls it *a* feast rather than *the* Feast. It was therefore probably the Feast of Tabernacles in September 28 AD because John refers to Passover 29 AD a little later on in 6:4.

[3] Since John says literally that the pool *is* in Jerusalem, some scholars argue that he must have written his gospel before 70 AD. However, like most Greek historians, John often uses the present tense to describe past events.

[4] N.T. Wright in *The Challenge of Jesus* (2000). Nineteenth-century scholars tried to deny this miracle and reduce Jesus to a teacher on the basis that no such ruins of a five-colonnaded pool had been discovered in Jerusalem. They were embarrassed in 1888, when archaeologists found the pool exactly as John had described it.

When the early Christians followed his example, they found each showdown resulted in converts and new churches. Paul told the Romans that his own fruit was simply *"What Christ has accomplished in me in leading the Gentiles to obey God by what I have said and done – by the power of signs and wonders."*[5] Sadly within a few generations, Christian writers started majoring more on how many were not healed at the Pool of Bethesda. It was presumptuous, therefore, they argued, to expect God to heal other people as he had that one man.[6] Some even began to treat the story as little more than an allegory of Israel – the man was thirty-eight years in the desert like Israel, there were five colonnades to correspond to the Law, and somehow (honestly, I can't work out how) the pool itself corresponded to Moses' Law. It may seem pretty far-fetched to us, but it's just as far-fetched to John that we should ever hope to win the world to faith in Jesus without a showdown with its gods. He gives us three key principles which worked in Jerusalem and which will also work for us if we try them in Jakarta, Johannesburg or New Jersey.

John tells us that healing comes *when we fix our eyes on Jesus*. The man at the pool had placed his confidence in the power of the water to heal him when it bubbled, but he and the rest of the invalids who crowded there had been waiting a long time.[7] Their faith in the waters had proved futile, but that changes as soon as Jesus comes along. All it takes is a short command and the man is instantly cured. No shouting at sickness and no long struggle with a demon. Healing begins when we fix our eyes on Jesus and remember that he has the power of the Living God.

John also tells us that healing comes when we look at Jesus *with expectant faith*. Bethesda was Aramaic for *House of Mercy*,

---

[5] Romans 15:18–19.

[6] In fact, it's their argument which is presumptuous. John only tells us about one healing but he doesn't say there were no others.

[7] Less reliable Greek manuscripts contain verses 3b–4, which say that God sent an angel to heal the first person who got into the pool. This text was added later – the man needed Jesus, not an angel.

but the man has so little hope that God is merciful that Jesus has to ask him outright, *"Do you want to get well?"* He is so full of excuses that it is no wonder that John only tells us about one healing if all of his friends had as little faith as he did.[8] Jesus isn't looking for perfect faith – verse 13 tells us that people can be healed without even knowing who he is – but he tells the lame man to stand so that a small act of faith can be used to perform a mighty miracle. Jesus doesn't see the man primarily as a platform for his preaching, but as someone towards whom he feels love and compassion. That's why you can also trust him to have the same compassion for people around you.

But John warns us that when healing comes *it does not guarantee conversion*. The man who is healed goes straight to the Temple, which is something, but Jesus finds him there to warn him that unless he stops sinning he will suffer a far worse fate in hell. Even then, the man seems to side with Jesus' enemies when he informs them that it was Jesus who broke their man-made Sabbath rules to make him well.[9] As for the Jewish leaders themselves, they ignore Jesus' signpost completely and criticize him for letting God out of their religious box again. Nevertheless, we will see in the rest of this section that his showdowns resulted in new believers. *"Believe because of the miraculous deeds,"* Jesus urges us. *"I tell you the solemn truth, the person who believes in me will perform the miraculous deeds that I am doing, and will perform greater deeds than these."*[10]

Let's end with the words of Peter Brown, history professor at Princeton University, on why he believes the Church is flourishing in nations where believers expect miracles but declining in those parts of Europe and America where they don't:

---

[8] Matthew 13:58; Mark 6:5–6; Hebrews 3:19.

[9] The Fourth Commandment forbade work on the Sabbath, but he was not a furniture removal man! The rule forbidding him to carry his own mat on the Sabbath was made up by the Pharisees.

[10] John 14:11–12 (New English Translation).

However many sound social and cultural reasons the historian may find for the expansion of the Christian church, the fact remains that in all Christian literature from the New Testament onwards, the Christian missionaries advanced principally by revealing the bankruptcy of men's invisible enemies, the demons, through exorcisms and miracles of healing.[11]

John sounds like he is talking sense. It sounds like it's time for a showdown.[12]

---

[11] Peter Brown, *The World of Late Antiquity* (1971).

[12] Wanting to see healings and actually seeing them are different. I will pick up on some lessons to help us as we prepare for a showdown in the chapter entitled "Why God Doesn't Heal".

Stop, Look, Listen
(5:16–20)

Very truly I tell you, the Son can do nothing by himself; he can do only what he sees his Father doing, because whatever the Father does the Son also does.

(John 5:19)

My house is on a very busy road in London. I have to help my children to cross it every morning on their way to school. *Stop, look, listen,* I tell them as we wait on the kerb. It's what John also feels he needs to tell us at this point in his gospel.

John has told us about three miraculous signs performed by Jesus: water into wine, the royal official's son and the lame man at Bethesda. He has given us three examples of Jesus' prophetic gifting: to Simon Peter, to Nathanael and to the Samaritan woman. It's so impressive that John knows he has to teach us quickly how Jesus ministered, or many of us will assume that we can't cross that road at all. Instead of following Jesus by ministering like him, we will settle for admiring him on the wrong side of the road.

Of course there is also another, opposite danger. John is concerned that we may leap into the road and try to minister in our own strength. That's as dangerous as leaping into busy London traffic, and it's why many Christians end up feeling physically exhausted and spiritually jaded. With our man-made mission statements and ambitious five-year plans, is it any wonder that many Christians end up crushed and bleeding by the roadside? John wants to teach us the secret of joyful

Christian ministry, so he brings us to the kerb and teaches us to *stop*, *look* and *listen*.

Jesus was only on a short holiday to Jerusalem, but already he had overstayed his welcome. The Jewish leaders were too angry to accept the signpost which heralded that he was the Messiah, because they considered him a blasphemer for calling God his Father,[1] and a lawbreaker for healing the lame man on a Sabbath. While they start plotting to kill Jesus, John starts teaching us to minister like him. He tells us that our destination is a life of similar fruitful ministry to Jesus, and that he can teach us to negotiate the traffic.

First, Jesus tells the Jewish leaders that he *stops*. That's ironic because his supposed crime is failure to take a Sabbath rest from his day job as a miracle worker.[2] Jesus reminds them that the Sabbath was never primarily about not working – if it were, God himself would be a Sabbath-breaker since *"My Father is always at his work to this very day."* No, the Sabbath was always about us downing tools to confess that the Lord is God and we are not. *"Stop your striving and recognise that I am God!"* is the command of Psalm 46:10.[3] Jesus never sabbathed better than when he stopped and fixed his eyes on God's work all around him. Unlike the Jewish leaders, who had turned the Sabbath into hard work, he had learned to turn hard work into Sabbath. We get tired in Christian service when we forget that God is God and think that we are.[4] Jesus tells us that we need to start by stopping.

---

[1] It was virtually unheard of for an individual to refer to God as his *Father*. However, Jesus addresses God as his Father in all but one of his twenty-one recorded prayers in the gospels (Mark 15:34).

[2] Typically for John, the account of the healing at Bethesda is unique to his gospel. However, it parallels another unpopular healing on the Sabbath in Matthew 12:9–14, Mark 3:1–6 and Luke 6:6–11.

[3] New English Translation. The NIV says simply *"Be still, and know that I am God."*

[4] Although fully God, Jesus chose to minister as a human being through the Holy Spirit to provide us with a model we could follow. When he says in 5:30

Next, Jesus tells the Jewish leaders that he *looks* and *listens*. He doesn't plan his own initiatives or plot his own path to fruitful service, but he simply fixes his eyes on the Father. It's as if being successful in Christian ministry means having really good eyesight. We see where God is working and then we join in. Even this act of looking and listening is easy, since the Father's love for us means that he gladly shows us what he is doing and invites us to get involved. That's what Jesus meant in 4:34 when he said that serving God should be like refreshing "food". We watch for the Father to beckon us to cross the road, and then we step out in faith that he will steer us through the traffic.

There is an example of this principle in action in Luke 19. Can you imagine the pressure on Jesus as he saw the crowds in Jericho? So many people to preach to and heal and deliver and help. He was as likely to be crushed by the needy crowds who lined the streets as my children are to be crushed by the heavy traffic in the road. But Luke tells us that Jesus isn't looking at the traffic. He has stopped to look and listen to what his Father wants to show him.

Zacchaeus is about the least likely person to warrant Jesus' attention. He is a chief tax collector, one of those traitors who cut a dirty deal with Rome and lined his pockets by extorting money from his fellow Jews. The people of Jericho despise him as a "sinner" and they are more surprised than anyone when Jesus plucks him out of the crowd. What had happened? Jesus had evidently remembered that Psalm 14 tells us that no one seeks God unless God seeks him first.[5] *Look at him,* Jesus thinks. *No one seeks God, but Zacchaeus has climbed up a tree to seek me. He is seeking me, and I'm God. Therefore the Father must be at work in his life!* Without hesitation, Jesus crosses the road and he isn't disappointed. By evening, Zacchaeus is repenting of his sin, accepting God's salvation and becoming part of his

---

that *"By myself I can do nothing"*, he means that we can't either.

[5] Paul teaches this from Psalm 14 in Romans 3:11, and Jesus teaches it again in John 6:44 and 65.

People. That's what happens when we stop, look and listen. It's what John, after a lifetime of following Jesus, says is the key to fruitful Christian ministry.

Even my two-year-old daughter has learned to stop, look and listen at the kerbside, but she very quickly forgets and needs constant reminders. It's exactly the same with us. A turning point in my Christian ministry came one morning several years ago when I read these five verses in John 5 and responded by praying: *"Lord, my diary belongs completely to you today. I'll keep my eyes open to watch wherever you are leading. Please reveal to me what you are doing in this neighbourhood."* Half an hour later, there was a knock at my door. A teacher had failed to turn up for classes at the Bible school across the road – would I be willing to take forty Bible students for the rest of the day? Before that day, I had no Muslim friends and little heart to reach Muslims, but I knew where the Muslim community lived and the simplest thing to do with forty volunteers was to knock on those doors and begin to make some friends. By the end of that unscheduled day, I was completely transformed by the discovery that many Muslims families were friendly and very interested in hearing about what Jesus, the most mentioned prophet in the Qur'an, had to say. We need to remember to pray that dangerous prayer every day. It's very easy for us to forget.

So why not pray that prayer yourself and fix your eyes on Jesus for the rest of today? Why not decide that you have had enough of living on the wrong side of the road to fruitful ministry and enough of being crushed by the burden of ministering out of your own strength instead of his? Let's learn to fix our eyes on Jesus and see what he is doing all around us. Let's be people who *stop, look and listen.*

Courtroom Drama
(5:21–47)

He has given him authority to judge because he is the
Son of Man.

(John 5:27)

The Ephesians loved a good courtroom drama. In a pre-
television age, it was some of the best entertainment in town.
They crammed into the public galleries at the city law courts to
catch a glimpse of the exciting twists and turns of Roman law.
John knows what his Greek readers are after, so he offers them a
courtroom drama better than anything that downtown Ephesus
had to offer.[1]

The Jewish leaders have placed Jesus in the dock and have
decided to try him for a capital crime. It is September 28 AD,
so it will be another eighteen months before they can actually
drag him into a real courtroom, but already they are trying him
in the courtroom of their hearts. They accuse him of Sabbath-
breaking and blasphemy, both of which are punishable by death
under Moses' Law, and they believe they have the witnesses to
secure a conviction. Their star witness is Moses, who can wield
Exodus 31:15 and Leviticus 24:16 as "Exhibit A" and "Exhibit
B". They are convinced that they have an open-and-shut case
against Jesus. But that is the stuff that great courtroom dramas
are always made of.

---

[1] Remember that even though John is a Jew he is writing for a largely Greek
audience. We can see this from the way he always translates and explains
Hebrew words and customs.

The action starts with the Jewish leaders playing both prosecuting attorney and judge. Their verdict appears certain unless Jesus can pull off a surprise, so he responds with a manoeuvre worthy of a John Grisham novel. He tells the Jewish leaders to look behind them and see who is actually sitting on the judge's bench. *"The Father judges no one,"* he warns them in verse 22, with a reminder that Daniel 7:13–14 promised that God would grant all *"authority, glory and sovereign power"* to the Messiah, the Son of Man.[2] Suddenly, they realize in horror that it is Jesus who is judge. The prosecutors begin to suspect that this courtroom drama may not go their way.

Now Jesus has gained the initiative, he runs rings around his accusers in verses 21–30. He knows that the Sadducees and Pharisees are at loggerheads over whether Scripture teaches that there will be a resurrection of the dead on the Last Day,[3] so he centres his defence speech not on the charge of blasphemy or Sabbath-breaking but on his promise of *"eternal life"* and the resurrection of the dead. For a moment, the Pharisees hope he might be about to endorse them as the orthodox interpreters of the Jewish Scriptures,[4] but while their guard is down he hits them with a promise that the resurrection will be for both the righteous and the wicked. Believing in the resurrection is not enough to save anyone unless they also believe in Jesus as God's Son. Otherwise, they will only be raised to share the same terrible judgment as the Pharisees. The Jewish leaders suddenly realize that it is they who are standing in the dock as the accused!

Jesus responds to their accusations in verses 31–37. Since Deuteronomy 19:15 stated that two or three witnesses were needed to establish a matter, and since he cannot act as his own

---

[2] He also promised this in Psalms 2:6–12 and 110:1–7.

[3] See Mark 12:18 and Acts 4:1–2, and the way that Paul turned this to his advantage in Acts 23:6–9.

[4] Martha's faith in John 11:24 was due to the traditional Jewish interpretation of verses such as Job 19:25–27.

witness because he is the judge, he therefore brings three star witnesses into the courtroom. There is John the Baptist, whose blazing ministry burned brightest when he testified in 1:34 that Jesus is the Son of God.[5] There are Jesus' miracles, seen most recently at the Pool of Bethesda, which also bear testimony that he has been sent by God. There is God himself, who bore audible testimony at Jesus' baptism that he is indeed the Son of God.[6] The Jewish leaders' case lies in tatters on the courtroom floor, and they barely have time to catch their breath before Jesus calls in three more witnesses to try his accusers.

In verses 37–44, the Jewish leaders ask both God and the Scriptures to take their side. Jesus cross-examines his accusers to show that neither will oblige. The very fact that they are trying to kill God's Messiah is proof they *"have never heard his voice nor seen his form"*. It also proves that their Bible studies are a superstitious clutching at salvation instead of a willingness to do what those Scriptures actually say.[7] Their compromise with Rome, with Herod, with the common people and with each other for the sake of human praise is further proof that they do not love God or his Word, but only themselves.

Now it is time for the biggest surprise of all, when Moses steps into the courtroom as the third and final witness. Here, at least, was someone whom the Sadducees and Pharisees could agree was the great Lawgiver, the great founder of the Jewish nation, and the source of their faith for salvation. As one of the Jewish leaders confessed to Jesus in Luke 10:25–27, they hoped to gain eternal life through their obedience to Moses' commands to *"'Love the Lord your God with all your heart and with all your soul and with all your strength and with all your*

---

[5] Jesus uses John the Baptist's testimony in verse 34 to repeat his warning in 3:3 that they are not saved.

[6] Matthew 3:17; Mark 1:11; Luke 3:22; John 1:33–34; 6:27; 2 Peter 1:17.

[7] Verse 40 says literally, *"You do not want to come to me."* The issue was not that they failed to understand the Old Testament Scriptures, but that they did not want to submit to what those Scriptures said.

mind,'" and, "'Love your neighbour as yourself.'" It is time for Jesus to ask their star witness to testify, and to end this great courtroom drama on a high.

Moses speaks, but it isn't what the Pharisees and Sadducees hoped that he would say. Instead of springing to their defence, he becomes a witness for the prosecution. *"Cursed is anyone who does not uphold the words of this law by carrying them out,"* Moses declares in Deuteronomy 27:26 – they have not simply failed to do this, they are even trying to murder God's Messiah for his message! *"Moses wrote about me,"* Jesus reminds them from Deuteronomy 18, since the one they are plotting to murder is the one Moses called *the Prophet*. Their hope that Moses will defend them is dashed in the final verses of the chapter, and the spectators gasp to see that their number-one defendant is in fact their bitterest accuser.

The courtroom is in uproar as the judge's gavel falls and marks the end of this thrilling drama. Jesus is acquitted, his accusers are condemned and the rift between Jerusalem's Messiah and its religious rulers grows ever wider. It is time for Jesus to take the road back north again to Galilee and to continue his ministry to "the bad" and "the ugly". The Jewish leaders have lost their first courtroom drama against Jesus. They lick their wounds and plot their strategy for a re-trial in months to come.

God's Calculator (6:1–21)

*He said to Philip, "Where shall we buy bread for
these people to eat?" He asked this only to test him,
for he already had in mind what he was going to do.*

(John 6:5–6)

John's Greek readers knew how to add and multiply. They were
really quite good at it. The great mathematician Pythagoras
had lived only a short boat ride away from Ephesus, and so
had Thales who is now known as "the father of science". John's
readers knew how to use an abacus as well as anyone, which is
why he starts talking numbers as he recounts Jesus' fourth and
fifth miraculous signs. He wants to teach us to appreciate who
Jesus really is and to challenge us to swap our old abacuses for
God's calculator.

Jesus is back at Lake Galilee and John fast-forwards the
story six months on from the end of chapter 5, to March 29 AD.[1]
Stopping briefly to tell us that Jesus performed many other
miraculous signs in Galilee,[2] he launches into a succession of
numbers: *5,000* hungry people, *8* months' wages, *5* loaves, *2* fish,
12 baskets and *3½* miles.[3] It's as if John is trying to provoke
us to get out our abacuses, going further than the other gospel
writers to emphasize that the loaves and fish were *small* and

---

[1] John calls the lake by its Greek name *Tiberias* here and in 21:1. Since this
name only became common after 70 AD, it helps date his gospel to the late
first century.

[2] John tends not to include signs which are in the synoptic gospels. These
two signs are the exception since Matthew and Mark record Jesus walking on
water, and Luke joins them in recording the feeding of the five thousand.

[3] If there were 5,000 *men*, then the entire crowd was probably over 10,000
people.

that the bread was made of inferior *barley* instead of wheat. If we want to know who Jesus really is, then we need to look and see what he is able to do with all these numbers.

John remembers Jesus asking Philip to suggest how to feed the five thousand, but he reflects that *"He asked this only to test him, for he already had in mind what he was going to do."* Philip fails the test by protesting that the numbers don't add up: it would cost 200 denarii, the equivalent of eight months' wages, for each person to be given even a mouthful.[4] Andrew fares a little better when he brings a boy to Jesus with a packed lunch of five loaves and two fish, yet even he has his eye on the abacus when he asks, *"How far will they go among so many?"*[5] The one who passes the test is the boy himself, since he alone among the crowd has no need of any miracle. The sums add up if he keeps his food to himself, but he throws away his abacus and hands his lunchbox to Jesus as an expression of his faith in God's calculator.

Jesus multiplies the boy's five loaves and two fish to feed five thousand, so we might have expected him not to care much about the leftovers. Instead, he decides to teach the disciples another lesson and tells them each to take a basket and gather a massive doggy bag of bread. He wants to make sure that they remember just how powerful God's calculator is. They can trust the Lord to defy the numbers whenever they face problems which can't compute in their tiny abacus world. *"It is more blessed to give than to receive,"* Jesus tells them.[6] We are to act like the little boy and put our faith in God's calculator.

---

[4] The other gospel writers stress that the crowd were too far away from the shops, but John stresses that the catering bill would have been too high regardless.

[5] Andrew brings the boy to Jesus in the same way that he brought his brother in chapter 1. This is important because God wants to work through *people* who use his calculator, and not just through their resources.

[6] Paul reminds the Ephesian elders of these words of Jesus in Acts 20:35, but they do not appear in any of the gospels. The boy's example makes this as likely a time as any for Jesus to have said them.

Jesus has not finished his maths lesson. The crowd are so impressed by his fourth sign that they start planning a military uprising to overthrow Caesar and enthrone their Messiah. Jesus quickly tells his disciples to row to the other side of the lake, then he withdraws to spend some time alone in prayer to his Father on the mountain.[7] Matthew 14:25 tells us that he spent over nine hours on the mountain, so it is just before dawn when he performs his fifth miraculous sign by walking on the water to his disciples.

It was about ten miles to the other side of the lake, and the wind was against them, so they have barely covered three-and-a-half miles in nine hours of rowing. At this rate, according to their abacuses at least, it will take another eighteen hours to reach the northern shore.[8] They are so exhausted that when they see Jesus walking on the water, they are terrified and think he must be a ghost. They didn't need Thales to tell them that what they saw did not add up, but Jesus is teaching them yet again that God's calculator refuses to play by this earth's rules. *Egō eimi*, he shouts to them – the Greek words for *"I AM"* – for he is Yahweh and therefore made the very sea he walks on as part of his work on the third day of creation. In case they still don't grasp this, he performs another miracle by transporting the boat seven miles across the sea in an instant so that they arrive on the northern shore with no need for a further eighteen hours of rowing. Life is often hard work with little progress when we try to forge our own way with a rusty abacus. John was in the boat and he tells us that everything changes in an instant when we start living life by God's calculator.

---

[7] Matthew 14:13 tells us that one of the reasons he prayed for so long was that he had just heard that John the Baptist had been martyred.

[8] Don't be confused that Mark 6:45 says they set off for Bethsaida and John says they set off for Capernaum. Both were on the northern shore of the lake, so it simply means the disciples rowed north. Matthew and Mark confirm that they landed in the land of Gennesaret, which simply means the northern shore.

You and I may live in world which has more technology than Pythagoras and Thales ever dreamed of, but it is still very much an abacus world spiritually. When we face challenges, we tend to run instinctively to human counting machines instead of trusting in Jesus and living by his calculator. Every time I see a sick person, I hear the words of my school biology teacher far more loudly than I do the promises of John 6:2 or 14:12. When I face financial challenges, I find it easier to do the sums like Philip or Andrew than to hand over what little I have to Jesus like the boy who believed. How about you?

When God calls you to do the equivalent of feeding 5,000 hungry people or walking on water, will you shift the beads on your human abacus or step out in faith that God's calculator will balance the sums for you? When you have opportunities to give money to support the increase of God's Kingdom, will you look at the five loaves and two fish you will lose or at the twelve baskets of leftovers you will gain? When you grow weary at the oars of life, will you stop rowing or call out to Jesus to step inside your boat and do for you what human strength cannot do?[9]

Your answer to these questions will shape your character and your destiny. John tells us to throw our abacuses away and to start living instead by the power of God's calculator.

---

[9] Psalm 107:24–30 encourages us to apply the lesson of this miracle to the storms of our own lives.

You Are What You Eat
(6:22–59)

*Then Jesus declared, "I am the bread of life.
Whoever comes to me will never go hungry, and
whoever believes in me will never be thirsty."*

(John 6:35)

You are what you eat. If you don't believe me, take a look at
Morgan Spurlock. He consumed nothing but McDonald's food
for thirty days to make his 2004 documentary film, *Super Size
Me*. His body weight rocketed 10 per cent in just twelve days,
and he started suffering from depression, lethargy, mood swings
and severe headaches. It's really not surprising that what we eat
affects our bodies. Now Jesus uses his fourth miraculous sign as
a platform to teach the Galileans that what we give our souls to
eat affects our spiritual lives too.

In verses 22–27, Jesus warns us not to feed our souls on
material things. There is nothing wrong with enjoying the good
things of life – as Jesus affirmed by providing dinner for the
five thousand and by producing fine wine instead of water in
Cana – but snacking on good things can stop us feasting on the
great. Jesus points out that the crowd are more interested in
being fed a second tasty dinner like the night before than they
are in exploring how he made it across the lake without a boat.
*"Man shall not live on bread alone, but on every word that comes
from the mouth of God,"* he had warned in Matthew 4:4, and now
he follows this up by commanding the crowd, *"Do not work for
food that spoils, but for food that endures to eternal life, which
the Son of Man will give you."* The bread and fish which filled

their bellies the night before should have left their souls feeling hungry for spiritual teaching from the Messiah.

In verses 28–29, Jesus also warns us not to try to feed our souls on *good works*. Understandably perhaps, since much of this discussion took place in the Pharisee-controlled synagogue in Capernaum,[1] the Galilean crowd assume that Jesus is telling them to behave a bit more like "the good" people of Judea. In fact, that is the very opposite of what Jesus is saying after clashing with self-righteous yet unsaved Jewish leaders in his courtroom drama in Jerusalem. Jesus is the one who performs all the good works that are necessary to achieve our salvation. The one good work which must form our daily diet is simply faith that he has earned our salvation so we don't have to.

In verses 30–33, Jesus warns us not to feed our souls on *miracle-chasing*. The God who gave supernatural manna to the Israelites, and loaves and fish to the Galileans, still loves to perform miracles in our lives. What he hates is the superficial miracle-chasing which never stops to consider what those miracles may signpost and simply craves miracles for the sake of miracles alone.[2] We are not to be blind like the Israelites who ate manna for breakfast then saw no conflict in spending the rest of the day worshipping a golden calf. Jesus is the true manna from heaven, and we must go out every day to fill our mouths with the sweet taste of his body which was crushed for us at Calvary.[3]

When the Galileans tell him in verse 34 that they want to feed their souls on this fine food, Jesus begins to list what will happen to those who empty their cupboards to live on a diet

---

[1] Verse 59. Remember that when John says *Jews* he means southern *Judeans*, so the Jews in verses 41 and 52 must be those who went as missionaries to plant synagogues among "the ugly" Galileans (Matthew 23:15).

[2] The Galileans' request for a sign is preposterous given the two signs he had performed on the previous day!

[3] God deliberately designed manna to require crushing in a mortar, and to taste sweet for all who did the work of gathering and crushing. See Numbers 11:7–8 and Exodus 16:31.

of his body every day. *"I am the bread of life,"* he declares as the first of his seven *"I AM"* sayings. *"Whoever comes to me will never go hungry, and whoever believes in me will never be thirsty."*

In verses 36–40, Jesus promises that those who eat and drink his crushed body have *a secure salvation*. As he told Nicodemus, if anyone looks with faith at the Son of God, they will be saved like the Israelites when they looked at the bronze snake. Those Israelites went on to die, but his salvation is far better, since *"I shall lose none of all those he has given me, but raise them up at the last day."* He is straightforward with the Galileans in verse 36 that they are infected with sin's venom and will remain as far from God as Nicodemus and his friends unless they change their diet straightaway.

In verses 41–51, Jesus promises that those who eat and drink his crushed body receive *a transformed destiny*. They may despise him as the local carpenter's boy who has more business mending broken furniture than laying out a Gospel banquet for the world, but those who eat his feast get to know God better than the synagogue rulers, because Isaiah 54:13 speaks about them when it promises that *"All your children will be taught by the Lord, and great will be their peace."*[4] They might not be able to preach about manna and the resurrection of the dead like the synagogue rulers, but they dine on better manna and experience eternal life today.

In verses 52–58, Jesus promises that eating and drinking his crushed body marks *the difference between the saved and the unsaved*. Far from back-pedalling and reassuring the angry Jews that they have misunderstood his metaphor, he pulls no punches as he tells them to stop arguing and to start feasting on his flesh and blood. *Do you think I'm using a clever allegory here?*, he asks. *You had better believe me when I tell you that my flesh*

---

[4] Don't miss the fact that this quotation from Isaiah 54:13 in verse 45 comes in the chapter immediately after the statement *"it was the Lord's will to crush him"*, and immediately before the invitation to *"Come, all you who are thirsty... come, buy and eat!... Why spend money on what is not bread?"*

and blood are real food and drink. There is clearly a link between this passage and what Jesus teaches about eating his body and blood in Matthew 26:26–28, but let's not forget that this warning about reducing his teaching to mere allegory is a warning for us as well. If we are not careful, then even participating in the Lord's Supper can degenerate into little more than a Christless superstition.

So let's renounce the secular or religious happy meals which prove so fatal to their eaters and which stop them from eating God's salvation. Let's feast deeply, daily and devotedly on Jesus.[5] We become what we eat, so let's draw our security, our destiny and our eternal life from him.

John Piper puts it this way:

> *If you don't feel strong desires for the manifestation of the glory of God, it is not because you have drunk deeply and are satisfied. It is because you have nibbled so long at the table of the world. Your soul is stuffed with small things, and there is no room for the great. God did not create you for this. There is an appetite for God. And it can be awakened. I invite you to turn from the dulling effects of food and the dangers of idolatry, and to say with some simple fast: "This much, O God, I want you."*[6]

---

[5] The word Jesus uses for eating his body is *trōgō*, which literally means *to gnaw* or *to crunch*. He expects us to chew on his sacrifice carefully, enjoying its every little texture and flavour.

[6] John Piper in *A Hunger for God: Desiring God through Fasting and Prayer* (1997).

Please Be Offended
(6:60–71)

Aware that his disciples were grumbling about this,
Jesus said to them, "Does this offend you?"

(John 6:61)

William Wilberforce made powerful enemies when he decided to make his life's work the elimination of slavery in the British Empire. One of the most persistent was Captain John Kimber. When Wilberforce accused him in a House of Commons debate of flogging to death one of his pregnant slave-girls, he developed an obsession with getting even with the young MP. He banged on Wilberforce's door to challenge him to a duel and, when he was denied entry, lay in wait to accost him in the street outside. His insults, violent threats and attempts at blackmail forced Wilberforce to employ an armed bodyguard, but he flouted the eighteenth-century rules of honour and declined the duel. He was convinced that his patient forbearance would prove to the world that Captain Kimber was guilty and that he himself was innocent of any crime.

Hold that thought, and let's return to Jesus' message to the Galileans in the final verses of chapter 6. The Galileans were so captivated by Jesus the previous day that they wanted to make him king by force, but now they are so offended that many of them walk away concluding that he is not the kind of Messiah they are looking for after all. Even the disciples are offended and perplexed that Jesus appears to have blown the perfect opportunity to become the most popular Jewish preacher since John the Baptist. The time has come for him to teach them what kind of Messiah he really is and to train them in how to preach his Gospel to the world.

Jesus begins by telling his disciples that *God deliberately sets out to offend*.[1] He does not respond to their complaints by softening his stance or by insisting that the crowds must have misunderstood him. On the contrary, he raises the stakes still further by proclaiming that he is the Son of Man who has come down from heaven and will very soon ascend back to the Father's side. *"Does this offend you?"* he asks, as he echoes what was probably his disciples' most stupid question in the synoptic gospels: *"Do you know that the Pharisees were offended when they heard this?"*[2] Jesus tells them that offence was precisely what he intended. As Smith Wigglesworth taught his apprentice evangelists: *"If you leave people as you found them, God is not speaking by you. If you are not making people mad or glad, there is something amiss with your ministry. If there is not a war on, it's a bad job for you."*[3]

Jesus is not just being awkward. He clarifies that *God offends people for a reason*. The best way to discover whether they are a Peter or a Judas, a William Wilberforce or a Captain Kimber, is to launch a full-scale attack on what they hold most dear. Kimber was acquitted by an English court of killing his slave-girl, but his violence towards Wilberforce proved to the world that he was very much a murderer at heart. Wilberforce was libelled and pilloried by his critics, but his refusal to respond to the captain's death threats proved that he was innocent of crime.

This is a very important principle for us to grasp, because God is determined to offend us as well. He finds the areas in our hearts where we are the least surrendered to his will, and

---

[1] The *disciples* who desert Jesus in verses 60–66 were not among the Twelve, but the fact that John mentions Judas for the first time in these verses shows that at least one of the Twelve was offended too.

[2] Matthew 15:12.

[3] Jack Hywel-Davies in *Baptised By Fire: The Story of Smith Wigglesworth* (1987).

he launches a fierce assault on our cherished views. For the Jews, he chose their food laws and their aversion to eating meat containing any blood. For us, he may choose sex outside of marriage, or homosexuality, or there only being one true religion in the world. It is only when God offends us that we discover the true shape of our heart – whether we will resist like Captain Kimber and Judas Iscariot, or let God use the offence to disciple us like William Wilberforce and Simon Peter. Offence simply reveals where God's Word crosses our own thinking, and our reaction simply reveals how much we are his true disciples.

Jesus explains that *God offends people because salvation depends on his sovereign choosing.* In verse 63, he repeats what he told Nicodemus in chapter 3, that no amount of human willpower or clever persuasion can make a person born again.[4] That depends on the sovereign work of the Holy Spirit, so Jesus gathers a large crowd through miracles and deliberately thins it down through radical teaching which exposes who in the crowd has actually been reborn through God's Spirit.[5] No smooth words. No stressing common ground. No holding back in telling them that they are not yet saved. No appeal to their flesh because *"No one can come to me unless the Father has enabled him."* That's the only way that Christian preachers can win true converts to the Gospel, but the side effect is that it also leads to Captain Kimbers and Judas Iscariots making bitter plans against them.[6]

To encourage us, John ends by reassuring us that *God offends people because salvation also depends on our choosing God.* John states the role of human choice as much as God's prior role in choosing us,[7] and he illustrates it here by giving

---

[4] So far, John has taught that salvation depends on God's initiative rather than our own in 1:13, 3:3–6 and 6:44.

[5] Humouring false disciples is not just dangerous for them; 6:15 warns us that it can also ruin the church.

[6] This is how we are to preach to people who believe they are saved. See the chapter "Bridges and Walls" in *Straight to the Heart of Acts* for a different way of preaching to those who admit they are unbelievers.

[7] For example, in John 1:29; 3:14–18, 36; 5:24, 40, 44; 6:35, 37, 40.

the example of what happens in the heart of Simon Peter. Peter recoils as much as anyone at the idea of switching diet to Jesus' body and his blood,[8] but when a person is truly born again the Holy Spirit gives them such a soft heart towards God that they willingly surrender to each point where he offends them. *"Lord, to whom shall we go?"* Peter asks, *"You have the words of eternal life. We have come to believe and to know that you are the Holy One of God."* William Wilberforce displayed the same renewed heart when he forgave his enemies for attacking him on the basis that their worst lies about him were nowhere near as bad as the truth he confessed before God: *"No man on earth has a stronger sense of sinfulness and unworthiness before God than I."*[9]

So don't be surprised when God offends you and invites you to discover through the furnace of his hard teaching what is in your heart. It is easy for us to convince ourselves that we are devoted followers of Jesus until he offends us and unearths a little Captain Kimber lurking in our hearts. He does so in order to produce a little William Wilberforce instead, who welcomes the offence as God's loving invitation to surrender further.

Yes, please be offended. It's the only way you can be saved and the only way you can grow in your salvation. And when you have been offended, go in the wisdom of the Spirit to offend others. Pay the price which has to be paid to call the world to look at Jesus and see the Living God.

---

[8] Acts 10:9–16; 11:4–10.

[9] William Hague in a biography simply entitled *William Wilberforce* (2008).

You Don't Vote for a King
(7:1–52)

The world cannot hate you, but it hates me because I testify that its works are evil.

(John 7:7)

It's expensive work trying to become president of the United States. In sixteen months of campaigning to become the Democratic nominee, Barack Obama raised and spent a quarter of a billion dollars. That was just the primaries. In five months of campaigning for the presidential election itself, he raised and spent a further half a billion dollars. Those who aspire to the highest office are normally forced to pay the highest price, which is why John wants to clarify that Jesus didn't need to kiss babies or charm the crowds to win his throne. He is God's Messiah, whether we like it or not, because his authority comes from his Father alone.

It is just as well. Jesus' message about God's holiness, human sin and the need for forgiveness didn't flatter the electorate or try to massage their egos. *"The world... hates me because I testify that its works are evil,"* he explained. John wrote for readers in an empire where only a small minority followed Jesus, and he did so to remind them that you don't vote for a king.

Even those closest to Jesus did not believe him. In verses 1–10, his brothers laugh at his talk of death threats, smirk at his claim to be the Messiah, and rib him that he ought to be out campaigning in the capital. Mark 3:21 tells us that they thought their older brother was *"out of his mind"*, and John confirms that they only tried to drag him back to Jerusalem because *"even his own brothers did not believe in him"*. If Jesus' brothers had been forced to put a cross on a ballot paper, none of them would have chosen him as their King.[1]

He isn't received any better when he arrives in Jerusalem.[2] In verse 12, some voters hail him as a good man and others hail him as a bad man, but neither group has grasped who he really is. The pundits declare that he is demonized in verse 20,[3] and they get angry in verse 23 when it becomes clear that he won't seek election by their rules. Democracy is based on the view that *vox populi vox Dei* – the voice of the people is the voice of God – but Jesus had already heard God's voice and it didn't sound very much like the crowd's. *"Stop judging by mere appearances, but instead judge correctly,"* he warned. He had come as God's Messiah and you don't vote for a king.

When the crowds begin to understand Jesus' claim to be Messiah – David's mighty King and Isaiah's suffering Saviour – they discuss the claim in verses 26, 40 and 41, before responding like angry talk-show hosts with a list of contradictory reasons why he will never get their vote.

Some argue in verse 27 that he cannot be the Messiah because nobody knows where the Messiah will come from. At the same time, others argue in verse 42 that he cannot be the Messiah because everyone knows the Messiah will come from Bethlehem! Others argue in verse 41 that the Messiah cannot come from Galilee, despite the fact that Isaiah 9:1–7 says Galilee is the very place that he will come from. *"Look into it, and you will find that a prophet does not come out of Galilee"*, they insist in

LOOK AT WHO JESUS REALLY IS

100

[1] They were technically *half*-brothers since Joseph was not Jesus' biological father. They would later be converted through Jesus' resurrection and go on to play a key role in the birth of the Early Church in Acts 1:14.

[2] Jesus did not deceive his brothers by going up later. He told them that he could not go up brashly on their terms because *"my time has not yet fully come"*. We saw in 2:4 that this refers to the timing of his death.

[3] Jesus was also accused of being demonized in 8:48 and in Matthew 9:34, 10:25 and 12:22–37. It was the only option open to his critics, since they knew that only a fool would try to deny his miracles were real.

verse 52, even though the great Old Testament prophets Jonah and Nahum were Galileans![4] Listening to the crowd reminds us of the novelist Robert Heinlein's lament that *"Democracy's worst fault is that its leaders are likely to reflect the faults and virtues of their constituents – at a depressingly low level, but what else can you expect?"*[5] The Jewish leaders are as ignorant as the crowd, but Jesus tells us we can expect a better way because God has the only vote in deciding who should be his Messiah.[6] In Jesus, he has sent us a perfect ruler of his own sovereign choosing.

God demonstrates that he has chosen Jesus as Messiah by performing supernatural miracles through him. Even the sceptics concede in verses 4 and 21 that he deserves a hearing because of *"the works you do"* and that they still have no explanation for the astonishing healing they saw a year earlier at the Pool of Bethesda. In fact, these miracles convince some voters to break ranks with the majority and put their faith in Jesus in verse 31, asking *"When the Messiah comes, will he perform more signs than this man?"*

God demonstrates that he has chosen Jesus as Messiah by granting him supernatural wisdom. Although Jesus received no formal training as a Jewish rabbi, he knew the meaning of Scripture like no other human teacher. When he heard the crowds marvelling in verse 15, *"How did this man get such learning without having been taught?"*, he replied *"My teaching is not my own. It comes from the one who sent me."* His words came from long hours spent in Bible study and prayer, which is why he told the crowds that *"I do nothing on my own but speak just what the Father has taught me"*. That's why *"even as he*

---

[4] 2 Kings 14:25; Nahum 1:1. Besides, Jesus was actually born in Bethlehem in Judea.

[5] Robert Heinlein in *Stranger in a Strange Land* (1961).

[6] The Jewish leaders admit in verses 48–49 that the majority of people are often wrong. They think their education means that they get the casting vote, but the Lord replies that the casting vote belongs to him.

spoke, many believed in him",[7] and even the soldiers sent by the Sanhedrin to arrest him returned in verse 46 believing that Jesus must be the Messiah because *"No one ever spoke the way this man does."*

God also demonstrates that he has chosen Jesus as Messiah by shielding him with supernatural protection. When the people of Jerusalem try to lynch him or arrest him in verses 30 and 44, they find that their majority is no match for God's single vote. John stresses God's sovereignty again and again in verses 6, 8, 30, 33 and 39 by telling us that Jesus will only be crucified when the Father decrees that "the right time" has come. It convinces Nicodemus to break ranks with the majority of the Sanhedrin and to side openly with God's anointed King.[8]

John wants you to make the same choice as Nicodemus, as the action begins to move swiftly into the final six months before Jesus' crucifixion. John tells us in verse 43 that *"the people were divided because of Jesus"*. People always are. Jerusalem is about to reject him, but as they nail him to a cross God puts his own cross in the ballot box and declares him Israel's King.

Jesus doesn't come to you with a begging bowl and try to charm you for your vote. He isn't after your cross on a piece of paper, because he has already been crowned King. His cross is a bloodied one on a hill outside the city, and he invites us to turn our backs on the majority in order to surrender to him as God's chosen King.

---

[7] John 8:28–30. The most reliable Greek manuscripts suggest that 7:53–8:11 was inserted into this story after John's death, so we should treat 8:12–59 as part of this same conversation.

[8] Nicodemus had once been gripped by the same fear as the crowd in verse 13. He sought Jesus out by night in chapter 3, but now he owns him by day in chapter 7.

How Faith Happens (7:17)

Anyone who chooses to do the will of God will find out whether my teaching comes from God or whether I speak on my own.

(John 7:17)

Neil Armstrong was a very brave man. Nobody knew for sure that man could walk on the moon until the moment he opened the door of his lunar module and took a short walk down the ladder. Visitors to the US National Archives can still read a copy of the speech which President Nixon prepared in case the astronauts died when they attempted the first human walk on the moon in July 1969:

> *Fate has ordained that the men who went to the moon to explore in peace will stay on the moon to rest in peace. These brave men, Neil Armstrong and Edwin Aldrin, know that there is no hope for their recovery. But they also know that there is hope for mankind in their sacrifice. These two men are laying down their lives in mankind's most noble goal: the search for truth and understanding. They will be mourned by the people of the world; they will be mourned by a Mother Earth that dared send two of her sons into the unknown.*[1]

Fortunately, President Nixon's speech was never needed. Neil Armstrong believed what he had learned in training and trusted in the NASA technical team – John would call it faith – and began

---

[1] The speech is quoted in full in Roger Bruns, *Almost History* (2001).

his short climb down the ladder onto the moon's surface. Relief sounded in his crackled voice as it broke the nervous silence: *"That's one small step for a man, one giant leap for mankind."*

John talks so much about faith in his gospel that he pauses for a moment here in verse 17 to explain how faith actually happens. It's easy for us to imagine that faith is an intangible feeling which God either drops or doesn't drop into our laps, so John feels he needs to clarify. Jesus didn't tell the crowds in Jerusalem to wait for a feeling or a sudden burst of enthusiastic zeal before turning their backs on their friends to follow him. He told them that the only way to discover whether he is truly King is to step out of the landing module and to take a walk down the ladder for themselves: *"Anyone who chooses to do the will of God will find out whether my teaching comes from God or whether I speak on my own."* He warns us not to wait for faith before we step out and obey. He tells us that when we start obeying, faith will swiftly come.

This has always been God's way. When Moses asked him at the burning bush for proof that he would definitely go with him to deliver the Israelites from their slavery, he simply promised in Exodus 3:12 that *"This will be the sign to you that it is I who have sent you: When you have brought the people out of Egypt, you will worship God on this mountain."* That wasn't very comforting to Moses. It meant he had to face up to Pharaoh in faith and wait for proof to come after he did so.

It was the same for Bethlehem's shepherds when an angel told them that their Messiah had just been born in a nearby stable. They wanted to go and see him, but they had a problem since they couldn't leave their sheep unguarded. How could they be sure that the angel was telling the truth and that he would protect their flocks while they were searching for their Messiah? *"This will be a sign to you,"* the angel reassured them in Luke 2:12. *"You will find a baby wrapped in cloths and lying in a manger."* What kind of reassurance is that? It meant that only after they had gone in faith would they finally know for certain whether the angel's words were true.

An English saying tells us that *"Seeing is believing"*, but Scripture insists that when it comes to faith it is always *"Believing is seeing"*.[2] John warns in verse 13 that *fear* keeps people from starting out to follow Jesus, or keeps them wallowing in spiritual shallows when they do. Neil Armstrong's destiny demanded that he throw aside fear and step outside his lunar module, and we must do the same if we are to walk the path God has laid out for us. Jesus doesn't offer us unassailable proof before he gives us the call to follow him. He always gives us the call of Psalm 34:8 – *"Taste and see that the Lord is good."*[3]

This has always been the believer's story. When Noah obeyed God's command to build an ark on dry land; when Abraham left the city of his birth to travel to a country he didn't even know; when Moses' mother built a papyrus boat and set her baby loose on the River Nile in faith that God would intervene; when Joshua told the priests to step into the Jordan; when David crossed the valley to face Goliath; when Daniel's friends refused the king's command and were thrown into the fiery furnace; when Esther risked everything for a chance to intercede with the king – every time that men or women put their faith in God it has always meant walking down the equivalent of Neil Armstrong's ladder. They always found their proof on the other side of stepping out in faith.

So let's not think it will be any different for us. My Christian life began when as an arrogant student I told the Lord: *"I don't know if you're real and I've many problems with the Bible, but I'm going to start living as if what you say in it is true. I'm not going to wait for faith to fall into my lap. I'm going to step out in the belief that you will be there to meet me if I set out on the journey*

---

[2] For further examples, see 2 Kings 19:29; John 11:40; 20:29.

[3] The apostles *reason* with people enough in Acts to demonstrate that faith and reason go hand in hand, but there is enough in John 7 to demonstrate that reason alone is never enough.

you are telling me to travel." If you have read this far into John's gospel but never prayed a prayer like that one, then perhaps now is the time for you to take a risk and take a walk down the ladder yourself.

On the other hand, if you are already a Christian but you have never stepped outside the comfort zone of safe religion, then perhaps it's time to take a walk with God through the highs and lows, the fear and comfort, the pain and thrills, the uncertainty and peace, of committing your whole life into God's hands.

Perhaps it's time to do what John himself did when Jesus found him mending nets in his father's fishing boat in Matthew 4. When Jesus told him, *"Follow me!"*, he took his own walk down Neil Armstrong's ladder onto the sands of God's adventure. Let's learn this simple lesson from the lips of Jesus. This is how faith always happens.

Rocks, Sticks and Rivers
(7:37–39)

On the last and greatest day of the festival, Jesus stood and said in a loud voice, "Let anyone who is thirsty come to me and drink."

(John 7:37)

John loved his Jewish feasts. He simply couldn't get enough of them.

Even though his gospel misses out huge sections of Jesus' three-year ministry as recorded in the other gospels, he makes sure to mention all three Passover feasts.[1] He explains why in 19:36, when he quotes from Exodus 12:46 to reveal that God had told the Jewish nation to celebrate the Passover as an annual picture of the future death of their Messiah. Jesus would be the true Passover lamb, and his blood would be smeared on the door frame of his People's hearts when he was nailed to a cross at Passover 30 AD. John can't get enough of talking about the Jewish feasts because he wants to use them to teach us who Jesus really is.

John also makes sure to mention the Feast of Tabernacles on two occasions. Jesus healed the lame man at Bethesda during the feast in September 28 AD, and John records what Jesus taught at the feast in September 29 AD in chapters 7–9.[2]

---

[1] 2:13; 6:4; 11:55. These three Passovers are crucial clues for dating Jesus' ministry.

[2] John does not specify that it was the Feast of Tabernacles in 5:1, but it cannot have been Pentecost since Mark 6:39 tells us that the events of chapter 6 took place before the hot and dry month of May.

This was the celebration where the Jews gathered for a week's holiday in Jerusalem to commemorate by living in temporary bivouacs across the city the forty years their ancestors had spent in the desert with Moses. On the last day of the feast, they drew water from the Pool of Siloam and poured it out on the altar to remember the time when the Lord brought water out of a rock in the desert to save the lives of his parched and dying People. John seizes that moment as a chance to teach his readers that the Feast of Tabernacles pointed to the coming of Jesus too.[3]

The 600,000 men plus women and children who had arrived at Rephidim in Exodus 17 needed to drink a lot of water: the equivalent of three Olympic swimming pools of water every day. When their water ran out at Rephidim, God saved their lives by telling Moses to hit a rock with his staff and create a miraculous river of water which gushed out from the rock in the middle of the desert. Jesus promised in 4:14 to cause living water to flow from his People to save a dry and dying world, so John uses the Feast of Tabernacles to teach us how Jesus fills his followers with the Holy Spirit.[4]

First, John warns that *ignorance* can be a major obstacle to our receiving the Holy Spirit. Jesus tells us in verse 38 that this promise is simply what *"Scripture has said"*, but many believers are unaware this is the Bible's teaching. They have no idea that Paul teaches in 1 Corinthians 10:4 that the rock was a picture of Jesus, Moses' wooden staff a picture of the cross, or the river of water a picture of the Holy Spirit.[5] They have no more idea than the Samaritan woman that they should come to Jesus and

---

[3] See Leviticus 23:33–43 and Nehemiah 8:13–18. Since the Jews also lit lamps to remember the pillar of fire in the desert, John also links this feast to Jesus healing a blind man at the Pool of Siloam and teaching that he is the Light of the World in 8:12 and 9:5.

[4] To explore this theme further, read the chapter "The River of God" in *Straight to the Heart of Revelation*.

[5] That is why Moses was shut out of the Promised Land for striking a second rock in Numbers 20. It denied that Jesus' death was a once-for-all achievement so that the Spirit could be poured out in every generation.

ask him to quench their spiritual thirst and make them into wells which water others. Yet Jesus warns us we will only experience this promise if we know enough to believe it and come to him and drink.

Second, John warns that *feelings of inadequacy* can be a major obstacle to our receiving the Holy Spirit. We may feel "bad" like the Samaritans or "ugly" like the Galileans, and therefore conclude that this great promise is not for us. That's why John plants these verses right at the heart of a chapter in which Jesus is rejected by the "good" Judeans and accepted by the weak and humble in the crowd. He wants us to understand that the gift of the Spirit is for anyone who admits their need for God to flood the dry and arid desert of their soul. He tells us that this promise is for *anyone* who is thirsty, for *whoever* believes and for all *those who believe.* Don't make the mistake of thinking that you need to reach a certain level of Christian maturity before you can receive the Spirit. The same God who was not ashamed to tabernacle in the body of a Galilean carpenter in 1:14 is not ashamed to tabernacle in the body of anyone he has saved.

Third, John warns that *self-indulgence* can be a major obstacle to our receiving the Holy Spirit. I lead a London church which has a reputation as a place for people to experience the outpouring of the Holy Spirit, so I have as much firsthand experience as anyone of the tendency of charismatic Christians to chase experiences so much that they actually grieve the Holy Spirit away. That's why John stresses in verse 38 that Jesus is looking for more than spiritual consumers who build bivouacs and get drunk on his water. He is looking for people who will let him turn them into little rocks so that *"rivers of living water will flow from within them."* In Luke 4, he told the people of Nazareth that the Spirit had anointed him to send him on God's mission, and he tells us here that the Spirit hasn't changed. The Holy Spirit is not looking for self-centred consumers. We will only receive the Spirit if we are willing to go out and give him away.[6]

Fourth, John warns that *complacency* can be a major obstacle to our receiving the Holy Spirit. Satan does not mind us having faith that this promise is for people in the past or for people in the future, but he trembles when God's People believe this promise in the present. John tells us in verse 39 that Jesus waited to pour out the Holy Spirit until after he was glorified through his death and resurrection, but now that we live on the other side of the cross we must let nothing else cause us to delay.[7]

Complacency can even hinder those who have been filled with the Holy Spirit in the past. Jesus uses a "present imperative" in Greek in verse 37, which can be translated, *"Let anyone who is thirsty **keep coming** to me and **keep drinking**."* John promised in 3:34 that the Lord *"gives the Spirit without limit"*, so we must not create limits of our own by being satisfied with anything less than daily drinking of the Spirit in the present. We need to notice Paul's use of another present imperative in Ephesians 5:18, where he tells us to *"**go on being filled** with the Holy Spirit"*.

So let's remember the Feast of Tabernacles, avoiding these four obstacles, and lay hold of the gift of the Holy Spirit afresh today. Let's find friends we can trust to increase our thirst and pray for one another to receive more of the promised Holy Spirit. When we do so, we find that the one who tabernacled with the Israelites in the desert and who tabernacled with Jesus in Jerusalem also tabernacles with us today.

Now that is a festival worth celebrating.

---

[6] The Greek word *koilia* in verse 38 means literally *belly* or *womb*, so it carries with it the promise of new life.

[7] Acts 2:33 also links the outpouring of the Holy Spirit to Jesus' death, resurrection and ascension.

The Victim (8:1–11)

"Neither do I condemn you," Jesus declared. *"Go now and leave your life of sin."*

(John 8:11)

Recently, one of my best friends came to see me in a rage. He had just discovered that his wife was having an affair. Normally mild-mannered, he was a picture of anger, yet I found his reaction perfectly reasonable. What I find unreasonable is that Jesus failed to react in the same manner in the passage which has been inserted into the account of his teaching at the Feast of Tabernacles.[1] When he looked at a woman who had been caught having an affair, his reaction was not one of anger but of unexpected grace and forgiveness. Jesus saw three things which we may not see and which show us what kind of Messiah he is.

The Jewish leaders looked at the woman who was caught in adultery and saw a criminal, but Jesus first and foremost saw *a victim*. I know that many of us don't like that, because we have had our fill of a justice system which treats criminals as victims instead of punishing them as wrongdoers. But note that Jesus isn't pretending that she is *just* a victim. *"Go now and leave your life of sin"*, he tells her straight. He reminds her that being caught red-handed in the act of adultery is just the tip of the iceberg in her whole secret lifestyle of sin. Jesus does not pretend that she isn't a sinner; he just looks a little further to see the reasons for her sin.

---

[1] This passage does not appear here in the oldest and most reliable Greek manuscripts, but that is not to say that these verses were not written by John and it is certainly not to say that they are not inspired Scripture.

As a church leader, I hear a lot of confessions. One came from a Christian teenager whose boyfriend kept pressuring her to give him her virginity. One evening, she gave in to his manipulative complaint that if she didn't give him sex then she couldn't truly love him. She cried as she remembered getting out of the bed afterwards and rushing to the bathroom to vomit in shame. The teachers of the law and Pharisees would have looked at her and shouted "Sinner!", but Jesus looks at girls like her and the first word he says is "Victim".

On another occasion, a man confessed to me that he was on the sex-offenders' register. He described his childhood, when he was abused by his schizophrenic mother for years as his spineless father looked on passively. He explained in tortured terms how it had left him too damaged to form friendships with his peers and that he had therefore bonded horribly and sinfully with children. While self-righteous critics cry out "Sinner!" and "Stone him!", Jesus looks at the man with eyes of love and the first thing he whispers is "Victim". We can quote lots of Bible verses which declare that such people are guilty, but we mustn't forget to include 2 Timothy 2:26, which tells us that Jesus came to help people like them *"come to their senses and escape from the trap of the devil, who has taken them captive to do his will"*.

This passage doesn't tell us the adulterous woman's full story, but it contains a clue which confirms that Jesus was right to see her as a victim. The religious leaders were right when they pointed out that Leviticus 20:10 demanded that she be stoned to death,[2] but they were very wrong when they failed to mention that it also demanded the stoning of the adulterous man alongside her.[3] They had caught her in the act, so the man had still been there. Was he so rich or well-connected that

---

[2] The Pharisees were trying to trap Jesus in verse 6. If he agreed that the Law of Moses demanded she be stoned, they could argue he was inciting them to break the law of Rome, which forbade Jewish stonings.

[3] They use a Greek feminine word which pretends the Law only commanded *such women* should be stoned.

they had let him slip away? The passage does not tell us, but it assures us that Jesus loves to step into the fray to take the side of Satan's victims.

Jesus saw a second thing when he looked at the woman. He saw her *humility*. She wasn't so humble an hour earlier, but it's funny how quickly things can change. With her love affair in tatters, her sin exposed and her life in danger, she provides an attractive contrast to the mouthy Pharisees. She stays silent and does not dare to speak to Jesus until he first speaks to her.[4] *"God opposes the proud but gives grace to the humble"*,[5] so Jesus warms to the way she doesn't try to protest her innocence. The "good" religious leaders are too proud to ask him for forgiveness, but this "bad" woman knows that he alone can save her. Jesus scribbles in the dust and then tells her accusers to go ahead and throw their stones if they have never sinned themselves, which suggests that what he scribbled was the Ten Commandments or another similar Scripture. He wants them to confess their own sin and grovel with the woman in the dust so that they can go home forgiven too.

Jesus can only forgive her because he sees a third and final thing which the religious leaders cannot see. He sees *his own blood*. Don't miss the imagery in these verses as Jesus stands between the deadly hand of justice and the sinner who deserves to die. Only six months later, these same religious leaders would crucify him as God's sacrifice for sin. Only two people are left standing after Jesus scribbles in the dust – the Saviour who obeyed God's standards to the full and the sinner who admits she deserves to die. Unless we grasp that the primary victim in this passage is not the woman but Jesus himself, we won't understand that *"Neither do I condemn you"* is the costliest sentence ever uttered. *Your blood is spared because my blood will be shed*, Jesus tells her. As John explained later in one of

---

[4] Verse 9 warns that such mouthy pride is a particular danger to younger men and women.

[5] Proverbs 3:34, which is quoted this way in James 4:6 and 1 Peter 5:5.

his letters: *"If anyone does something wrong, we have a Friend to help us. He speaks to God for us. He is Jesus Christ who does what is right. He himself is the sacrifice God offered to pay for the wrong we have done."*[6]

That's why these three things which Jesus saw make this passage one of the most comforting, and most frightening, passages in John's gospel. It is comforting because it offers reassurance that there is no sin we can commit which places us beyond the reach of God's love and forgiveness, but it is frightening because it warns we might think we are too "good" to need that love and forgiveness ourselves. If we are not careful, we will be like the religious leaders who were not saved themselves yet used God's Word to condemn others.

So Jesus ends this passage with an invitation for each one of us to confess our sin and receive his forgiveness like the woman caught in adultery. He became an innocent victim because we became guilty victims of the Devil. He became a victim so that he can speak over our lives: *"Neither do I condemn you. Go now and leave your life of sin."*

---

[6] 1 John 2:1–2 (Worldwide English Translation).

Step Out of the Cave
(8:12–36)

I am the light of the world. Whoever follows me will never walk in darkness... If the Son sets you free, you will be free indeed.

(John 8:12, 36)

The Feast of Tabernacles; Plato's cave; the Hindu festival of Diwali; the movie *The Matrix*. Every culture has its own way of expressing the victory of light over darkness.

The Matrix tells the story of a computer programmer named Neo who discovers he is living in a cyber version of Plato's cave. A mysterious stranger named Morpheus steps into his world to warn him that all he sees is merely an elaborate computer program through which evil machines keep the human race captive as docile pawns in their power games. *"You are a slave, Neo,"* he tells him. *"Like everyone else you were born into bondage. Born into a prison that you cannot smell or taste or touch. A prison for your mind."*[1] If you have seen *The Matrix*, then keep that scene in mind. It will help you to understand what Jesus teaches in John 8.

On the first day of the Jewish Feast of Tabernacles, golden lamps were lit in the Temple courtyards as a reminder that God led the Israelites through a pillar of fire for forty years in the desert.[2] On the last and greatest day of the Feast, those lamps

---

[1] *The Matrix* (Warner Bros. Pictures, 1999).
[2] Exodus 13:21–22; Numbers 14:14. There is some evidence that the lamps were lit and extinguished near the treasury box in the "court of women". If so, then verse 20 is more than just an aside.

were extinguished to mark the end of the week of celebration. We therefore need to understand that these verses carry on from where Jesus left off in 7:37–39. He told the crowds that he is the true rock in the desert, and now he adds that he is the true pillar of fire as well. His second *"I AM"* saying is the claim that *"I am the light of the world. Whoever follows me will never walk in darkness."* God promised to send a messenger in Isaiah 42:6, 49:6 and 60:1–3 who would lead all nations to salvation. That messenger is Jesus, and he says it's time for each one of us to step out of the cave.

"Welcome to the real world," smiles Morpheus to Neo, but the Jewish leaders aren't smiling back at Jesus. They understand that he is claiming to be the Messiah in verse 12, so they quote his words back at him from 5:31 and retort that his words cannot be trusted because he isn't one of them. Since none of their clique of Jewish rabbis has believed in him, then it must be him who is deceived.[3] In reply, Jesus ups the ante by declaring that they have so misunderstood the Scriptures that it is now *"your own Law"*, not God's Law, and by stating that God is his Father and bears testimony that his words are true.[4] This is like a red rag to a bull and they retort, *"Where is your father?"*, using his miraculous conception as a reason to doubt his message instead of hailing him as the one God promised in Isaiah 7:14.[5]

Jesus is not discouraged by their spiritual blindness. As in Plato's cave, he knows most of his hearers would rather attack him than leave their shadow-life behind. *"You are from below; I am from above. You are of this world; I am not of this world,"* he squares up to his listeners before telling them plainly in

---

[3] When they say this in 7:48–49, it provokes their colleague Nicodemus to prove them wrong in 7:50–52.

[4] This was extraordinarily offensive to the Jewish leaders, who prided themselves on being teachers of God's Law. Jesus repeats it, however, in 10:34 and 15:25.

[5] John clarifies in verse 41 that the Jewish leaders asked this question in order to accuse Jesus of being an illegitimate bastard. They were as blind to God's warnings as King Ahaz in Isaiah 7.

verses 24 and 26 that they are unsaved and hurtling towards God's judgment.[6] *"I told you that you would die in your sins,"* he reminds them. *"If you do not believe that I AM, you will indeed die in your sins."*[7] They need to confess their darkness and let him lead them out of the cave. They need to receive forgiveness for the penalty of sin and let him free them from the residual power of sin.

Like all good preachers, Jesus leaves his audience divided. Those watching the lamps being snuffed out in the Temple courtyard know that he is claiming to be someone far greater than the other Jewish rabbis. The Jewish leaders get angry and repeat their insult in verse 41, but many in the crowd choose to believe what he says in verse 30.[8] They look to him as their ancestors did when they followed the pillar of fire. They are transfixed as he tells them how to step out of the cave in verses 31–36.

First, he tells us that we step out of the cave by *holding on to his teaching*. Faith means filling our minds with Jesus' teaching until we recognize this world's lies for the shadows that they really are. *"I gain understanding from your precepts... Your word is a lamp for my feet, a light on my path,"* says Psalm 119:104–105. If we say we believe in Jesus but neglect his Word, we cannot wonder if we still find ourselves languishing in spiritual darkness.

Second, he tells us that we step out of the cave by *co-operating with him as he sets us free*. The Jewish leaders would rather rewrite the history books in verse 33 and ignore Israel's

---

[6] Don't misunderstand Jesus' statement in verse 15 that he will not judge anyone. He says in 9:39 that his appearance is enough to expose hard hearts and reveal which people are heading for God's judgment.

[7] Although 9:9 reminds us that *"I am"* need not carry deep spiritual meaning, John expects us to spot what Jesus is saying when he hints three times that he is the *"I AM"* in verses 24, 28 and 58.

[8] Don't misunderstand verses 31–33 to mean that all of these believers were false ones. I will explain in the next chapter that Jesus' teaching proved which of his Judean converts were genuine and which were false.

slavery in Egypt in order to lie that they *"have never been slaves of anyone"*. *"Everyone who sins is a slave to sin,"* Jesus insists, but *"If the Son sets you free you will be free indeed."* If we repent of our sin, renounce its hold on our lives and renew our minds through God's Word by the power of his Holy Spirit, Jesus promises that the Gospel which forgives us from sin's penalty will also free us from its power. Paul explains: *"The grace of God has appeared that offers salvation to all people. It teaches us to say 'No' to ungodliness and worldly passions, and to live self-controlled, upright and godly lives in this present age."*[9]

Third, he warns us that when we step out of the cave, he will *send us back inside*. Jesus says he is the Light of the World while he is in the world in 9:5, but he adds in Matthew 5:14 that we are the light of the world now that he has gone back to heaven. That's why Paul takes the prophecy of Isaiah 49:6 and applies it in Acts 13:47 to the followers of Jesus. Jesus isn't inviting us just to step out of the cave like Neo. He is warning us that he will send us back inside the cave, like Morpheus, to rescue those who are still chained to the wall.

Let's step out of the cave like those in the crowd, and not be like the stubborn Jewish leaders who clung to the chains of wrong thinking which kept them tied to the cave wall. Morpheus continues: *"I'm trying to free your mind, Neo. But I can only show you the door. You're the one that has to walk through it."*

A far better saviour than Morpheus is calling. It's time for us to step out of the cave.

LOOK AT WHO JESUS REALLY IS

118

---

[9] Titus 2:11–12. The Hebrews had also been slaves to the Philistines, the Arameans, the Assyrians, the Persians, the Macedonians, the Seleucids and now the Romans!

John Was Jewish (8:37–59)

I know you are Abraham's descendants. Yet… if you were Abraham's children… then you would do what Abraham did.

(John 8:37, 39)

"We all know that a religion of race-consciousness is being propagated in Germany, involving the glorification of one race – the Teutons, and the vilification of another – the Jews." So warned one English church leader in 1938 during the rise of Adolf Hitler's regime. He continued:

> *Many may be shocked to learn that a favourite text-book of anti-Jewish propaganda is the Gospel according to St. John. Here, say the Nazis, is a piece of Scripture which needs no editing to bring it into line with our views. In it Jesus and the Jews confront each other in antagonism and hatred. The feud between them brought Him to death. To continue that feud is to perpetuate His spirit.[1]*

The Nazis are not the only Jew-haters who have tried to twist John's words to dress him up as one of their own. Many modern scholars use verses like these ones at the end of chapter 8 to paint the Christian faith in corrosive colours. They accuse John of racist stereotyping and argue that Christianity itself is inherently anti-Jewish and at odds with our modern, multicultural society. That's why we need to read verses like these ones very carefully – not just to reassure ourselves that John didn't hate his fellow

---

[1] Rev. Francis Evelyn in an article in the *Expository Times* in June 1938, entitled "The Supra-Racial Gospel".

Jews, but to learn from him what it means for us to truly love the Jewish nation.

John was Jewish. That might sound obvious, but it's easy to forget it amidst the cries of anti-Semitism. He wasn't just Jewish – he was so passionate about his nation that he once tried to persuade Jesus to annihilate a Samaritan village that showed a lack of respect for pilgrims heading to Jerusalem. He was one of the disciples who tried to persuade Jesus to restore David's great Jewish empire after his resurrection. He was on such friendly terms with the Jewish high priest that he was let into his courtyard on the night of Jesus' arrest and trial.[2] That's the irony when John is accused of anti-Semitism. Even though he now lived in pagan Ephesus, he was still as Jewish as a bagel at a Bethlehem bar mitzvah.

Note, however, that John makes a distinction between the northern Jews of Galilee and southern Jews of Judea. We noted this as the key to his statement in 4:44 that Jesus' home country was Judea and that the Judeans there ought to have welcomed him as warmly as the Galileans. Although John sometimes uses the Greek word *Ioudaioi* to mean *Jews* in general, he also uses it to distinguish between "the ugly" Galileans and the "good" Judeans (for example, 4:45 and 7:1 tell us that *"when he arrived in Galilee, the Galileans welcomed him"*, but *"he did not want to go about in Judea because the Judeans were looking for a way to kill him"*).[3] In fact, these verses at the end of chapter 8 make no sense unless *Ioudaioi* means *Judeans*. Verse 20 tells us that this encounter took place by the treasury box which was in a courtyard barred to anyone but Jews. Everyone in the crowd was Jewish, but those who opposed him were Judeans.

When we grasp this distinction, we find that John is actually eager to place Jesus in a Jewish context. *"Salvation is from the*

---

[2] Luke 9:51–56; Acts 1:6; John 18:15–16.

[3] The 2011 revision of the NIV text actually paraphrases this to read *"the Jewish leaders"* in order to make it clear John is talking about a specific group of southern Jews and not about Jews in general.

Jews", Jesus teaches in 4:22, and John's gospel refers to Abraham and Moses as many times as Matthew and Mark put together. Even when the southern Judeans despise Jesus' breeding and call him a Samaritan in verse 48, John still insists in 1:49 and 12:13 that Jesus is *"the King of Israel"*.

John's agenda in passages like this one is to convince his readers – both Jew and Gentile – that Jewishness is not a matter of genealogy but of *faith*. When he tells us literally that Nathanael is *"truly an Israelite"* in 1:47, he means to teach us that there are many false Israelites who masquerade as part of God's People. In case we miss this, he quotes Jesus' words in Revelation 3:9 to teach that many *"claim to be Jews though they are not, but are liars"*. In doing so, he simply continues the teaching of John the Baptist and of Jesus that many ethnic children of Abraham are spiritual children of the serpent Satan. He simply agrees with Paul's teaching in Galatians 4 that ethnic Jews can be Gentiles like Hagar and ethnic Gentiles can be Hebrews like Sarah.[4]

If that still strikes you as anti-Semitic, you need these verses to teach you how to truly love the Jewish nation. You need to turn to Romans 9–11, where Paul tells us that he loves the Jews so much that he would gladly go to hell himself if it means he can save them, and where he tells us that God wants to make ethnic Jews jealous through this message in order to provoke them to salvation. Jesus, John and Paul are all determined to kick away the ladder of false hope from under the feet of their fellow countrymen because it is the only way to make them lay hold of the outstretched arms of the Messiah who came to save them.[5] If you prefer to indulge your Jewish friends in their Christless religion, it doesn't make you more pro-Jewish than John. It's actually as anti-Jewish as it gets.

---

[4] Matthew 3:7; 12:34; 23:33; Galatians 4:21–31.

[5] That's why John doesn't even mention the destruction of the Temple in 70 AD. The closest he comes is in 4:21–24, where he warns Jews not to let the Temple distract them from worshipping God as he truly desires.

It therefore shouldn't surprise us that John records eight statements from Jesus in verses 42–59 which he knows will be abhorrent to Jewish ears: that he knows God intimately as his Father; that he has been sent by God,[6] is utterly sinless,[7] speaks the very words of God and is the focus of God's glory; that he is the giver of eternal life, the one Abraham saw in his theophanies[8] and – most shocking of all – none other than Yahweh himself, the great *"I AM"* of Exodus 3:14. The Jews may pick up stones to lynch him in verse 59, but it isn't for anti-Semitism. It is because he claims to be the Jewish Messiah, and they prefer to celebrate God's dealings with Israel in the past to surrendering to God's dealings with Israel in the present.

I hope you love the Jewish nation. I hope you love them as much as Jesus and John and Paul and the other New Testament writers. I hope you love them enough to tell them that their Jewishness can't save them. I hope you love them enough to tell them that they need to bow their knee to the Messiah who was born in Bethlehem in Judea.

---

[6] Interestingly, by accusing Jesus in verse 48 and 7:20 of being demonized, the unbelieving Jews affirm that his miracles are real. They know he has been sent by someone. The only debate is over whom.

[7] Don't miss the astonishing nature of this claim. The Jews have scrutinized Jesus' lifestyle for over two years, yet he dares challenge them to identify one single sin which he has committed.

[8] God's appearances to the patriarchs in Genesis are known as "theophanies". Paul tells us in Galatians 3:8 that through them God *"announced the gospel in advance to Abraham."*

What a Blind Man Saw
(9:1–41)

*Whether he is a sinner or not, I don't know. One thing
I do know. I was blind but now I see!*

(John 9:25)

When John wanted to explain what Jesus meant when he said *"I
am the Bread of Life"*, he recounted how he used five small barley
loaves to feed five thousand hungry mouths. He said this was a
miraculous sign which illustrated what Jesus meant through his
first *"I AM"* teaching. Now he helps us to understand what Jesus
meant when he said *"I am the Light of the World"* by recounting
another miraculous sign which he performed as an illustration.

Don't be fooled by the chapter division between chapters
8 and 9. John gives us plenty of clues to link this miracle to the
teaching which goes before. *"I am the Light of the World"*, Jesus
repeats in verse 5 as he sends the blind man to the Pool of Siloam,
the pool from which the water came which prompted his teaching
on the Holy Spirit in 7:37–39.[1] The themes of blindness and sight,
night and day, darkness and light, pervade this whole passage
and John expects us to understand that to step out of the cave we
must also see the things this blind man saw.

The Pharisees can see, but John shows us their spiritual
blindness in verses 1–3 and 13–16. He opens the chapter with
some of the Pharisees' teaching which the disciples had picked

---

[1] Siloam means *Sent* in Hebrew, and Nehemiah 3:15 tells us that the pool
was already known by this name. Jesus sent the blind man there to illustrate
7:37–39 as well as 8:12 – to show that he healed through the power of the
Holy Spirit.

up from their synagogues. They look at a blind beggar and assume that his sickness must be the result of God's judgment on either his sin or that of his parents. The Pharisees have used Scripture verses to teach that God judges people with sickness if they are less devoted to Moses' Law than they themselves are,[2] but they have completely missed the teaching in Scripture that no one – not even a Pharisee – is good enough to escape God's judgment.[3] Jesus dismissed their distorted view of Scripture by referring to *"your own Law"* in 8:17. As if to confirm it, they criticize Jesus for breaking the Sabbath without seeing that they are calling God himself a sinner for saving people on a Saturday![4] *Open your eyes and see the Living God!*, Jesus warns them. God doesn't go round striking beggars for not being as perfect as the Pharisees. He lets them reap the fruit of Adam's sin so that he can glorify the Father by enabling the blind to see.[5]

The beggar may be blind, but John tells us that he can see more than the Pharisees. When Jesus restores the blind man's sight,[6] the Pharisees dismiss him as a Sabbath-breaker, but the man sees through their blinkered logic and points out in verse 16 that anyone can see that Jesus has been sent by God. The Pharisees deny the facts and bully the key witnesses into silence in verses 18–24 – anything to support their preordained

---

[2] See Genesis 19:11; Deuteronomy 28:28; 2 Kings 6:18; Zephaniah 1:17. See also Acts 9:8; 13:11.

[3] Sickness entered the world through sin, but this does not mean that sick people are more sinful than the healthy. Jesus would correct this smug blindness again in Luke 13:1–5, since it compounded a sick person's main course of physical pain with an unnecessary side order of spiritual guilt.

[4] This clash over the Sabbath links Jesus' sixth sign at the Pool of Siloam in south Jerusalem to his third sign at the Pool of Bethesda in north Jerusalem in chapter 5.

[5] Although we can glorify God by the way in which we bear our sickness, Jesus clarifies in 11:4 and 14:11–12 that what he means here is that God made the man blind in order to glorify himself by healing him.

[6] Note that Jesus does not pray for the man to be healed, but he simply commands him to take a step of faith that he has been healed. It is as he acts in faith that he comes back seeing.

conclusion that Jesus is a sinner – but the man insists on the visible facts and tells them: *"One thing I do know. I was blind but now I see!"*

Morpheus warned Neo that *"You have to understand, most of these people are not ready to be unplugged. And many of them are so inured, so hopelessly dependent on the system, that they will fight to protect it."* Plato tells us that Socrates also warned that

> *When any of them is freed and suddenly forced to stand up and turn his neck round and walk and look towards the light, he will suffer sharp pains; the glare will distress him... Will he not fancy that the shadows which he formerly saw are truer than the objects which are now shown to him?*

Therefore it shouldn't surprise us when the blind Pharisees get angry and abusive towards the beggar who can see what they cannot. They rush back to their darkened understanding of Moses in verse 28 in order to avoid having to look at the one greater than Moses who stands before them. They hide behind their studies and diplomas to argue in verse 29 that Jesus is untrustworthy because he lacks proper accreditation.[7] They shield their eyes with the same false teaching which Jesus debunked in verse 3, throwing the healed beggar out of their cave with a cry that *"You were steeped in sin at birth; how dare you lecture us!"*

Jesus has already healed the man physically, but the chapter ends with him completing his work of spiritual healing. The man already sees more than the Pharisees do when he confesses Jesus is a godly prophet sent by God to do his will by exposing the blindness of Israel's leaders. He recognizes that

---

[7] Verse 29 cannot mean that the Pharisees did not know Jesus' background, since that would not fit in with 7:15, 27, 41 and 52. Rather, they are dismissing Jesus because he has not been accredited by any of their rabbinic schools. Acts 2:22 tells us that his accreditation came from a far better school.

Jesus' accreditation is not like the Pharisees' certificates but comes in the form of his unprecedented miracles. They prove that he is the Messiah about whom the Lord prophesied in Isaiah 42:5–9: *"I will take hold of your hand. I will keep you and will make you to be a covenant for the people and a light for the Gentiles, to open eyes that are blind, to free captives from prison and to release from the dungeon those who sit in darkness."*[8] Jesus therefore fulfils these words by helping the man to see that he is Daniel's Son of Man and Isaiah's messenger who would blind proud eyes and enlighten the eyes of the humble.[9] The chapter ends with the beggar worshipping Jesus in wide-eyed faith as Yahweh[10] and with Jesus accusing the Pharisees of a blindness which is made all the more grievous by their loud claims that they can see.[11]

"You see, but you do not observe," Sherlock Holmes tells Dr Watson, is the key to his great ability to solve crime. *"I make the point of never having any prejudices and of following docilely wherever fact may lead me."*[12]

We all have prejudices, backgrounds and beliefs which can stop us from looking at Jesus and seeing who he really is. John turns to each of us at the end of chapter 9 and urges us to throw them aside like Sherlock Holmes, or like a humble beggar, so that we can see what a blind man saw.

---

[8] Jesus is referring to these verses and to Isaiah 29:18, 35:5 and 61:1 when he urges John the Baptist in Matthew 11:5 to take his healing of the blind as proof that he is the Messiah prophesied by Isaiah.

[9] John explains this further at the end of part two of his gospel, by quoting from Isaiah 6:10 in 12:39–41.

[10] The word *kurios* in verse 38 could simply mean *Master* or *Sir*, but it was also the normal Greek word for *the Lord*. Since Jews knew that they must worship Yahweh alone, the rest of the verse forces the latter reading.

[11] By claiming that they could see enough to judge Jesus, the Pharisees actually passed judgment on themselves.

[12] This is an amalgamation of two quotes from Sir Arthur Conan Doyle's short stories – one from *A Scandal in Bohemia* (1891) and another from *The Reigate Squires* (1893).

David, Only More So
(10:1-30)

I am the good shepherd; I know my sheep and my sheep know me.

(John 10:14)

Moses wasn't the only spiritual hero that the Jewish leaders hid behind. They were also blinded by pride in their region's strong links back to King David. Jerusalem had been *"David's city"* and nearby Bethlehem *"David's town"*. The elders of Judah had been his friends while Saul pursued him, and they had received him as God's anointed king while the other tribes chose Saul's son. They comforted themselves that, unlike the Galileans or Samaritans, they southerners had a pretty good track record when it came to recognizing God's Messiah.[1]

That's why, after healing the blind man, Jesus continues his clash with the Pharisees by showing them that they cannot hide behind their links with David any more than behind their links with Moses (note the clue in verse 21 that this passage belongs with chapter 9 despite the chapter divisions). Although he doesn't mention David by name, he draws such clear parallels between himself and Israel's shepherd-king that he simply doesn't have to. He demonstrates to the Pharisees that he is like David, only more so.

David was a *shepherd-boy* who was overlooked by his brothers but chosen by God. Psalm 78:70–72 saw the climax of

---

[1] 1 Samuel 20:6; 30:26; 2 Samuel 2:1–3:1; 1 Chronicles 11:4–8; Luke 2:4, 11; John 7:42. The Hebrew word which is used repeatedly in 1 and 2 Samuel to describe David as God's anointed king is *messiah*.

Israel's early history as the moment when God *"chose David his servant and took him from the sheep pens; from tending the sheep he brought him to be the shepherd of his people Jacob, of Israel his inheritance. And David shepherded them with integrity of heart; with skilful hands he led them."* The prophets had used David as the benchmark for any future leader of Israel, contrasting his blind and self-centred successors with the Messiah who would come to shepherd them lovingly like David.[2] The Pharisees knew those verses well enough to see that Jesus was claiming to be the Messiah when he told them in verse 11 that *"I am the good shepherd."*[3]

David was a man who *divided and defined* Israel. He proved a rallying point for those who truly loved the Lord during Saul's reign, and he provoked people to fierce loyalty or gross treachery when he succeeded Saul. Even after the death of his son, the Israelites split over whether they should submit to the anointed dynasty of David or manufacture rival rulers of their own. When Jesus told the Pharisees in verses 7 and 9 that *"I am the gate for the sheep... whoever enters through me will be saved"*, he was warning that they should expect him to divide the sheep from the goats in Israel, just like David.[4] These third and fourth *"I AM"* sayings were a claim that he was God's Messiah and was like David, only more so.

David was a man who *risked his life to save* God's People. He told Saul that he often chased after lions and bears which attacked his flock, despising his own life in the hope of snatching his precious sheep from their jaws. He displayed the same willingness to lose his life to save God's People when he fought the giant Goliath, when he pursued and attacked a much

---

[2] See Isaiah 40:11; Jeremiah 23:1–6; Ezekiel 34:1–31; 37:24; Micah 5:4; Zechariah 13:7. The Messiah would be the Great Shepherd whom David described in Psalm 23.

[3] Their failure to understand Jesus in verse 6 was due to the spiritual blindness which Jesus rebuked in chapter 9.

[4] Jesus will expand on this theme through his sixth *"I AM"* saying in John 14:6.

bigger Amalekite army, and when he rode to conquer each of the foreign armies which had long oppressed Israel. Jesus picks up on this when he tells the Pharisees that *"the good shepherd lays down his life for the sheep"*, and when he tells them that the gate of the sheep pen does more than let sheep in – it also keeps thieves and robbers out.

If we understand this context, then we find a lot more in these verses than tender words of comfort. We grasp why Jesus spoke them in a way which loaded them with deliberate confrontation.

When he tells the Jewish leaders that *"I am the good shepherd"*, he is also telling them that they are strangers, thieves and robbers. They are like the self-serving shepherds of Judah who were condemned by the prophets, since they are robbing and murdering the people they lead by preventing them from receiving his offer of life to the full.[5] When they threaten the crowd or the blind man and his parents into shutting their ears to Jesus, they rob them of God's salvation in order to safeguard their own position. For all they hide behind Judea's long links back to David, they have failed to recognize David's greater Son, and they have acted like the lions and bears which David had to chase and kill.

When Jesus tells the Jewish leaders that *"I am the gate"*, he is also telling them that they themselves are shut outside the sheep pen. Jesus said this plainly in the words he spoke at the Feast of Tabernacles in September 29 AD, but John also tells us from verse 22 onwards that he taught this even more plainly when he returned to Jerusalem for the Feast of Dedication that December.[6] He returned to his theme of shepherding and told them, *"You do not believe because you are not my sheep. My sheep listen to my voice;*

---

[5] Although the first half of verse 10 is a good description of the aims of the great Thief, the Devil, Jesus actually intends it to describe the Pharisees as the thieving agents of the Devil.

[6] Literally the *Feast of Renewal*, it celebrated the rededication of the Temple by Judas Maccabaeus in December 165 BC. Nowadays, it is more commonly known as Hanukkah.

I know them, and they follow me."[7] For all they boast that their ancestors were faithful supporters of David, they are more like Saul's supporters, or like Shimei and Sheba who cursed David and rebelled against him. Since the Judeans reject their own Messiah and refuse to step out of the cave to receive his offer of salvation, he will gather *"other sheep that are not of this sheepfold"* – sheep like the Samaritans and Gentiles that they despise.[8]

When Jesus tells the Jewish leaders that he is willing to lay down his life to save God's sheep, he is also predicting how his clash with them is going to end. He will not leave God's sheep to predators like themselves, as a hired hand might do, but will act like David, only more so. He will let them kill him as the price of plucking God's People from their jaws.[9] He tells them in verses 17–18 that they will only kill him because he will let them do so and that once they have done their worst to him he will return from the grave to protect and preserve his flock forever.[10]

John wants us to search our own hearts to check that we are not like the Pharisees – resisting God's shepherd and seeking another gateway to salvation. He wants us to be sure that we are not still blind to who Jesus really is.

For Jesus is standing before us like the great Old Testament hero David, only more so.

---

[7] Although this passage is confrontational, it also comforts us with a promise of deep intimacy with God if we believe, particularly in verses 3–4, 13–15 and 27–28.

[8] Comparing verse 23 with Acts 5:12 reveals that the first meetings of the Church which would fulfil this global mission actually took place in the very place where Jesus clashed here with the Jewish leaders!

[9] This should be a challenge to any church leader. Pastoring means selflessly pouring out our lives to serve God's People, not using them as a means to gain position. Farm shepherds may only breed sheep for the slaughter, but Jude 11–13 warns that church shepherds ought to be willing to be slaughtered for the sheep.

[10] Since John 6:44 and 65 assure us that we only choose God because he first chose us, we can trust him to protect us and enable us to persevere in that choice till the end. Our assurance of our salvation stems from the goodness of our shepherd, not from our own goodness as sheep.

Blinder than a Pharisee (10:31–42)

> *"We are not stoning you for any good work,"* they
> replied, *"but for blasphemy, because you, a mere
> man, claim to be God."*
>
> (John 10:33)

"Almost everything our fathers taught us about Christ is false," says
Sir Leigh Teabing in *The Da Vinci Code*, with that peremptory tone
which is the hallmark of Dan Brown's novels. *"Jesus was viewed
by His followers as a mortal prophet... a great and powerful man,
but a man nonetheless... Jesus' establishment as 'the Son of God'
was officially proposed and voted on by the Council of Nicaea... A
relatively close vote at that."*[1] Even though *The Da Vinci Code* is
sold in the fiction section of bookstores, it is amazing how many
educated readers read it as fact. They pride themselves on being
smart, but they are blinder than a Pharisee.

The Jewish leaders disliked Jesus' teaching, but even they
were not blind enough to miss what he was saying. As early
as 5:18, they tried to kill him for *"calling God his own Father,
making himself equal with God"*. He taught so plainly in the rest
of chapter 5 that he was God the Judge, the giver of eternal life
and the central focus of the Old Testament Scriptures that he
knew if he returned to Jerusalem openly with his brothers he
would surely die. When he followed them up to the Temple later,
the Jewish leaders were so aware of what he meant in 8:58 that

---

[1] Dan Brown in *The Da Vinci Code* (2003).

they picked up stones to execute him for blasphemy.[2] Here in 10:33, they tell him that *"We are not stoning you for any good work, but for blasphemy, because you, a mere man, claim to be God."* Jesus claimed repeatedly to be fully man and fully God. For Dan Brown or anyone else to fail to grasp that is for them to be blinder than a Pharisee.[3]

But people do fail to see it. The preface to John's gospel in one tenth-century manuscript says that *"The apostle John, whom the Lord Jesus loved most, wrote this gospel last of all at the request of the bishops of Asia against Cerinthus and other heretics."*[4] Cerinthus was a very clever scholar with a highly developed "adoptionist" view of Jesus, which claimed that he was neither fully man nor fully God. That's why John fills his gospel with details that stress the full humanity of Jesus – he gets tired and hungry and thirsty and angry and sheds tears[5] – and with passages like this one which stress his full divinity. Dan Brown's novels might not have been on sale in downtown Ephesus, but the city was nevertheless home to many ancient teachers who were just like him.

C. S. Lewis famously tackled this issue in his book *Mere Christianity*. He points out that all four gospels show that – whatever little else they had in common – the disciples, the Pharisees and the crowd all understood that Jesus claimed repeatedly to be God. Other prophets talked about the Lord and said *"he is..."*, but Jesus talked about him and said *"I AM..."* Other rabbis taught people how to find forgiveness from God, but Jesus personally granted forgiveness as if he were the God

---

[2] They tried to stone him to death because Leviticus 24:14–16 stipulated this as the penalty for blasphemy.

[3] The reason the Jewish leaders crucified Jesus in 19:7 was *"because he claimed to be the Son of God"*.

[4] This is in the preface of the *Codex Toletanus*, a manuscript from early medieval Spain.

[5] John 2:14–17; 4:6, 8; 11:35–36; 19:28. Although this chapter defends the full divinity of Jesus, John also warns us not to deny his full humanity by singing sentimental nonsense such as *"the little Lord Jesus, no crying he makes"*.

they had offended. Other preachers told their listeners how God created the world and would visit it with Final Judgment, but Jesus looked back to *"the glory I had with you before the world began"* and claimed that *"the Father judges no one, but has entrusted all judgment to the Son."* Other saintly leaders helped their followers to worship God, but Jesus encouraged his followers to worship himself.[6] In view of this great weight of evidence, C. S. Lewis argues, we only have three options open to us: either Jesus claimed to be God but knew he wasn't (he was therefore a liar), or he claimed to be God but didn't know he wasn't (he was therefore a lunatic), or he claimed to be God because he was God.

So take your choice. Was Jesus a liar? Or does John eliminate this as an option when he tells us that Jesus' disciples and his enemies scrutinized his life to see whether John the Baptist had been right when he hailed him as the sinless Saviour of the world, and Jesus challenged them confidently after two long years of scrutiny: *"Can any of you prove me guilty of sin?"*[7]

Or was he a lunatic? Were the Pharisees right when they accused him of being a madman in 10:20, or is the fact that they accused him repeatedly of being empowered by a demon a tacit admission that they knew his miracles must be more than just delusion?[8] Ancient heretics and modern novelists might attempt to deny the historicity of John's seven miraculous signs, but it is significant that for the first few centuries of AD history Jesus' enemies only dared challenge the source of his miraculous power and not the fact of the miracles themselves.[9]

BLINDER THAN A PHARISEE (10:31–42)

---

[6] John 5:21–30; 6:62; 9:38; 17:5; 20:23; 20:28–29. He makes similar claims in the other three gospels too.

[7] John 1:29; 8:46.

[8] John 7:20; 8:48, 52; 10:20–21 or Matthew 9:34; 10:25; 12:22–32.

[9] Jesus himself points out in 10:37–38 that his amazing miracles preclude the idea that he is a liar or a madman.

C. S. Lewis therefore concludes with a challenge to anyone who has fallen for the teaching of Cerinthus, Arius, Muhammad, the Mormons, Unitarians, Jehovah's Witnesses or Dan Brown:

> *I am trying to prevent anyone saying the really foolish thing that people often say about Him: "I'm ready to accept Jesus as a great moral teacher, but I don't accept His claim to be God." That is the one thing we must not say. A man who was merely a man and said the sort of things Jesus said would not be a great moral teacher. He would either be a lunatic – on a level with the man who says he is a poached egg – or he would be the Devil of Hell. You must make your choice. Either this man was, and is, the Son of God: or else a madman or something worse. You can shut Him up for a fool, you can spit at Him and kill Him as a demon; or you can fall at His feet and call Him Lord and God. But let us not come with any patronising nonsense about His being a great human teacher. He has not left that open to us. He did not intend to.[10]*

As John approaches the end of this second section of his gospel with its call to look at who Jesus really is, he therefore wants us to pause and recognize why the Jewish leaders picked up stones.[11] He doesn't want us to swallow the flawed speculations of false teachers or fiction writers. He tells us in no uncertain terms that, if we do so, we are blinder than a Pharisee.

---

[10] C. S. Lewis in his chapter "The Shocking Alternative" in *Mere Christianity* (1952).

[11] The verse Jesus quotes from Psalm 82:6 in verse 34 is quite obscure. He does not quote it to explain its meaning but to prove to the Jewish leaders that they understand Scripture far less well than they think.

Why God Doesn't Answer Prayer (11:1–15)

*Now Jesus loved Martha and her sister and Lazarus.
So when he heard that Lazarus was ill, he stayed
where he was two more days.*

(John 11:5–6)

Oh, come off it. Let's get real. It's all very well for John to tell us who Jesus is – the healer, the provider, the satisfier and the deliverer – but we all know that he often feels like none of those things at the moment we most need him. Our experience is more like that of Nikabrik in *Prince Caspian*, another book by C. S. Lewis. The cynical dwarf gives full vent to his anger at the Saviour's long delay:

> *Either Aslan is dead, or he is not on our side. Or else
> something stronger than himself keeps him back...
> Anyway, he was in Narnia only once that I ever heard of,
> and he didn't stay long. You may drop Aslan out of the
> reckoning.*[1]

It's all too easy for us to get cynical like Nikabrik. John had been tempted to succumb to the disappointment of unanswered prayer when God freed Peter from death row with a mighty miracle but left John's brother James to die there.[2] That's why

---

[1] C. S. Lewis in *Prince Caspian* (1951). Aslan represents Jesus in the Chronicles of Narnia.
[2] See Acts 12. John was therefore supremely qualified to teach on this subject.

he slows down to tell us about the last of Jesus' seven miraculous signs in a bit more detail. He wants to use two sisters and their unanswered prayer to encourage us that Jesus is who this section says he is, even when he doesn't feel much like it straightaway.

Mary and Martha had placed their trust in Jesus.[3] When their brother was struck with a fatal sickness, they had managed to get their prayer request through to him in time. Jesus had even sent back an encouraging promise that *"This illness will not end in death. No, it is for God's glory so that God's Son may be glorified through it."* It sounded so much like the promise about the blind beggar in 9:3 that they must have told their friends and neighbours that they were certain their brother would not die. Imagine, then, standing in their shoes as they wept at their brother's funeral.[4] People have walked away from the Christian faith over disappointments far smaller.[5]

John explains why Jesus didn't do as they expected, although if you rush over these verses you will miss it. The NIV translation used to do so, rendering verses 5–6 as *"Jesus loved Martha and her sister and Lazarus. **Yet** when he heard that Lazarus was sick, he stayed where he was two more days"*. The revised edition recognizes that the little Greek word *oun* at the start of verse 6 actually means *therefore*, and renders it *"Jesus loved Martha and her sister and Lazarus. **So** when he heard that Lazarus was ill, he stayed where he was two more days."* It's important, because John isn't telling us that Jesus loved the two sisters in spite of their unanswered prayer. He is telling us that Jesus delayed his answer precisely because he loved them.[6]

---

[3] Luke 10:38–42 describes the sisters' close friendship with Jesus.

[4] Jewish funerals took place within twenty-four hours of death, so Lazarus' corpse was well and truly buried and decaying by the time Jesus arrived at Bethany. See verse 39.

[5] Some fall away by leaving church altogether. Others fall away by continuing with church but growing spiritually cold on the inside.

[6] God is never callous in his slowness to answer prayer. Jesus weeps with the sisters in verses 35–36.

I wish I had muscles like my best friend Nick. When I acted as his groomsman, we both went to the same tailor and my measurements seemed pitifully puny next to his. But the truth is I don't want bigger muscles as much as I pretend, because if I did then I would join him in the gym where he puts in hours and hours of weightlifting to develop them. That's the challenge which John wants to lay down for us as he continues his explanation in verses 14–15. Jesus adds, *"Lazarus is dead, and for your sake I am glad I was not there, so that you may believe."* Glad? Glad that he lingered two days so that Lazarus died before he made it back to Judea?![7] Yes, because only by exercising our faith muscles in the gym of unanswered prayer will we ever develop the kind of belief that moves a mountain.

Jesus wanted to train his disciples not to respond to unanswered prayers by *growing bitter*. Martha reproaches Jesus in verse 21 when he arrives too late in Bethany by pointing out how much better things might have been "if only" he had come straightaway. Mary does the same in verse 32 when she uses another "if only" to blame him for her brother's death. It's all too easy to let "if only" rob us of our faith in who Jesus is, when he actually wants to use unanswered prayer to do the very opposite. He could have easily mapped out his strategy to the sisters beforehand, but he wanted to teach them and his disciples to trust that he is who he says he is, even when all the evidence suggests he isn't.[8] He promised them that Lazarus' illness would not *end* in death. When our circumstances do not match up with God's promises, it simply means we have not yet reached the end of the story.

WHY GOD DOESN'T ANSWER PRAYER (11:1–15)

137

---

[7] Typically, John covers Jesus' three months of ministry in Perea from January to March 30 AD in just three verses in 10:40–42 – ministry which warranted six chapters in Luke! John just wants to get back to Judea and he uses a reference to *the light of this world* in verse 9 to remind us that the Judeans tried to kill Jesus on his last visit.

[8] When we let disappointment make us doubt God's love towards us, we become like the cynical crowd in verse 37 instead of like Martha in verse 27.

Jesus wanted to train his disciples not to respond to unanswered prayers by *dumbing down the Word of God*. When Jesus tells Martha that her brother will rise again, she immediately spiritualizes what he says so that it applies to the future instead of to the present. Is it just a coincidence that the unanswered prayer in this chapter is for *healing* and for *the resurrection of the dead*? Aren't some of the hardest unanswered prayers to bear those that we pray for a loved one who needs his body restored or her soul reborn?[9] Jesus responds to our discouragement in praying for the sick or in sharing the Gospel by insisting in his fifth *"I AM"* saying that *"I am the Resurrection and the Life"*. He warns us not to let delays make us downgrade God's precious promises to little more than Monopoly money.

Jesus wanted to train his disciples not to respond to unanswered prayers with *passivity*. Do you remember how Jesus taught the servants at the wedding in Cana that it required a simple act of faith on their part to trigger a mighty miracle? That is how faith happens, and this time is no exception. Jesus commands the funeral guests to remove the stone which seals the tomb, to stop making excuses and to believe so they can see. When they do so, he has to shout *"Lazarus, come out!"* because such faith was enough to raise many corpses unless he specified which one! If you grow cynical like Nikabrik, you will see nothing, but if you believe like the sisters and the disciples, *"you will see the glory of God"*.

Fourteen years later, in 44 AD, the Lord would rescue Peter from death in response to the Church's prayers, but not John's brother James. Through this delay in healing Lazarus, Jesus had prepared his beloved disciple for that dark day of disappointment. Whatever unanswered prayers we may experience, he wants to use them in the same way to make us

---

[9] Martha had to call her sister aside privately in verse 28 because their friends approved of their weeping at their brother's grave but not of their going to Jesus in faith for healing.

ready for what lies ahead. He wants to strengthen our faith so that we bring him more glory tomorrow than we ever could have brought him without delayed answers to prayer today.[10]

---

[10] John tells us in 11:48 and 12:9–11 that because the delay made Jesus' final miracle more dramatic and more public, it resulted in far more conversions than if he had answered the sisters' prayer straightaway.

Why God Doesn't Heal
(11:16–44)

Then Jesus said, "Did I not tell you that if you believe, you will see the glory of God?"

(John 11:40)

Jesus healed people. A lot. Three of John's seven signs involve healing and one involves raising the dead. So what should surprise us is not that John tells us in 14:12 that God wants to continue to heal people through us,[1] but that we often come away unsuccessful when we try to do so. John wants to help us by finishing his teaching on why God doesn't always answer prayer with some specific teaching on why he doesn't always heal people either.

John wants to teach us that we often fail to see people healed because *we lack God's passion*. He begins by telling us in verse 4 that God is passionate to be glorified and, in verse 40, that miracles are a vital way to display *"the glory of God"*. He tells us in verses 45–48 and 12:18–19 that this miracle was a signpost which successfully pointed many crowds to God. So if Jesus was so passionate about God's glory that he risked looking foolish in front of the people of Bethany,[2] and if the apostles were so passionate about his glory that they risked looking foolish all across the world, then we can hardly be surprised

---

[1] This promise ties in with Matthew 10:7–8, Mark 16:17–18 and Luke 10:8–9, and with scenes like Acts 8:4–8.

[2] This Bethany in Judea was different from the northern Bethany on the other side of the River Jordan where John the Baptist had ministered in 1:28.

that we see so few miracles when we tend to play it safe instead. John Wimber's healing breakthrough came when

> *I resolved in my heart at that moment that from that point out I was going to do the foolish thing in the eyes of the world. I didn't know it was going to be the foolish thing in the eyes of the church too, but I determined that night that if Christ was worth coming to at all, he was worth coming all the way with.*[3]

Apart from God's glory, John tells us that Jesus' other passion was for people. He tells us in verses 3, 5 and 11 that Jesus performed this miracle because he loved Lazarus and his family, and that even the cynical crowd in verses 35–36 remarked on his tears, saying *"See how he loved him!"*[4] Fruitful healing ministry invariably begins with God filling our hearts with the same love which characterized Jesus' healing ministry.[5] Mahesh Chavda remembers that his own breakthrough came when *"The Lord broke off a little piece of his heart and placed it inside me... I was learning that the power of God was to be found in the love of God... The healings came almost as a by-product. I learned that only love can make a miracle."*[6]

141

John wants to teach us that we often fail to see people healed because *we lack God's perspective*. Whereas we look at sickness as a physical problem, Jesus saw it as the hallmark of Satan's hatred of humankind.[7] John uses the strange Greek verb

---

[3] John Wimber speaking in 1985 at the "Signs and Wonders" conference in Anaheim, California.

[4] Verse 35 is the shortest verse in the Bible. It stresses Jesus' tender love and full humanity.

[5] See Matthew 9:35–36; 14:14; 20:34 or Mark 1:41; 5:19.

[6] Mahesh Chavda in his autobiography, which he entitled *Only Love Can Make a Miracle* (1990). We also see Jesus' love in the tender way he follows up on the healing in verse 44.

[7] He even calls back problems "Satan's prison" in Luke 13:16. Peter has the same perspective in Acts 10:38.

embrimaomai in verses 33 and 38, which means literally that he *snorted like a horse* eager to get into battle. He uses another verb, *tarassō*, in verse 33 to tell us that when Jesus saw the grieving mourners and the tomb, his heart was *churned up* like the sea. The truth is that we tend to put up with the existence of sickness all around us, offering little godly challenge to the pretended authority of Satan. The great healing evangelist John G. Lake said that his breakthrough came when he saw his sister dying and

> *A great cry to God, such as had never before come from my soul, went up to God. She must not die! I would not have it! Had not Christ died for her?... No words of mine can convey to another soul the cry that was in my heart and the flame of hatred for death and sickness that the Spirit of God had stirred within me. The very wrath of God seemed to possess my soul!*[8]

John wants to teach us that we often fail to see people healed because *we lack God's power*. Verse 41 is the closest Jesus ever comes to praying for someone to be healed in the gospels, because the rest of the time he simply commands sickness to leave or tells the sick person to do the thing their sickness stops them from doing. Note, however, that on closer examination this actually isn't a prayer for healing at all. He simply tells the crowd that because he has spent long hours alone in prayer, he is sure that even death cannot resist his command.[9] The one who called the Twelve *"that they might **be with him** and that he might send them out to preach and to have authority to drive out demons"*, and who told them to give themselves to *"prayer and fasting"* if

---

[8] John G. Lake in *Adventures in God* (c.1930).

[9] In doing so, Jesus reminds us that, when we pray in public, we should consider those who are listening.

they wanted to heal the sick, still calls us to prayer in private as the pathway to power in public.[10]

John wants to teach us that we often fail to see people healed because *we lack God's perseverance*. God never gives up when circumstances stand against him, and neither does Jesus as he stands outside Lazarus' tomb. Despite the fact that the man is four days dead and his body stinks of decay, Jesus reminds the crowd that faith begins by stepping out in obedience despite all evidence to the contrary. *"Did I not tell you that if you believe, you will see the glory of God?"* he asks, quashing the idea that seeing is believing. Jesus did not give up when a blind man was not fully healed the first time round in Mark 8:22–25, and neither must we. When we have prayed for someone and they have not been healed, when their symptoms persist, and when those round us give up in despair, even then God promises to heal through us if we have faith to *"Take away the stone"*.

Does that mean there is never a time when we should stop praying for people to be healed and start preparing them for death? No. Jesus suggests in verse 4 that God decrees a time when people will die of sickness,[11] but this passage warns us that we reach that conclusion far too readily. God wants to heal people far more than we imagine.

John Wimber continues:

> *I was praying for the sick, not because I had seen the sick healed but because that was what Scripture teaches Christians to do. Over the course of the next ten months, week in and week out, I prayed for people – and not one person was healed... God spoke clearly to me: "Do not preach your experience. Preach my word."... At the end of*

---

[10] Mark 3:14–15; 9:29. We need to understand from Luke 5:17 and 24:49 and Acts 2:22 and 10:38 that Jesus healed the sick because God's was power with him, and that he promises God's same power to us.

[11] 2 Kings 13:14 and 21 tell us that Elisha was full of God's healing power and yet still died of an illness.

> *this ten-month period, when I was at my lowest point, a woman was healed... This was the beginning of a trickle that soon became a steady stream.*[12]

Jesus promises that if we share God's *passion* to display his love and glory; if we share his *perspective* that sickness is the spiteful work of Satan; if we receive his *power* through times of focused prayer and fasting; and if we *persevere* with faith when healing does not come straightaway – then we will also see that steady stream of healing miracles flowing through us too.

---

[12] John Wimber in *Power Evangelism* (1985).

This Man Must Die
(11:45–12:19)

He did not say this on his own, but as high priest
that year he prophesied that Jesus would die for the
Jewish nation.

(John 11:51)

We have now read all seven of John's miraculous signs. We have read five of Jesus' seven *"I AM"* sayings. We have almost reached the end of this second section of John's gospel, which tells us to look at who Jesus really is. Now, to help us grasp not only who Jesus is but also what he came to do, John gives us three unexpected prophecies from three most unlikely prophets. Together, they offer us one uniform conclusion. There is no doubt about it: Jesus has to die.

The first unlikely prophet is the Jewish high priest Caiaphas in 11:45–57, and John wants us to understand that he speaks for his nation as a whole.[1] He addresses the Sanhedrin – the full assembly of Israel's top seventy-one religious leaders – and the Greek word John uses in verse 47 to describe its being *called together* is *sunagō*, the root of the word *synagogue*.[2] This, then, was the gathering of both the chief priests and the Pharisees, both the rulers of the Temple and the rulers of the synagogue.

---

[1] Caiaphas was high priest from 18 to 36 AD, but his father-in-law Annas was the power behind the priesthood. The Romans deposed Annas as high priest in 15 AD, but he was succeeded by five sons and one son-in-law.

[2] He also uses this word in verse 52 to describe God *calling together* a true Synagogue from every nation.

They endorse his prophecy and make a national decision that this man must die.

The Sanhedrin are blind to the identity of Jesus. They know his miracles are signposts pointing to who he really is, but their eyes are too focused on preserving their political power to read what is written on the signs. Rome had granted them authority to rule over internal Jewish affairs, and if Rome heard rumours that the crowds were rallying to their Messiah then the Sanhedrin feared that Rome would *"come and take away both our temple and our nation"*.[3] Caiaphas rudely interrupts with his own prophetic solution: *"It is better for you that one man die for the people than that the whole nation perish."*[4] He meant that even God himself must not be allowed to threaten their grip on power, but John explains in verse 51 that he spoke far more truly than he knew. As high priest, he was the man who offered sacrifices in the Temple, and through the Holy Spirit he had identified the perfect sacrifice to save God's People. Instead of looking at Jesus' power to raise Lazarus and repenting, he looked at Jesus as a threat to his own power and made a resurrection grounds for murder.[5]

The second unlikely prophet is Mary of Bethany, the sister of Lazarus, in 12:1–11. A few months earlier in Luke 10:38–42, Jesus had commended her for prioritizing fellowship with him over ministry for him. Now at a banquet in Jesus' honour at their house, Martha is still serving and Lazarus is reclining, but Mary gets up and starts worshipping instead.[6] She breaks a flask of expensive perfume, pours it on Jesus' feet, then wipes them

---

[3] The Jewish leaders literally say *"take away our place and nation"*, but Acts 6:13–14 and 21:28 show us that by *place* they mean the Temple.

[4] Caiaphas lost his position as high priest anyway in 36 AD, and the Romans destroyed Jerusalem and its Temple in 70 AD. When we reject God's leading because we love an idol more, he destroys that idol anyway.

[5] John mentions the fairly obscure village of Ephraim in 11:54 as another little proof he was actually there.

[6] Matthew 26:6 suggests that Martha served because she was the wife or widow of Simon the Leper.

dry with her hair. Judas Iscariot is incensed that the perfume might have been sold for a year's wages, feigning concern that three hundred denarii could have helped the poor but actually thinking about how much it could have helped himself.[7] John was a guest at the banquet and still remembers, as he explains to us what her lavish act of worship prophesied, the way that the fragrance of her perfume filled the whole house.

Mary was saying that Jesus was her *King*, since nard had to be imported from far-off India and could only be afforded in royal palaces. The beloved bride in Song of Songs expresses her love for King Solomon by telling her friends that *"While the king was at his table, my nard spread its fragrance,"* so – whether consciously or unconsciously – Mary re-enacts that scene for all to smell.[8]

She was also saying that Jesus was her *Saviour*, since she was copying a similar act of worship for Jesus performed by a prostitute who repented a year earlier in Luke 7.[9] Jesus had responded to the sinful woman's tears by declaring to all the dinner guests that *"her many sins have been forgiven"*. Now Mary loosens her hair like a prostitute herself, and performs the same act of worship to make a confession: For all that she is one of "the good" people of Judea, she needs Jesus to be her Saviour as much as did a sinful Galilean.

Finally, Mary was saying that *Jesus must die*, since the Jews anointed corpses with perfume before they buried them. She may not have known what she was doing, but Jesus explains this in verse 7 – a wise man brought him myrrh at his birth to

---

[7] John 12:8 is not an excuse for churches to renege on helping the poor. Jesus tells us that true churches will always have the poor among them – if they don't, they are more like Judas than like Jesus.

[8] Although some translations of Song of Songs 1:12 render the Hebrew word *nayrd* as *perfume*, it is exactly the same Hebrew word which is translated *nard* in Song of Songs 4:13 and 14.

[9] Matthew 26:6–13 and Mark 14:3–9 emphasize that she anointed his *head* to link back to 1 Samuel 16:1–13, but John emphasizes that she anointed his *feet* to link back to Luke 7:36–50. She had enough perfume to do both.

prophesy that he had been born to die, and now a wise woman has brought him nard to prophesy that the time has come for this to happen.[10] He is only six days away from death, and the Holy Spirit has led her to focus her worship on the fact this man must die.[11]

The third unlikely prophet is the fickle crowd in 12:12–19.[12] They hear that Jesus is entering the capital city and they unwittingly quote the prophecies about the Messiah in Psalm 118. John makes it clear in verse 16 that they simply thought back to the triumph of Judas Maccabaeus in 165 BC. When he had entered the capital, their forefathers had waved palm branches and shouted worship from the Psalms.[13] As they do the same for Jesus now, John tells us that they were doing more than they knew.

They were proclaiming that Jesus was the *Saviour* when they shouted from Psalm 118:25 the Hebrew word *Hosanna*, meaning *"Save us!"* They were proclaiming that he was their *King* when they carried on the quote and declared that he came in the name of the Lord. They proclaimed he was their *Messiah* when they cut down branches from the trees to worship him as decreed in verse 27 of the psalm. John makes this explicit by changing the words that they shouted in Matthew 21:9, calling him *"the Son of David"*, and explaining for his Gentile readers that this meant he was *"the king of Israel"*. He also adds his own quotation from Zechariah 9:9 to tell us that they proclaimed *this man must die*, since Psalm 118:22 also prophesied that the Jews would reject him and Psalm 118:17 prophesied his resurrection from the dead. John reminds his readers that Zechariah

---

[10] Matthew 2:11; Luke 23:55–24:1; John 19:39–40.

[11] Matthew and Mark record this event as if it happened *after* Jesus entered Jerusalem on a donkey. They do so to show it triggered Judas' decision to betray Jesus, but John sticks to strict chronology instead.

[12] They are fickle, because only a few days later their cries of *"Hosanna"* turn to cries of *"Crucify!"*

[13] 2 Maccabees 10:7.

promised that the Messiah would not enter the capital on a mighty charger, but on a humble donkey.

Caiaphas; Mary; the fickle crowd. They didn't understand in full what they all prophesied, but they all teach us who Jesus really is. The one who has told us repeatedly that he is God's own Son has ridden into the capital because he is God's only Saviour. Let's follow the example of Mary and bow down in worship. Yahweh has become a man, and has decreed this man must die.

Seeds, Snakes and Sunlight
(12:20–36)

Very truly I tell you, unless a grain of wheat falls to the ground and dies, it remains only a single seed. But if it dies, it produces many seeds.

(John 12:24)

The hero never dies in a good action story. Even my five-year-old son can tell you that.

"Heroes never die," claimed Mickey Spillane, the bestselling author of the Mike Hammer detective series, *"otherwise you don't have a hero. You can't kill a hero."* Sylvester Stallone's Rambo agreed, claiming that *"Heroes don't die. They just reload."*[1] So when John turns his full attention to the fact that Jesus must die, he thinks we are going to need an explanation. He thinks we need to hear what Jesus says about seeds, snakes and sunlight.

Verses 20–26 begin with Jesus at the height of his popularity. Not only are the Jewish leaders scared in 11:48 that *"everyone will believe in him"* and, in 12:19, that *"the whole world has gone after him"*, but now even the Greeks are trying to book an appointment with him.[2] They go to Philip (perhaps because his name suggested some Greek ancestry), and he goes to Andrew (perhaps because he also had a Greek name and because the two of them began their ministry in chapter

---

[1] Mickey Spillane speaking in an interview with *Crime Time* magazine in 2001; Sylvester Stallone in *Rambo* (Lionsgate, 2008).

[2] Up until this moment, Jesus has warned in 2:4, 4:21, 4:23, 7:30 and 8:20 that his time has not yet come. His announcement that the time has now come marks a turning point in the story, leading to 13:1 and 17:1.

1 simply by bringing people to see Jesus). The arrival of these Greeks prompts Jesus to teach the crowds why it is now vital that he should die. Note that John tells us that it is *in reply* to the Greeks' request that Jesus announces that his time has finally come.[3] He tells the crowd that *"Unless a grain of wheat falls to the ground and dies, it remains only a single seed. But if it dies, it produces many seeds."*

Remember, John has told us six times so far that Jesus' time has not yet come.[4] We therefore need to see this as a major turning point in his gospel, which prepares us for the theme which will dominate its third section. John repeats in 13:1 and 17:1 that it is time for Jesus to die, and he packs chapters 13 to 17 with instruction for Jesus' followers on how to co-operate with his plan to continue his ministry through them when he has gone.[5] Remember that John's original readers were looking back with sad nostalgia to the glory days when Jesus and his apostles walked the earth. He tells them to shift their eyes back onto Jesus alone and to recognize in verse 23 that Jesus' death was his glory day! Because that one seed died, he caused many seeds to sprout through whom he carries on his global mission. John wants his readers in Greek-speaking Ephesus, and also us, to wake up to the fact that Jesus died so that we could live and take his message to the world.[6]

Naturally, this talk of death makes Jesus' heart very troubled in verses 27–33. Like us, he struggled with his destiny,

[3] John does not call them *Hellēnistai*, or *Greek-speaking Jews*, as in Acts 6:1 and 9:29. He calls them *Hellēnes*, meaning *Greek Gentiles*, albeit those interested enough in Judaism to come to the Passover.

[4] John 2:4; 7:6, 8, 30, 39; 8:20.

[5] The equivalent of verse 25 can be found in Matthew 10:39 and 16:25, Mark 8:35 and Luke 9:24 and 17:33 with regard to *discipleship*. John resets the emphasis here, talking more about the work of *global mission*.

[6] Some readers also see a hint of Romans 9–11 in this metaphor. The Jewish nation had to be made jealous through the Gentiles before many Jews could be saved. Although possible, this isn't John's primary meaning.

knowing he would die a painful death.[7] He therefore returns to the passage which he shared with Nicodemus in 3:14–15, when he said that *"Just as Moses lifted up the snake in the wilderness, so the Son of Man must be lifted up, that everyone who believes may have eternal life in him."* He tells the crowd not to be surprised when he dies a bloody death. The very reason he came into the world was to be raised up on a cross to die and so undo once and for all the work of the great snake Satan.[8] Just like in verse 23, he insists that nothing is more glorious than this message. He cries out for it to glorify his Father, and his Father booms back that he will be glorified as much through Jesus' death as he has been through Jesus' life.[9] The cross would not just be the place where Jesus bore God's judgment. It would also spell out judgment for the *"prince of this world"*, Satan. The Greeks who sought out an audience with Jesus through Philip were simply the foretaste of a new era when he promised to *"draw **all people** to myself."*

The crowd are still confused in verses 34–36, having learned the verses in the Old Testament which promised that the Messiah would reign forever, but not having understood the ones which prophesied that his reign would come through death and resurrection. Jesus therefore returns to his recurring theme of light and darkness, of day and night, and of calling his listeners to step out of the cave. He reminds them that he has dwelt among them as the Light of the World and warns that a moment is coming which 13:30 will label *"night"*. The word he uses to describe darkness overtaking his listeners is *katalambanō*, the same word which John used in 1:5, and he

---

[7] Very little of John's third section is repeated from the synoptic gospels, so verse 27 is a counterpart to Matthew 26:37–44, Mark 14:33–41 and Luke 22:41–44.

[8] John expands on this in 1 John 3:8 and Revelation 12:9–11 and 20:2.

[9] John tells us that many in the crowd explained away God's booming voice as thunder. This mixed crowd of Jews and Greeks reminds us that blind unbelief is not just a Jewish problem.

urges them to believe and become *children of light* in the same way that John described in 1:12.[10] The darkness which could not overcome him would overcome them unless they fixed their eyes on who he really is and stepped out of the cave. If his death seemed foolish to their minds, then they must trust him that it was only because they had been living in the cave for so long. His death would be like the moment when the final curtain falls on a play and the stage lights dim to tell the audience that it is time to stop watching and time to start walking.

As if to demonstrate this, Jesus ends his message abruptly and suddenly hides from the Passover crowds. With the exception of verses 44–50, he will never again in John's gospel preach another message to the crowds. They have heard enough to grasp who Jesus is and what he came to do. All that remains is for them to make their final faith decision.

Jesus turns to us as we come to the end of John's second section and asks us the same question: Will you accept what John tells you about who Jesus really is? Will you step out of the cave? Will you look and see the Living God?

---

[10] People are only *children of God* in the loosest sense before they are saved (Acts 17:28–29). They are described literally as *children of disobedience* or *children of wrath* in Ephesians 2:2–3 and Colossians 3:6, because only faith in Jesus' death and resurrection gives us authority to be reborn as children of God (John 1:12 and Galatians 3:26).

Choose the Right Cup
(12:37–50)

Even after Jesus had performed so many signs in
their presence, they still would not believe in him.

(John 12:37)

We started this second section of John's gospel by talking about the famous scene from the end of the movie *Indiana Jones and the Last Crusade*. Indiana is forced to leap across stepping stones that spell out God's name, and we likened this to the challenge which John sets us of fixing our eyes on who Jesus really is. Indiana passes this test and two other tests which lie before him – one which requires him to get on his knees in humble penitence before God, just as John told us we must do in the chapter "Please Be Offended", and one which requires him to take a leap of faith into a chasm before he sees the bridge beneath him, just as John told us we must do in the chapter "How Faith Happens".

At the very end of his quest, Indiana Jones is forced to make a final life-or-death decision based on what he knows of Jesus. He stands in a room filled with goblets, flanked by the Nazi traitor Walter Donovan and the hoodwinked victim Elsa Schneider, and they are told to choose which of the antique goblets belonged to Jesus. The premise of the scene may be a bit silly, but it helps us to understand the way in which John ends the second section of his gospel.

Walter Donovan chooses first, and he is like the Jewish leaders and crowd in verses 37–41. He ignores the Jesus that John describes in these chapters and takes the largest gold chalice which is encrusted with jewels. *"It certainly is the cup of the King of kings,"* he drools as he takes a drink from the cup he has chosen. Seconds later, he discovers that his Jesus was a Messiah of his own making. He lies dead on the floor.

John has no pleasure in telling us that the same thing happened to most of his fellow countrymen. They had witnessed Jesus' signs, but had refused to let their eyes follow the direction in which those signs pointed. When Jesus healed people, they had objected that he did so on the Sabbath, and when he raised the dead they had plotted to kill him for jeopardizing their hold on power. When they heard his *"I AM"* sayings, they had picked up stones instead of falling down in worship. John tells us in verse 41 that Isaiah repented when he saw a vision of Jesus' glory in the Temple in Isaiah 6, but that the Jewish leaders plotted murder instead when Jesus actually came.[1]

Perhaps John feels the need to explain how the Jews who received Jesus as Messiah in 12:13 could reject him only a few days later in 19:15. Perhaps he feels the need to explain to his readers in Ephesus how Jesus could be the Jewish Messiah and yet be rejected by the majority of the city's Jews. Either way, he reminds us in verse 38 that Isaiah 53:1 had always predicted that Israel would despise, reject and kill their Messiah, and he reminds us in verse 40 that Isaiah 6:10 had also predicted that they would be blind and unresponsive towards him in their hearts. Sure enough, the Jews had twisted the facts, browbeaten the witnesses into silence, and accused Jesus of being anything from a Samaritan to a demonized madman. Each time they did so, God had responded to their stubbornness by making their eyes a little blinder and their hearts a bit more calloused.[2] They

---

[1] Paul quotes these same verses in Acts 28:25–27 and tells us that *God the Holy Spirit* spoke in Isaiah 6:9–10. Like Abraham in 8:56, Isaiah therefore saw God in his Triune glory long before Jesus became a man.

[2] These verses warn that each time we push aside the Gospel we make ourselves blinder and more calloused for the next time. Respond to Jesus while you can today. You cannot be sure of being able to do so tomorrow.

had betrayed their race like Walter Donovan, and they would pay the same price as he did.

Elsa Schneider is an art professor who has been blinded by the wealth and power of the Nazis. *"It would not be made out of gold,"* she advises as she helps Indiana Jones to choose the right cup, but she is so infected by the values of her friends that she fails to follow through on the implications of her find. She also dies, not for failing to grasp what Jesus is like, but for failing to give up everything to follow him. She is like the group of Jews that John turns to next in verses 42–43.

John has told us in these chapters that many Jews believed that Jesus was the Messiah,[3] but that many of them kept their faith a secret, *"for fear they would be put out of the synagogue; for they loved human praise more than God".*[4] Like Elsa Schneider, when God shone the light of faith into their hearts, they let their culture block it out behind a blackout blind of fear. We can do the same when we take John's portrait of Jesus and modify it to make him more palatable to the soothing voice of peer pressure and the tyrant drumbeat of popular opinion. Now John tells us what happened to many of these would-be believers who failed to follow through on their faith. Jesus warns in verse 48 that *"the very words I have spoken will condemn them at the last day".*[5] Elsa Schneider ends up as dead as Walter Donovan, because verbal faith in Jesus cannot save us unless we prove our faith by our radical obedience to his call.[6]

---

[3] John 2:23; 3:2; 6:14; 7:31, 40–41; 8:30–31; 9:16; 10:42; 11:45, 48; 12:13.

[4] John 7:13; 9:22. John probably mentions the threat of being excommunicated from the synagogues in 9:22 and 12:42 as a direct appeal to the Jews of Ephesus that such a price was worth paying to follow Jesus.

[5] Verse 48 ties in with Matthew 11:20–24 to tell us that God will judge us based on the amount of revelation we have received. Now that you have read John 5–12 and seen who Jesus really is, you are even worse off than you were before you read it unless you actually respond to what John says.

[6] Matthew 3:7–10; Acts 26:20; James 2:17–26. The fact that this statement is in any way controversial to many Christians is a sign of just how like Elsa Schneider our Christianity can be.

Indiana Jones reaches out his hand and takes a simple pewter cup. *"That's the cup of a carpenter,"* he says. John ends his second section with verses 44–50 and Jesus' promise of what will happen if we reach out our hands and do the same. He promises in verse 45 that *"The one who looks at me is seeing the one who sent me."* If we look in faith to Jesus as he really is, then we will see the Living God.

"I have come into the world as a light, so that no one who believes in me should stay in darkness," Jesus explains as he tells us yet again that we must step out of the cave. If we refuse to believe in Jesus then we drink from the same cup as Walter Donovan and share his fate. If fear of family or friends causes us to hesitate or try and modify John's picture of Jesus, then we drink from the same cup as Elsa Schneider and perish too. But if we accept Jesus as John knew and loved him, and turn our faith into action, then eternal life is ours.

Indiana Jones puts the cup to his lips and tells himself, *"There is only one way to find out!"* John ends this section by telling us to do the same. He tells us what will happen if we drink from the cup he has given us. He promises us eternal life if we drink from Jesus as the Living God.

Part Three:

Look at What Jesus Has Given You

(Chapters 13–17)

A Briefcase from Q
(13:1–17:26)

*Jesus knew that the hour had come for him to leave
this world and go to the Father. Having loved his own
who were in the world, he loved them to the end.*

(John 13:1)

James Bond is quintessentially British, and often ridiculously
so. My favourite moment is in *From Russia with Love* when he
knows another agent cannot possibly be British because he
orders red wine instead of white wine to go with fish. Bond then
fights the Russian impostor using items which were given him
earlier in a briefcase by Q, the MI6 master of equipment. Each
one of the many items which we saw Q give him in the briefcase
will prove vital in his efforts to defeat the enemy and complete
his mission. Now, as John moves into part three of his gospel
and records Jesus' handover to his disciples, he lists ten items
which Jesus' followers need to carry on his mission. Having told
us to *Look at Jesus alone* and *Look at who Jesus really is*, he now
hands us a briefcase and says, *Look at what Jesus has given you*.

John assumes that we have read the synoptic gospels, so
he doesn't waste time in repeating the events from Passion
Week which they have already recorded. There is no cursing of
the fig tree, no cleansing of the Temple,[1] no lengthy clashes with
the Jewish leaders and no detailed prophecy about end times.
John assumes that we already know all this, so he gives us five
straight chapters of Jesus' hitherto-unrecorded teaching on the

---

[1] Instead, John told us about the time that Jesus cleansed the Temple earlier
at Passover 28 AD in 2:13–17.

night of his betrayal. He tells us that Jesus handed his ministry over to his disciples, telling them in 13:20 and 17:18 that he was sending them just as the Father had sent him.[2] In order that they might continue his ministry on earth, he gives them ten essential items which would overturn the overwhelming odds which stood against them.

The first two items in chapter 13 focus on the *character* of Jesus' followers. Whereas modern conferences on church growth and evangelism have a tendency to focus on the kind of methods we employ, Jesus starts his handover by focusing on the kind of men that he will use. He tells us in verses 1–16 that we must display the same *humility* as he does and, in verses 17–36, that we must also share his *loving obedience*. General Norman Schwarzkopf, who commanded the military coalition which won the First Gulf War, had a similar approach as he prepared his troops for victory. He told them, *"Leadership is a potent combination of strategy and character. But if you must be without one, be without the strategy."*[3]

The next three items in chapter 14 focus on our *equipment*. These are some of the clearest verses in the Bible about how we can be filled with the power of the Holy Spirit for God's mission. Having taught us that godly character comes first, Jesus now explains how we can unleash the power of the Gospel and of miracles. General Schwarzkopf won a very one-sided war because, unlike the Iraqis, his men had state-of-the-art GPS technology and thermal sights and laser rangefinders. His tanks could find and destroy their Iraqi counterparts while still over a mile outside the range of their inferior guns. Jesus tells us that we have weapons which are just as devastating to the Devil. He will not just continue his mission through us if we let him; he will also equip us with all the spiritual weaponry that we need.

---

[2] Jesus states this even more explicitly later in John 20:21.

[3] Quoted by James Charlton in *The Military Quotation Book* (2002).

Items six and seven in chapters 14 and 15 focus on the disciples' *communication* with God. Jesus reminds us that it is God's mission, not our own,[4] and that we need to keep in close communion with him through prayer and the Holy Spirit. General Schwarzkopf began his invasion of Iraq with a series of air strikes which knocked out all communication between the frontline Iraqis and their headquarters in Baghdad, and Jesus warns us that the Devil will also try to disrupt our connection to our Master. Instead, we must be like Schwarzkopf when he used sophisticated satellite systems to co-ordinate ground, air and naval forces so thoroughly that air support and cruise missiles were targeted exactly where his ground troops radioed that they needed them. As a result, he was able to rejoice that *"Saddam's military forces suffered a crushing defeat... and lost face in a humiliating military rout."*[5] John tells us that we will see such victories as well, if we stay connected to Jesus as we go and let his Spirit bear fruit through us.

Finally, items eight to ten focus on our vital need for *courage under fire*. Jesus warns in chapters 15 and 16 that times of heavy persecution and stubborn opposition lie ahead. That's why we need to wear the *body armour* of his name and find protection in the *unity* for which Jesus prays in chapter 17. General Schwarzkopf's victory relied on the unity of a coalition of thirty-four nations, bringing together such unlikely allies as the Saudis and Swedes, the Koreans and Qataris. He united his troops and invested them with courage under fire by telling them: *"True courage is being afraid, and going ahead and doing your job anyhow, that's what courage is."*[6]

---

[4] The Lord taught Joshua the same lesson as John 15:26–27 in Joshua 5:13–15.

[5] General Norman Schwarzkopf in his autobiography *It Doesn't Take a Hero* (1992).

[6] Quoted by Kelly Nickell in *Pocket Patriot: Quotes from American Heroes* (2005).

Given how vital these five chapters are for our mission, it seems surprising that the three synoptic gospel writers did not include them before. Perhaps they felt such lessons were still fresh enough in the minds of the first generation of Christians. Whatever the reason, John clearly felt as the last surviving one of the Twelve that this teaching must be preserved for future generations like our own too. He wanted to ensure that believers from the second century onwards did not hark back to a Christian golden age, when Jesus had handed them the same briefcase with the same ten items in it. He tells us we have all we need to complete the same mission today.

John's teaching was so successful that one Christian writer could reflect 130 years after he wrote his gospel that:

> *If we consider how powerful the Gospel has become in just a few short years, making progress through persecution and torture, through death and confiscation – a fact made all the more surprising by the small number of Gospel preachers and their lack of skill – and if we consider that the Gospel has been preached throughout the earth so that Greeks and barbarians, the wise and foolish, surrender to worship Jesus, then there can be no doubt that human might and power have not caused the words of Jesus Christ to conquer the minds and souls of all men with faith and power. This is what Jesus predicted would happen, and it is what He has established through divine answers to prayer.*[7]

John hands us part three of his gospel and tells us to treat it as a briefcase for our mission. Jesus is about to fill it with the ten items we will need.

---

[7] Origen writing in c.230 AD in *De Principiis* (4.2). This is a translation of Rufinus' Latin paraphrase.

Item One: Humility (13:1–16)

Now that I, your Lord and Teacher, have washed your feet, you also should wash one another's feet.

(John 13:14)

In John's younger days, he had been a bit like Madonna. Don't get me wrong, he wasn't an early Galilean fashionista, but he had shared her unbridled passion to take centre-stage. *"I have the same goal I've had ever since I was a girl. I want to rule the world,"* she confessed to a reporter. *"To me, the whole process of being a brushstroke in someone else's painting is a little difficult."*[1]

John had struggled with letting anyone – even God – hold the paintbrush, because he had so many glorious colours of his own for his life's canvas. He had tried to paint them in Mark 10:35–45 when he told Jesus he should make him and his brother sit beside him on the podium of his Kingdom. John's lust for glory-next-to-Jesus had been embarrassing to say the least, but everything had changed a few days later in this chapter in the upper room. That's why the first item which John places in our briefcase is a lesson in humility, as he explains to us the four things he saw which changed his attitude completely.

This was the night when John *saw how Jesus acted*. He had grown used to Jesus telling people that his hour had not yet come, but he only truly understood when Jesus leapt to his Father's call in verse 1. If Jesus was willing to let the Father

---

[1] These two quotes come from interviews with *People* magazine on 27th July 1992 and *Vanity Fair* magazine in April 1991.

hold the paintbrush,[2] then who was he to think he could refuse? He finally grasped that a self-assertive follower of Jesus is as contradictory in terms as a teetotal wine-taster. As he watched Jesus responding to the Father's guidance that his hour had come, John decided to stop struggling and let God do the painting from now on.

This was also the night when John *saw who Jesus was* and saw how his self-awareness changed everything. He tells us in verses 3–4 that Jesus washed his disciples' feet because he *"knew the Father had put all things under his power, and that he had come from God and was returning to God"*. None of the disciples had been willing to do such a lowly servant's job because they were still busy jockeying for position.[3] Jesus refused to grab the paintbrush from the Father's hand to paint his own path to glory because he was secure in who he was and in who the Father had promised him he would be.

To her credit, Madonna has admitted it is insecurity which drives her craving for attention and her desire to hold the paintbrush in her hand:

> *All of my will has always been to conquer some horrible feeling of inadequacy... I push past one spell of it and discover myself as a special human being and then I get to another stage and think I'm mediocre and uninteresting... Again and again. My drive in life is from this horrible fear of being mediocre. And that's always pushing me, pushing me. Because even though I've become Somebody, I still have to prove that I'm Somebody. My struggle has never ended and it probably never will.*[4]

---

[2] This is essentially what Jesus says through his submissive attitude in 5:19, 5:30, 7:6, 8:28 and 12:49–50.

[3] The other disciples were as bad as John, growing indignant in Mark 10:41 because they craved glory too.

[4] This comes from the same interview in *Vanity Fair* in April 1991.

In the upper room, John's struggle ended when he saw Jesus so secure in who he was.

This was also the night when John *saw who he was*, as Jesus passed heaven's verdict on his life. John was a sinner who needed cleansing, and he heard Jesus tell Peter that *"Unless I wash you, you have no part with me."*[5] He felt ashamed of his clutching ambition when he saw the gulf between God's character and his own. Although he reclined at the table that night with his head on Jesus' chest in verses 23–25, he was beginning to grasp the glory of Christ which culminated in his experience in Revelation 1:17 – *"When I saw him, I fell at his feet as though dead."* He saw himself as the dirty sinner that he was, and his self-deluded ambition died.

At the same time, as Jesus washed his feet John also grasped that the Lord had counted him worthy of cleansing.[6] *"You are all clean,"* Jesus proclaimed in verse 10, except for Judas who persisted in snatching the paintbrush from God's hand. If Jesus was willing to stoop down to cleanse him, he could not respond by trying to trample his way to the top. The only natural response was to say with John the Baptist at the end of John 3 that *"The one who comes from above is above all"*. He must say with the one who had first pointed him to Jesus that *"He must become greater; I must become less."*

Finally, this was also the night when John *saw how he must act*. Jesus had washed his disciples' feet in order to *"set you an example that you should do as I have done for you"*,[7] and if such lowly work was not beneath their Lord and Rabbi, then he could not refuse to follow his lead as a slave to the others.[8] God alone

---

[5] Peter found letting Jesus wash him very humbling, but this is at the heart of the message of the cross.

[6] Unlike Pilate in Matthew 27:24, Jesus used a basin of water to take responsibility. Since the Greek of verse 1 can mean Jesus *"showed them the full extent of his love"*, he did it to point to his imminent death on the cross.

[7] See similar teaching in Matthew 10:24–25, Luke 6:40 and John 15:20.

[8] Interestingly, the word translated *messenger* in verse 16 is same the word usually translated *apostle*.

must hold the paintbrush and paint whatever colours he chose on John's canvas. He would serve Peter's lead in Acts 2–4, serve the Samaritans he once despised in Acts 8, serve God's sovereign plan when his brother was executed in Acts 12 and fade into the background of Acts thereafter. He wants us to see this attitude as vital to the successes of the Early Church, of his own time in Ephesus and of our own place in Church history today. God is still looking for humble servants who remember that their lives belong to him and who let him do the painting. He still says in Isaiah 48:11: *"For my own sake, for my own sake, I do this... I will not yield my glory to another."*

In 1929, a tiny eighteen-year-old Albanian girl named Agnes arrived in India. Motivated by her love for Jesus and the same attitude which John learned in this chapter, she visited the poorest families in Calcutta's slums to wash the sores of lepers, love the crippled, clothe the naked, feed the hungry and care for those the city had discarded as unwanted refuse. She devoted the rest of her life to serving them until she died in 1997. Known to the world as Mother Teresa, she attracted the world to her Saviour like few others in her generation, but she told Time magazine, *"I don't claim anything of the work. It is his work. I am like a little pencil in his hand. That is all. He does the thinking. He does the writing. The pencil has nothing to do with it."*[9]

Take it from John, who once snatched at God's paintbrush like Madonna, that if you want to play a role in God's mission, and if you want to see fruit that will last to the Father's glory, you must also take this same downward path to greatness. You must adopt the humble spirit of a common slave.

---

[9] Interviewed in *Time* magazine in December 1989.

Item Two: Loving Obedience (13:17–38)

Now that you know these things, you will be blessed if you do them.

(John 13:17)

When Bill Clinton became president of the United States in January 1993, he became custodian of the world's largest arsenal of nuclear weapons. Except for Russia, his stockpile of 12,000 warheads gave him several times more nuclear firepower than the rest of the world combined. So it was rather disconcerting when the Chairman of his Joint Chiefs of Staff confessed a decade after leaving office that for several weeks Bill Clinton had lost the nuclear launch codes. *"We were both terrified that we might open up The Washington Post the next day to find the front-page headline 'PRESIDENT LOSES KEY TO NUKES – LAUNCHES IMPOSSIBLE',"* he remembered. *'This is a big deal – a gargantuan deal.'"*[1] And in verse 17, John agrees.

John is concerned we may have stockpiled knowledge about Jesus in parts one and two, but done nothing more. That's why he tells us in verse 17 that Jesus cautioned his disciples: *"Now that you know these things, you will be blessed if you do them."* Not if they knew them. Not even if they believed them. Their stockpiled knowledge about Jesus would be of no gain to them unless they actually triggered its power through the launch code of *loving obedience*.

To help us see this, John turns the spotlight onto Judas Iscariot in verses 18–30. Judas had far more information

---

[1] General Hugh Shelton in his memoir *Without Hesitation* (2010).

about Jesus than we have, but John reminds us in verses 11 and 18 that this didn't stop him going to hell.[2] We can miss the shock of Judas' betrayal through familiarity with this story, but we must remember none of the Eleven even suspected in 12:4–6 that Judas was dipping his hand into their money bag. When he got angry with Mary of Bethany for "wasting" her perfume on Jesus, the synoptic gospel writers tell us that the other disciples took his side. Most shockingly, John tells us that when Jesus revealed that one of the Twelve would betray him, no one's eyes turned to Judas as the obvious candidate, even when Jesus spelt it out by passing bread to his betrayer. He had such a fine reputation that they assumed he must be on an errand for Jesus or on his way to help the poor. John wants to show us that it doesn't matter how large our stockpile of knowledge may be, unless we respond with loving obedience and therefore trigger its power.

Judas looks like a believer on the outside, but on the inside he hasn't changed. He still thinks he can serve both God and money, and he is blind to where such a double-minded pilgrimage will end. Jesus pleads with him tenderly by washing his feet as a sign that he loves him as much as the other disciples, with a warning that he is well aware that a disciple stands on the brink of betrayal. He encourages Judas to confess that his head-knowledge is no substitute for obedience, but instead of repenting and triggering his stockpile, the stubborn Judas presses on.[3] Jesus pleads a second time with him by quoting from Psalm 41:9 with a second warning – that he knows the

---

[2] John 17:12 is even more explicit about this, and we read similar statements in Matthew 26:24 and Acts 1:25.

[3] Note John's repetition of the themes of part two. Jesus hints that he is the *"I AM"* who spoke to Moses at the burning bush in verse 19, and Judas goes out into the dark night in verse 30. The Passover dish contained a bitter sauce of raisins and vinegar which represented slavery in Egypt and linked back to 8:31–47.

exact identity of his betrayer.[4] He hands him a piece of bread so that he can choose either to betray him and fulfil that verse or to obey him and turn his knowledge into action.[5] Tragically, Judas takes the bread and as he does so Satan enters him.[6] John demonstrates that without loving obedience no amount of head-knowledge can save us.

Now John switches the spotlight onto Peter in verses 36–38 to show that talk is no substitute for loving obedience either. It didn't matter that, unlike Judas, Peter truly wanted to make his stockpile count or that he claimed to be willing to follow Jesus even to the death.[7] He fell into the all-too-common trap of thinking that loud verbal profession of faith is the same thing as obedient action. It doesn't matter how loudly we sing worship songs, debate theology or talk of plans for global mission. If we don't put Jesus' teaching into practice then our words are merely empty chatter. Jesus adds in 14:15–24 that *"Whoever has my commands **and keeps them** is the one who loves me,"* and that *"Anyone who loves me **will obey** my teaching."* Without the launch code of loving obedience, then noisy praise and protestations have no power to detonate our stockpile of knowledge.[8]

In between his dealings with Judas and Peter, Jesus states this principle more positively in verses 31–35. He talks five

---

[4] David probably wrote this psalm when his wife's grandfather Ahithophel betrayed him in 2 Samuel 15. Jesus quotes it as an ancient prophecy that Judas would also betray the Messiah.

[5] Matthew and Mark tell us Judas dipped his own bread in the bowl with Jesus, but John clarifies that Jesus dipped his bread in the bowl with Judas and fulfilled Psalm 41:9 by offering him his own piece of bread too.

[6] Satan had already entered Judas in Luke 22:3, but he entered more completely when Judas chose the role of Ahithophel by taking the bread as a rejection of Jesus' loving overtures.

[7] It appears that Peter protested over dinner that he would never betray Jesus (Luke and John), and was so convinced that he carried on protesting as they walked outside to Gethsemane (Matthew and Mark).

[8] 14:31 tells us that one of the purposes of Jesus' cross was to show us what loving obedience truly looks like.

times about his glory in just two verses, and tells his disciples that if they put his teaching into action then they will make his glory visible to the world. *"A new command I give you: love one another,"* he says before explaining why loving obedience must be the second item in our mission briefcase. *"By this everyone will know that you are my disciples, if you love one another."*[9]

The first two items which John has put in our briefcase both emphasize character because he had proved Jesus' promise for over sixty years. When John and the other early Christians triggered the stockpile of their knowledge in Jerusalem after Pentecost, they saw thousands of people converted to the Lord. When they stepped out in miracles with great courage and told the Sanhedrin defiantly to *"Judge for yourselves whether it is right in God's sight to obey you rather than God"*, they found that even their enemies noticed the power of their lifestyle and *"were astonished and they took note that these men had been with Jesus"*.[10] From Jerusalem to Samaria and from Antioch to Ephesus, when Jesus' followers triggered the stockpile of their knowledge about Jesus through loving obedience, they saw God's glory on display.[11]

Perhaps that's why Jerome told his readers in around 388 AD that in John's extreme old age he only preached one sermon. *"Little children, love one another,"* he repeated, and when they complained that they had heard him preach this message before he replied that *"This is what the Lord commanded, and if this one thing shall be obeyed then it shall be enough."*[12]

So let's put item two in our briefcase and not settle for

---

[9] The command was *new* in the sense that love is the Law of Christ's new Kingdom (James 2:8; John 15:12, 17). It also links to the fact that Luke 22:20 tells us Jesus taught about his New Covenant at this time.

[10] Acts 2:42–47; 4:13, 19; 5:14.

[11] Paul also writes in Titus 2:1–10 that our loving character will convince the world that the Gospel is true.

[12] Jerome in his *Commentary on Galatians*, remarking on 6:10. Jerome is not always reliable but this story certainly ties in with what we know of the repeated message of 1 John.

stockpiled knowledge like Judas or for empty words like Peter. Let's trigger a mighty detonation of God's stockpiled blessings. John tells us that the launch code is:

L-O-V-I-N-G O-B-E-D-I-E-N-C-E.

Item Three: The Holy Spirit (14:1–31)

I will ask the Father, and he will give you another advocate to help you and be with you for ever – the Spirit of truth.

(John 14:16–17)

Ancient Israel had a secret weapon in their army. It was a weapon which turned weak and helpless soldiers into mighty warriors.

Gideon was a humble farmer in around 1200 BC. He was so scared of Midianite invaders that he threshed his wheat in hiding and waited till his neighbours were in bed before he went up against their idols. Yet when the Holy Spirit – Israel's secret weapon – came upon him in Judges 6:34, he defeated a Midianite army thousands of times bigger than his own.

Samson was a surly young man in around 1140 BC. He was so weak naturally that when his girlfriend shaved his hair, he was powerless to resist being captured and blinded and chained to a millstone like a common donkey. Yet when the Holy Spirit came on him in Judges 14:6 and 15:14, he was able to kill a lion with his bare hands and a whole army of Philistines with just the jawbone of a dead donkey.

David was a teenager in around 1020 BC who was more used to playing soft music on his harp and nursing baby lambs than stepping onto a battlefield. Yet when the Holy Spirit came on him in 1 Samuel 16:13, he became such a potent military threat that he killed a mighty giant and routed an invading army with just a slingshot and stones.

There was no doubt about it, the Holy Spirit was Israel's unstoppable secret weapon. The only problem was that he came on very few individuals and for very little of the time.

John's gospel focuses on the Holy Spirit more than the other three gospels. Clement of Alexandria described it as a *"spiritual gospel"* or a *"gospel of the Spirit"*.[1] John expects us to know that the Old Testament prophets foresaw a time when this limited experience of the Holy Spirit would change through the Messiah – men like Jeremiah who predicted that *"No longer will they teach their neighbour, or say to one another, 'Know the Lord,' because they will **all** know me, from the least of them to the greatest,"* and men like Joel who relayed God's promise that *"I will pour out my Spirit on **all** people. Your sons and daughters will prophesy, your old men will dream dreams, your young men will see visions. Even on my servants, both men and women, I will pour out my Spirit in those days."*[2] Those were the verses which John had in mind when he identified Jesus as the Messiah in 1:32–33 by telling us that the Holy Spirit came on him and remained on him.[3] He referred to them in 7:37–39 when he said that Jesus promised to fill each one of his followers with the Spirit, *"as Scripture has said."* In 7:39, he told us that this would not happen until Jesus was glorified. Now that Jesus prepares to die, he teaches us in chapter 14 that the Holy Spirit is the indispensable third item in our briefcase.

John tells us that Jesus taught that the *Holy Spirit is God himself.* He is not an intangible power supply, rather like the ch'i in kung fu or the force in *Star Wars*, but a person just like him. The Greeks had two words – *allos* and *heteros* – to distinguish between *another of the same kind* and *another of a different kind*. Jesus chooses the first one in verse 16 to teach that the Holy

---

[1] I gave the full quote from Clement in the introduction to this book.

[2] Jeremiah 31:31–34; Joel 2:28–29. See also Ezekiel 36:26–27.

[3] The other gospel writers also make this same link in Matthew 3:11, Mark 1:8 and Luke 3:16.

Spirit is another person of the Trinity, just like him.[4] He is God as much as the Father and the Son, which is why Jesus can say in verses 18 and 23 that when the Spirit comes then the Father and the Son also come as well.[5]

Since *spirit* is a neuter noun in Greek and ought to take the pronoun "it", Jesus further emphasizes that the Holy Spirit is a person by almost always using the pronoun "him" instead.[6] He calls him the *paraklētos*, which means *one who comes alongside to help*, and which was a word used by the Greeks to describe a helpful slave, an advocate, a defence attorney or an adviser. Their soldiers also used it when they buddied up before pitched battles as the name for the person with whom they would stand back to back during the melee which ensued. Jesus therefore teaches in this chapter that the Holy Spirit is the third person of the Godhead and that he stands with us to intertwine his life with ours. He conveys this amazing privilege by telling us in verse 20 that *"I am in my Father, and you are in me, and I am in you."*[7]

John also tells us that Jesus taught that *the Holy Spirit is for all people and for all occasions.* Unlike in the days of Gideon and

---

[4] Note the overlap between the three persons of the Trinity as Jesus teaches in verses 6 and 17 that the Son is the Truth and the Spirit is the Spirit of Truth. John is the only New Testament writer to use the Greek word *paraklētos*, and he does so four times in this chapter to describe the Holy Spirit and once in 1 John 2:1 to describe Jesus. No wonder Luke calls the Holy Spirit *"the Spirit of Jesus"* in Acts 16:7.

[5] Don't be confused by this, like the fourth-century heretic Arius, who misunderstood verse 28 to mean that Jesus is inferior to the Father. Don't get caught up either in the ancient dispute over whether the Spirit proceeds from the Father alone or also from the Son. John 1:33, 7:37 and 20:22 stress that Jesus is the Baptizer in the Holy Spirit.

[6] We needn't be pedantic about this, since Jesus does call him "it" once in verse 17. We simply need to remember that he is a person, who *chooses* and *speaks* and can be *tested* and *lied to* (Acts 5:3, 9; 20:28; 21:11).

[7] Although some readers interpret verse 28 as a reference to Jesus' resurrection, the context of the chapter makes it far more likely that he is promising to come back to his followers through the Holy Spirit.

Samson and David, when the Spirit only came on a few people for a fixed period of time, Jesus promises in verses 16 and 23 that his Spirit will come to each one of his followers for every moment of their lives.[8] He promises in verse 17 that, while the Holy Spirit has lived *with* them for the past three years in the person of their Master, after Pentecost that same Spirit will live *inside* them too. Their mission might be as hopelessly oversized as Gideon's, Samson's and David's, but with the Holy Spirit on the inside they would prove more than a match for Satan's ugly horde.

When John and the early Christians applied the message of this chapter, they found that the Holy Spirit strengthened them, encouraged them, and gave them rapid advance with the Gospel, just as Jesus promised.[9] When later generations forgot this third item in their briefcase, they saw corresponding weakness and decline. That's why the Puritan preacher, Robert Traill, warns us as he did his own seventeenth-century English church:

> *Men, brethren, and fathers, you are called to a high and holy calling. Your work is full of danger, full of duty, and full of mercy. You are called to the winning of souls... What can be the reason of this sad observation: That when formerly a few lights raised up in the nation did shine so as to scatter and dispel the darkness... [yet] now there are more, and more learned men amongst us, the darkness comes on apace? Is it not because they were men filled with the Holy Ghost and with power; and many of us are only filled with light and knowledge?*[10]

---

[8] Jesus is careful to continue his teaching about loving obedience in this chapter, emphasizing in verses 15, 21, 23 and 24 that the gift of the Spirit is for true believers, not for false stockpilers of unused knowledge.

[9] See for example Acts 9:31, Romans 15:18–19 and 1 Corinthians 2:4–5.

[10] Robert Traill (1642–1716) preached this in October 1682 in a sermon entitled "By what Means may Ministers Best Win Souls?" A copy can be found in Volume 1 of *The Works of Robert Traill* (1775).

House Swap
(14:1–4, 22–24)

Anyone who loves me will obey my teaching. My Father will love them, and we will come to them and make our home with them.

(John 14:23)

In the Mark Twain novel *The Prince and the Pauper*, a young commoner from one of London's vilest slums comes face to face with Edward, the only son of King Henry VIII.[1] Tom Canty looks so similar to Prince Edward, but for the contrast between the rags and royal clothes, that Edward invites him into the palace and they swap clothes for fun. Their fun quickly turns sour, however, when the palace guards mistakenly throw out Edward as an intruder. Tom Canty finds himself as a prince in the king's palace, while the future Edward VI finds himself begging in the alleyways of London.

Hold that thought and you can begin to appreciate what Jesus told the disciples in this chapter. He promised them a house swap which exceeds anything conjured up by fiction. Jesus told them that item three in their briefcase meant that God wants to relocate to live with them on earth, and he has invited them to relocate to live with him in heaven.[2] We need to slow down to digest this before rushing on to John's fourth item. It is

---

[1] Published in 1881, the novel has inspired countless similar stories, from *Trading Places* to *Freaky Friday*.

[2] Unlike a human house swap, Jesus' house swap enables both parties to reside in two places at once.

a promise of such magnitude that it puts what passed between Tom Canty and Prince Edward firmly in the shade.

Jesus begins by telling us in verses 1–4 that his Father's house in heaven has many rooms. The word is *monē*, which simply means *dwelling place*, so some older translations render it *mansions*.[3] What matters is not the size of the dwelling place, but where Jesus tells us that it is located. Although his own heart was troubled in 13:21, he tells the disciples that their hearts need not be troubled at all. They can trust him as much as they trust the Father,[4] and can believe that his death, resurrection and ascension are all vital components of God's relocation service. There is plenty of space for all his followers to sit with him in heaven, and in the context of verses 19–21 this simply cannot be restricted to the promise of heaven when we die. Jesus is promising his disciples that, when he comes back from the dead, he will make his ragtag bunch of followers into an army of Prince Edwards, reigning with him in heaven both in this life and in the next. Paul explains in Ephesians 1:20–21 and 2:6:

> *He raised Christ from the dead and seated him at his right hand in the heavenly realms, far above all rule and authority, power and dominion, and every name that is invoked, not only in the present age but also in the one to come... And God raised us up with Christ and seated us with him in the heavenly realms in Christ Jesus.*

That's the first half of the story. Now Jesus turns to the second half in verses 22–24. John told us in 7:39 that the time would not come for God to pour out his Holy Spirit until Jesus was glorified. Now Jesus promises the disciples that through his forthcoming

---

[3] It is the noun of the verb *menō*, which means *to dwell* or *remain* in verses 10, 17 and 25, and throughout chapter 15.

[4] The word *pisteuete*, used twice in verse 1, is a "present imperative" which can mean *go on believing*. They were to go on trusting in God the Father and the Son, even during the trauma of the next three days.

death, resurrection and ascension that longed-for moment will finally arrive.[5] The Father and Son would also relocate through the Holy Spirit to their new dwelling places (it's the same Greek word, *monē*) which Jesus had purchased with his blood. It was only half of their plan for us to dwell with Jesus in the heavenly realms. They were also getting ready to dwell with us on the earth too. Paul excitedly celebrates this truth in 2 Corinthians 6:16, telling his Christian readers that *"We are the temple of the living God. As God has said: 'I will live with them and walk among them, and I will be their God, and they will be my people.'"*[6]

So how should we respond to a house swap such as this?

First, we must be *confident in our authority*. Jesus says in verse 30 that Satan styles himself the "prince of this world", but in reality he has no hold over Jesus and therefore no hold over anyone who dwells in him.[7] In the Old Testament, God talked of heaven as his Throne and the room where the Ark of the Covenant was housed in the Temple as the footstool to his Throne.[8] Jesus wants us to grasp that this house swap now means that we sit with him on God's Throne in heaven and that he makes us the new footstool to his Throne on earth. He wants us to remember that Jeremiah 3:16–17 prophesied that at his coming, *"People will no longer say, 'the ark of the covenant of the Lord.' It will never enter their minds or be remembered; it will not be missed, nor will another one be made. At that time they will call Jerusalem The Throne of the Lord."* This house swap has given us authority to rule with Christ on his throne. We can attack Satan's crumbling kingdom as those who have the upper hand.

---

[5] Luke describes how this happened in Acts 2:33.

[6] Paul's quotation is a mixture of Leviticus 26:12 and Ezekiel 37:27 in order to teach that what we now enjoy through the Holy Spirit is the fulfilment of what was foreshadowed by Old Testament Judaism.

[7] Jesus is saying here that he is entirely sinless. Positionally, through the cross, so are we.

[8] See 1 Chronicles 28:2; Psalm 132:7; Isaiah 66:1; Lamentations 2:1. Compare this with King Solomon's royal throne in 2 Chronicles 9:18.

Second, we must be *confident in our power*. Jesus told Nathanael in 1:51 that he is Jacob's Ladder which connects heaven's power to earth's need. Our house swap means that Jesus uses each of us as a little ladder too, seating us with him in heaven and going about with us on earth to make us God's channel for heaven's power supply.

Third, we must be *devoted to God's mission*. Since we dwell in heaven with Jesus, we must cast away sin and obey him as he commands in verses 23–24,[9] and since we host Jesus on earth we must be eager to put our feet in every unreached place to act as the foot of God's Ladder which carries heaven's blessing.

Fourth, we must be *devoted to God's presence*, and not treat the house swap which cost Jesus so dear as if it were just another pleasant fiction story. Mark Twain begins *The Prince and the Pauper* by stating that *"It may have happened, it may not have happened: but it could have happened."* In contrast, Jesus tells us that the house swap he describes in this chapter is unassailably true. God has made us into his earthly dwelling place – not his office, not his workshop, not his war room, but his home – and he has invited us to dwell with him and to make his heaven our new home.

The writer to the Hebrews warned his readers not to forget this:

> *So, friends, we can now – without hesitation – walk right up to God, into "the Holy Place." Jesus has cleared the way by the blood of his sacrifice, acting as our priest before God. The "curtain" into God's presence is his body. So let's do it – full of belief, confident that we're presentable inside and out. Let's keep a firm grip on the promises that keep us going. He always keeps his word.*[10]

---

[9] We do not earn God's presence through obedience (Galatians 3:2, 5), but the more we obey him the more we enable ourselves to experience the fullness of his presence (John 1:16; 3:34; 8:29; 14:21; 15:4).

[10] This paraphrase of Hebrews 10:19–23 comes from *The Message*.

Item Four: The Gospel (14:6)

Jesus answered, "I am the way and the truth and the life. No one comes to the Father except through me."

(John 14:6)

Many people think that John was out of touch with twenty-first-century culture. Why else would he ruin such a beautiful chapter with such a jarring verse? When 65 per cent of American Christians believe that more than one religion can lead to God,[1] and when even the front cover of *Time* magazine reports that many Christian leaders doubt the reality of hell,[2] what does John think he is doing by telling us to put a statement such as verse 6 into our mission briefcase? For many modern readers, it just sounds frankly ignorant.

But let's stop for a minute and remember where John wrote this gospel. It wasn't in Jerusalem but in Ephesus, a pluralist city with as many gods as taverns and which was home to the magnificent pagan temple of Artemis, one of the seven wonders of the ancient world. The sneering words he told us Pilate used to dismiss Jesus in 18:38 – *"What is truth?"* – must have been hurled at him many times since then in his city's Roman forum. No. John knew exactly how controversial Jesus' sixth *"I AM"* statement would be to pluralist ears, but he also knew it would win us a hearing. He tells us that if we want to make people mad or glad, then we need this item four.

---

[1] Taken from the Pew Forum survey on American Religion and Public Life in 2008.

[2] *Time* magazine, 25th April 2011.

We need it because *pluralism is dishonest.* The playwright George Bernard Shaw famously stated that *"There is only one religion, though there are a hundred versions of it"*,[3] but when he came to die he found he wasn't pluralist at all. He left strict instructions in his will that no memorial to him must *"take the form of a cross or any other instrument of torture or symbol of blood sacrifice"*. George Bernard Shaw's show of tolerance masked a hatred of the cross and a desire to draw his own religious line. It was the same across the Roman Empire and it is still the same today.

We also need it because *pluralism is arrogant.* Though our culture claims to tolerate any view, it is just as determined to draw its own religious line as George Bernard Shaw was. It excludes manipulative cults and hate-preaching mullahs (thankfully), and it excludes any view which refuses to toe a multifaith line. With breathtaking arrogance, it thinks it can snatch the religious paintbrush out of God's hand. That's why Jesus couples his statement *"I am the Way"* with the sister statement *"I am the Truth"*, to remind us that it is God who draws the line. Jesus exposed as a lie in 3:7 the Jewish hope of impressing God with good works, and he will expose as a lie in 18:37 the Greco-Roman hope of being saved through philosophy and polytheism. To resist him when he exposes our own pluralism as a lie is simply to be as blind as a Pharisee.

We need it because *pluralism is ignorant.* It never stops to define what God is like, much less what salvation means or what it means for us to get there. Its line is drawn with all the precision of a child playing pin-the-tail-on-the-donkey. That's why Jesus adds a third statement, telling us that *"I am the Life"* as well. He isn't just repeating his fifth *"I AM"* statement which he spoke on his way to Lazarus' tomb. He is telling us that salvation means far more than being forgiven and given a Paradise full of

---

[3] He wrote this in his preface to the second volume of *Plays Pleasant and Unpleasant* (1898).

virgins, and far more than being given a better reincarnation on our way to achieving moksha. It is the intimate, life-giving union with himself which he describes in this chapter as a marvellous house swap, and describes in 10:10 as *life, and life to the full*. The world's religious leaders were able to *show* the way and *teach* the truth and *explain* the lesser life they peddled, but Jesus alone could describe such a mind-blowing divine master plan and tell his listeners that he *is* the Way, he *is* the Truth and he *is* the Life of God. After Jesus has defined the depth of human need and set our hearts on the heights of divine provision, it is obvious that we can only bridge this gulf by travelling on a pathway of God's own making, not a makeshift pathway of our own.

We also need it because *pluralism is lazy*. *"What is truth? said jesting Pilate, and would not stay for an answer,"* observed the philosopher Francis Bacon,[4] and John warns that our own culture can be every bit as flippant with Jesus as his. The pluralist scoffs that the only reason Christians believe in Jesus is that they were born in a Christian country, yet he never stops to consider that he only thinks that way because he was born in a pluralist one. Instead, the pluralist rushes on to his second objection, that of course everybody nowadays knows that there can't just be one way to God. There may indeed be many people who believe that in twenty-first-century London, but the pluralist never stops to think that such an appeal to the majority view would yield a very different result in the London of 200 years ago or in the Riyadh of today.

Finally, we need it because *pluralism is unproven*. It is the mere speculation of people still chained to the wall in Plato's cave, who interpret the shadows with the help of their fellow prisoners. In stark contrast, Jesus has proven through his death and resurrection that his *"I AM"* statements are all true. When we come to this fork in the road of our lives, should we

---

[4] Francis Bacon (1561–1625) wrote this in the chapter "On Truth" in his book of *Essays* (1625).

ask directions from Buddha, who died of dysentery and was cremated; from Muhammad, who died of fever in the arms of one of his dozen wives and then was buried in the grave to rot there; from George Bernard Shaw, whose best advice in later life was *"Do not try to live forever. You will not succeed"* and *"The last word remains with Christ"*?[5] Should we not rather ask directions from the one who proved he is the Way, the Truth and the Life by passing through the gate of death ahead of us and then returning so that he can lead us on?

Here's a really strange thing: When John and his friends preached this message in all its uncompromising, offensive glory across the world, they found it made them foes and followers in equal measure. When he and Peter told Jerusalem in Acts 4:12 that *"Salvation is found in no one else, for there is no other name under heaven given to mankind by which we must be saved"*; when they both confronted the folk religion of Samaria with some similar straight-talking in Acts 8:20–23; and when John told the people of Asia in Revelation 5 that there is no other Saviour under heaven but Jesus Christ – they quickly discovered why Jesus had told them to treasure this message as the fourth item in their mission briefcase.

So don't tone down, dial down or water down this Gospel you have been given. If you preach Jesus as the only Way, then you will provoke the same reaction which won over the pagan world.

---

[5] In *The Doctor's Dilemma* (1911) and *On the Rocks* (1933).

Item Five: Miracles
(14:11–12)

Very truly I tell you, whoever believes in me will do the works I have been doing, and they will do even greater things than these, because I am going to the Father.

(John 14:12)

Sharing the Gospel can often feel a bit like World War One. We start our Christian lives like the soldiers who went merrily to war in August 1914, convinced that their mission would be easy and they would be home for Christmas. We share Jesus with anyone who will listen, and we wait expectantly for friends and family to start falling to their knees. But it doesn't happen; at least not quite as we expected. Our experience starts to feel a bit more like the Somme in 1916, where the Allies lost almost two thirds of a million soldiers in order to advance a mere two miles. Some of us stay positive, rather like Hugh Laurie's character in *Blackadder Goes Forth*, but the majority of us are more like Blackadder himself. We realize that the enemy's obstacles and weaponry are just too strong. We start hiding in our church buildings, like trenches, in the hope that someone else will go and accomplish our mission instead.

Sound familiar? You're not alone.

Now imagine you are in the trenches at Cambrai. It's November 1917 and three years of stalemate have robbed you of any hope of punching through the enemy lines. As you ready yourself to go over the top again, you hear that today is different. A new invention has arrived on the battlefield, and you will have 500 tanks supporting you. Sure, the new tanks had teething problems at Cambrai, and there were setbacks as well as successes, but with their help you gain as much ground in six hours of fighting as you did in the previous three months combined. Once perfected, the tanks help you again at Amiens in August 1918. They help you to advance four times further in one day than in six months at the Somme. World War One is as good as over. Your mission is accomplished.

Jesus never told his disciples that their mission would be easy. He simply told them that he would give them all the heavy weaponry they needed. He taught them how to perform miracles as part and parcel of their preaching, and helped revive their discouraged spirits whenever they failed.[1] On the night of his betrayal, he told them that miracles were going to be the fifth item in their briefcase. He told them in verse 12 that *"whoever believes in me will do the works I have been doing, and they will do even greater things than these"*.

Sure enough, after the Day of Pentecost the disciples found they could advance as quickly as the Allies at Amiens. Peter healed people with his shadow, and the rest of the apostles found that when they laid their hands on sick people *"all of them were healed"*. There were some setbacks and failures, but with this fifth item in their briefcase the apostles spread the Gospel throughout Cyprus and Asia and Macedonia and Greece and Italy in the space of only a few years.[2] Paul was able to write in Romans 15:18–19 in 57 AD that they had made converts across the Empire *"by the power of signs and wonders, through the power of the Spirit of God"*.[3]

---

[1] Jesus equipped them to perform miracles in Matthew 10:1–8 and Luke 10:9. He taught them to cope with the both the highs and lows of attempting the miraculous in Mark 9:17–29 and Luke 10:17–20.

[2] Examples of successes are in Acts 5:12–16, 9:32–42, 13:6–12, 19:11–20 and 28:1–10. Examples of failure to see healing, at least at first, are in Galatians 4:13–15, Philippians 2:25–27 and 2 Timothy 4:20.

[3] Like the other gospel writers, John 11:12 uses the verb *sōzō*, or *to save*, to describe healing. Therefore Paul adds in Romans that unless he had attempted

During the two centuries which followed, the Christians kept using this heavy firepower. Miracles and Christianity were so connected in the public eye that Justin Martyr used them as a major argument when he told the Roman Senate to look at Jesus and see the Living God.[4] Tertullian preached to non-Christians that they should follow Jesus because the miracles which his followers performed were much more exciting than attending the theatre or the gladiatorial games![5] Origen tells us that the most ordinary believer still had a share in the fun, writing that miracles came *"by prayer and simple requests which the most ordinary person can offer, because for the most part it is uneducated people who perform this work... [It does] not require the power and wisdom of those who are mighty in argument."*[6]

Sadly, after the conversion of the Emperor Constantine in 312 AD, the Church started relying more on man-made weapons such as money and promise of advancement, and the heavy weaponry of miracles grew rusty from disuse. Evangelism became more like the Somme than the breakthrough at Amiens, and the rapid growth of Christianity stalled.[7] From time to time, certain generations rediscovered the power of miracles, and none more so than certain parts of China, Africa and South America today, where the power of signs and miracles has transformed nations in a short time. Those of us who live in the developed world need to look to them and learn. We need to rediscover this fifth item instead of *"having the appearance of godliness, but denying its power"*.[8]

---

miracles, he would have been preaching an incomplete Gospel.

[4] See his *Dialogue with Trypho* (82 and 88) and his *Second Apology* (6), both written in around 150 AD.

[5] See his *De Spectaculis* (29), written in *c.*200 AD.

[6] Writing in *Against Celsus* (7.4) in 248 AD.

[7] John 10:41 reassures us that we can still see some Kingdom advance without any miracles, but verses such as 11:47–48 remind us that we need to persevere in faith for miracles if we want to save large crowds.

[8] 2 Timothy 3:5 (English Standard Version).

I wish I could tell you my own experience is always like Amiens, but at least it's beginning to look a bit more like the early days at Cambrai. Four years ago, a friend challenged me to study this verse, and the more I studied it the fewer and fewer my excuses became. I saw that in the context the word *works* must mean the *miracles* described in verse 11,[9] not just preaching and character and willingness to serve. I saw that this promise is one of scope as well as of scale – Jesus is not just saying that there are lots of us and only one of him, since the Greek says literally that *"he who believes in me, the works which I do, that one will also do, and greater than these shall he do"*. I also saw that this promise cannot just be for the disciples' generation, since Jesus links it to his going away to the Father and therefore to the day of his return.

Armed with this verse, I went as a visiting speaker to another church and let them advertise me as having a healing gift as well as a preaching one. During the worship time, I invited anyone who needed healing to come to the front so that I and others could pray for them as the congregation sang. When a man was healed instantly of a long-standing knee injury, he was surprised but nowhere near as surprised as I was. Another two or three out of the twenty that we prayed for were healed – as at Cambrai, there were setbacks too – but when I preached the Gospel and called people to respond, more people came forward than in the whole of my previous year's preaching put together.[10]

Are there still setbacks? Yes, all the time. But I've kissed the Somme goodbye. From now on I'm using this fifth item in my briefcase. Come and do the same by asking God to send his heavy weaponry to the trenches where he has called you to play your own part in his mission.

---

[9] This word *erga*, or *works*, is also used to refer to miracles in 5:36, 7:3, 7:21, 10:25, 10:32, 10:38 and 15:24.

[10] This is simply what John promised would happen in 2:11, 10:38, 11:47–48, 12:11, 14:11 and 20:30–31. God uses miracles to generate saving faith in the heart of unbelievers, helping them to look and see the Living God.

Item Six: Prayer (14:13–14)

I will do whatever you ask in my name, so that the Father may be glorified in the Son.

(John 14:13)

Olaf of Norway had a problem. His enemies the Danes had outwitted the English king Aethelred the Unready and their invading army had succeeded in capturing London. It occupied the city on both sides of the river, and unless Olaf could drive it out he knew that Norway was next on the Danish shopping list.

Olaf's plan was so clever that we still celebrate it a thousand years later in a children's nursery rhyme. When he saw that the Danish army was split across both sides of the river, he led his fleet of ships to the single wooden bridge which joined the two halves of the city. It was low tide, and he ordered his men to tie their ships securely to the bases of the wooden piles which had been driven into the river bed to support the bridge. High tide was many hours away, and the Danes made use of the time to pelt the ships with a barrage of missiles from above, but Olaf had built protective roofs on the ships and his men held firm. The river rose, the power of the tide dislodged the piles from the river bed, and Olaf ordered his men to row up river and collapse the now unstable bridge. The Danish army was split in half and London quickly fell to the English army.

Jesus isn't any less clever than Olaf, and he has a similar plan in mind as he offers us the sixth item in our briefcase. The cities of the world may seem resistant to his mission, but he tells us they will fall if we dislodge the piles of Satan's bridges through our prayer. He knows we find prayer hard and that

Satan attacks us when we pray, so he promises us seven times in this third section of John's gospel that he answers prayer. The first two are here in verses 13 and 14: *"I will do whatever you ask in my name... You may ask me for anything in my name, and I will do it."*[1]

These verses help us to pray prayers of *faith*. The reason we pray as little as we do is that it takes faith to shut ourselves away and pray to someone we can't see.[2] He reassures us that the Father wants to glorify the Son by responding to prayers offered by his People. Like the power of the tide which dislodged London Bridge, he promises that prayer will break down any mighty obstacle which stands against us. Hudson Taylor discovered this when he put his faith in these seven promises and ignored advice which told him not to try to preach the Gospel in inland China. He later reflected, after seeing thousands of Chinese people saved, that *"It was to me a very grave matter, however, to contemplate going out to China, far away from all human aid... How important, therefore, to learn before leaving England to move man through God by prayer alone."*[3]

These verses help us to pray prayers with *authority*. The three words *"in my name"* may sound insignificant, but they are more than an invitation to tag Jesus' name onto the end of our prayers. They remind us that the Gospel has turned us from paupers into princes,[4] that we sit at the Father's right hand in Christ and that we can therefore lay our requests at his Throne as if Christ laid them there himself. It doesn't matter if a policewoman is only five feet tall; if she knocks on your door "in

---

[1] The other five are in 15:7, 15:16, 16:23, 16:24 and 16:26. These seven promises about prayer go alongside John's seven signs and his seven *"I AM"* sayings.

[2] Jesus does not talk here about the need to find a time and place for prayer, but he teaches us to do so in Matthew 6:6, 14:23 and 26:36. Prayer requires discipline as well as desire.

[3] James Hudson Taylor in his autobiography *A Retrospect*, written towards the end of his life in 1894.

[4] Jesus emphasizes that we must act like princes when we pray in 16:26–27.

the name of the law", you respond to her badge and not to her. It doesn't matter if you feel like a second-rate Christian or that your prayers lack the punch of other people at your church. Jesus assures you in 15:16 that your authority comes from the fact that *"You did not choose me, but I chose you and appointed you so that... whatever you ask in my name the Father will give you."*[5]

These verses help us to pray for *specific things*. We will not receive the answers that we crave through vague prayers that God will bless this or take care of that. Jesus tells us that God will answer *anything* and *whatever*, and therefore encourages us to get specific. E.M. Bounds writes that

> *The secret of unanswered barren prayers is found in the weakness of our desires... Though one may pray without desire, there can be no true praying if desire is absent... Desire is intense and narrow. It cannot spread itself over a wide field. It wants a few things and it wants them badly, so badly that nothing but God's will can content it with anything else... Do not our prayers often lie in the sickly regions of a mere wish or the feeble expression of a memorized concern or want? Sometimes our prayers are but stereotyped editions of set phrases and decent proportions whose freshness and life went out years ago.*[6]

These verses help us to *persevere* in prayer. When answers fail to arrive, Jesus tells us to check that what we are asking is truly *"in my name"* and for his glory. If he himself let the Father choose the right plan (5:19–20) and right timing (7:6), then it shouldn't surprise us when he tells us that God is wise enough

---

[5] These seven promises contain a mixture of encouragement to pray directly to *Jesus* and to pray to *the Father through the Son*. Acts 4:24–30 and 7:59–60 show us that we can pray both ways.

[6] E.M. Bounds in a sermon preached in October 1890, preserved in *Prayer and Revival* (1993).

to recognize when our prayers are foolish. However, he tells us in 15:7 that the more we get to know him and his Word, the more our prayers will be in wise accordance with his will. It may well be that the piles supporting the Devil's bridge are so firmly embedded that it will require a concerted period of prayer before they come crashing down,[7] but Jesus promises that if we strap as many prayers to them as Olaf strapped ships then the Devil will simply have no power to resist our tide of prayer.

So let's remember this sixth item in our briefcase, and let's allow these seven promises to form a roof to protect our faith from Satan's missiles as we pray. Let's respond to this final warning from Charles Spurgeon:

> *The condition of the church may be very accurately gauged by its prayer meetings. So is the prayer meeting a grace-ometer, and from it we may judge of the amount of divine working among a people. If God be near a church, it must pray. And if he be not there, one of the first tokens of his absence will be a slothfulness in prayer.*[8]

---

[7] Daniel 9:20–23 and 10:12–13 teach that prayer is always heard immediately but may take a little while to achieve a victory in the heavenly realms. Delay does not mean that God is not answering our prayers!

[8] Charles Spurgeon in a sermon preached in 1873, preserved in the *Metropolitan Tabernacle Pulpit*.

Item Seven: Partnership (15:1–17)

I am the vine; you are the branches. If you remain in me and I in you, you will bear much fruit; apart from me you can do nothing.

(John 15:5)

I'm not sure that the person who described being filled with the Holy Spirit as being like touching a live electric wire had actually touched one. I've touched a live mains circuit by mistake while renovating my house, and I can tell you it's really painful.

That said, the person was onto something when they likened God's power to an electrical circuit. As Jesus leaves the upper room in 14:31 and starts walking with his disciples to the Garden of Gethsemane,[1] he evidently spots a vine on the way and gives his seventh and final *"I AM"* saying: *"I am the true vine... you are the branches."*[2] It was the perfect illustration for first-century winemakers of what it means to partner with God, but if he'd flicked off an electric light switch as he left the upper room he might have chosen that instead. Vines, electric circuits: the principle is the same. *"If you remain in me and I in you, you will bear much fruit; apart from me you can do nothing."*

---

[1] He doesn't actually reach the garden until 18:1. He speaks the whole of chapters 15–17 on the way.

[2] Jesus only says *"I am the vine"* in verse 5, but says *"I am the true vine"* in verse 1. Since Israel was called God's vine in Psalm 80:8–16 and Isaiah 5:1–7, but had refused its gardener's hand, Jesus is saying that he obeys where Israel failed and that his followers need to partner with God as "true Israelites" like him (1:47).

There are two mistakes we can fall into as we embark on Jesus' mission. We can succumb to *pride* and assume that our own talents are sufficient, or we can succumb to *despair* when we quickly discover that there are some pretty real obstacles standing in our way. Like most Christians, I can find myself lurching between both extremes, which is why I love this seventh item in our briefcase, which serves as antidote to both. It reminds us that God has called us into a partnership with him. Disconnected from him we can achieve nothing, but connected to him nothing can stand in our way.

Jesus tells us that we need this partnership even to know the first thing we should *say*. He refers in verse 3 to *"the word I have spoken to you"*, because he gives the model of ministry we are to follow. Remember, he told us in 7:15–16 that *"My teaching is not my own,"* and in 8:26–28 that *"I do nothing on my own but speak just what the Father has taught me"*. He now tells us this is the same way that we must preach his message to the world. Are you unsure what to say to win your friends and family to Christ? That's no problem for a mere vine branch or for an electrical appliance. Jesus reassured us in 12:49–50 that even he needed the Father's guidance over what to say to people.[3] *"The Father who sent me commanded me to say all that I have spoken,"* he explained. *"So whatever I say is just what the Father has told me to say."*

As someone God has called to share the Gospel, this should strike you as very good news, and particularly if God has granted you the privilege of preaching. Jesus is promising that if we partner with him, he will tell us what to say. If we write messages of our own, he warns us to expect about as much fruit as a branch which has fallen off a tree or an electrical appliance which has been unplugged. But if we do as he commanded

---

[3] Don't be surprised by Jesus saying he relied entirely on the Father for what to say. Isaiah 50:4–5 always prophesied that the Messiah and his followers would minister this way. Jesus models the route that we must follow, and he promises in 17:8 that when we do people will accept what we have to say.

in Matthew 10:27 – *"What I tell you in the dark, speak in the daylight; what is whispered in your ear, proclaim from the roofs"* – and if we trust his promises in 14:26, 15:7 and 16:13–15 that he will speak to us as we read his Word, we will find ourselves sharing with such divine wisdom that people are converted and built up by what we say.[4]

N. T. Wright confesses that this has been at the heart of his own successes: *"The first time I preached a proper sermon, my mentor gave me some good advice: your praying and your preaching should be of the same length. You don't want to find yourself limping with one leg shorter than the other."*[5]

Jesus also tells us that we need this partnership in everything that we *do*. He freely confessed that none of his own successes were due to the fact that he is God, but due to the fact that the Father had anointed him with the Holy Spirit as a man.[6] He told us in 5:30 that *"By myself I can do nothing"*, and in 14:10 that *"it is the Father, living in me, who is doing his work"*. So if even Jesus the Vine could not succeed in his mission without being plugged into the Gardener, how can we presume to achieve anything without being plugged into the Vine? My angle grinder can cut through thick sheet metal when it is plugged into the mains, but it can't even cut through butter from the fridge when I cut off its electricity supply.

That's why Jesus tells us in verse 11 that this seventh item in our briefcase should make us very happy. If we can truly achieve nothing, nada, zip, zilch and zero without him, then the pressure is off. If our calling is not to *produce* fruit, but simply *bear* fruit, then the burden is on him, not on us. All we have to do is to stay connected to him through faith, prayer, Bible reading and

---

[4] Examples of this are in Matthew 10:19–20, Acts 6:8–10 and Acts 9:17–22.

[5] Tom Wright shares this secret to his preaching ministry in *Surprised by Hope* (2007).

[6] This did not make Jesus any less God. It simply meant he relied on the Father to empower him through the Spirit in order to give us a model we could follow. See Acts 10:38 and Luke 5:17 and 11:20.

loving obedience[7] in order to discover what God can do through ordinary partners like us. We will discover why he doesn't call us servants or workers in verse 15, but his *friends*.[8]

It's also why Jesus tells us to be happy when we feel the Father disciplining us. Vines need pruning and circuit boards need cleaning, because anything which dilutes or resists God's power means we are less fruitful in his hands. The words for *cutting off* and *pruning* are both sister words in Greek,[9] because every single one of us has to feel the sharp edge of the Father's knife one way or the other. Jesus encourages us that if the Father is pruning us, then it is proof we are true disciples and our fruit is on its way.[10] Our pride may not like God's pruning, but it ends all our despair. It proves that Jesus has spoken his word over our lives: *"I chose you and appointed you so that you might go and bear fruit – fruit that will last."*[11]

Talk about taking the pressure off us as we step out on mission! No wonder Jesus tells us this should make us very happy! Let's learn to stay connected to Jesus like branches on a vine, or like a power tool in God's own hands, plugged into his great power supply.

---

[7] John defines what he means by *remaining* in Jesus in John 6:56 and 15:4 and 1 John 4:16. The Greek word for *remaining* is *menō*, the verb of the noun *monē*, or *dwelling place*, which we looked at in the chapter "House Swap".

[8] David and Job were called "servants of God" as a great honour (Psalm 18:1; Job 42:7–8), but Jesus tells us that we have a greater honour as "friends of God" (James 2:23).

[9] *Airō* means *to cut off* and its compound *kathairō* means *to prune* or *purify*. When Jesus talks about us being *cleansed* in verse 3, it can therefore also be translated *pruned*.

[10] Jesus doesn't make a distinction between faithfulness and fruitfulness. He promises that if we are faithful then he will ensure we are fruitful too. In fact, verse 6 suggests that fruitless Christians are false Christians.

[11] Verse 16 tells us that Jesus has appointed us to *"go"* and bear fruit. If you are unfruitful, it may be because you have yet to *"go"* where he has called you on his mission.

Item Eight: Courage under Fire (15:18–16:4)

If the world hates you, keep in mind that it hated me first.

(John 15:18)

John was the only one of Jesus' twelve disciples still alive. And the Christians at Ephesus knew the deaths of the others hadn't been pretty.

Peter, Andrew and Philip had been crucified. John's brother James had been beheaded. The other James and Thaddaeus had both been stoned. Nathanael had been flayed alive. Simon the Zealot had been shot with arrows. Thomas had been disembowelled with spears in India. Matthew had been stabbed to death somewhere in the Caucasus.[1] Now the Emperor Domitian's persecution of Christians had reached Ephesus as well. It was time for John to tell his readers that they needed courage under fire.

Jesus had been entirely up front with his disciples. He had told them they were going to need this eighth item in their briefcase, and need it often. Rather than soothing them with promises of safety, these verses are like the sign which Napoleon Bonaparte erected at the Siege of Toulon in 1793. Napoleon knew that the British could be defeated if he placed a battery of cannon in a place where those who manned it were very easy prey to enemy fire, so he raised a sign which declared that those cannon were the *"Battery for Men without*

---

[1] Most of this is Church tradition, based largely on the early writings of Hippolytus and Eusebius.

Fear". People queued for the honour of manning that battery, and as Jesus describes the perilous mission he has laid out before us, he expects our devotion to the Gospel to exceed an artilleryman's devotion to France.

In 15:18–19, Jesus tells us that being a Christian means taking on *new citizenship* in heaven. When he told his disciples that the Father would relocate his followers to sit with him in heavenly realms, he wasn't just using a vivid metaphor. He tells us that he really meant it and that he has taken us out of the world. We are no longer citizens of our native countries, but citizens of heaven, and we must not be surprised when our friends and neighbours therefore treat us like foreigners. It's nothing but a lie when preachers try to win converts with promises of comfort and prosperity through the Gospel. Jesus tells us that Christian conversion means switching to the other side in a war.

Brother Yun is a Chinese house-church leader. On his way home from a Christian meeting in December 1983, he was arrested by government agents and asked his name and address as a prelude to their forcing him to betray the identities of the other local Christians. *"I am a heavenly man!"* he replied in a loud voice. *"I live in Gospel village! People call me Morning Star! My father's name is Abundant Blessing! My mother's name is Faith, Hope, Love!... I don't know where the meetings took place because I'm a heavenly man! I'm not from this earth!"* His shouting warned the other Christians to run and hide, but it also earned him four years in a prison labour camp.[2]

In 15:20–27, Jesus adds that being a Christian means taking on a *new sovereign ruler*. It is a wonderful thing to be seated with Jesus in heavenly places and to be authorized to make requests to the Father in his name, but he reminds us in verse 21 that if we want to be princes through his name then

---

[2] Brother Yun tells this story in his autobiography *The Heavenly Man* (2002).

we must be persecuted for it too.[3] If our new sovereign is Jesus, and the Psalms predicted that he would be hated without reason,[4] then it should come as no surprise for Jesus to repeat the teaching of 13:16 in verse 20 to remind us that they will hate us too. We must expect people to love us or hate us, just like Jesus, reminding ourselves that their hatred for us is really hatred towards God.[5] We must hold on to Jesus' promise in 16:33 that in the end it will be our ruler whose Kingdom wins the day.

A few years ago, my wife and I went on a backpacking holiday through China. We took a ten-hour train journey through inland China and fell into conversation with an old man and his son. Towards the end of our journey, I reached into my bag and brought out a Chinese Bible as a gift for them. *"Where did you get this?!"* the old man interrogated me, as if I had restored to him a long-lost friend. Then he told me his story. He had only been a child when the government agents had arrested his father for his work as a travelling evangelist. He remembered little about his father, since he had never returned from the labour camp they took him to. He only remembered his mother's tears and what it felt like to grow up in poverty, his family blacklisted by the government for daring to suggest that Jesus Christ was Lord and not Mao Zedong. I learned on that train journey what it means to be a follower of Jesus. As I handed the Bible to that evangelist's son and grandson, I also learned that King Jesus never forgets the sacrifices his subjects have made for his cause.

In 16:1–4, Jesus warns us that being a Christian means taking on a *new commission*. Persecution, prison and even

---

[3] Paul had already taught this in 2 Timothy 2:11–13 while Timothy was stationed at Ephesus.

[4] This quotation could come from either 35:19 or 69:4 because it is such a recurring theme in the Psalms.

[5] Jesus is not saying in 15:22 and 24 that people are innocent before they hear the Gospel, but that our arrival with the Gospel and with miracles reveals their guilt by exposing them for the God-haters that they are.

death are no reason to practise faith in private or keep the Gospel to ourselves. Jesus tells us that public persecution and widespread conversions are two sides of the same coin. As Brother Yun's wife remembers from her husband's years in prison: *"Despite the hardships – or rather because of them – the church experienced rapid growth. Revival fires from the Lord ignited all across China."* Yun adds: *"The Christians still in prison found their witness was empowered because of the many fervent prayers for us. Consequently, countless prisoners came to know the Lord. Many government officials and Communist Party members received Jesus at that time. Some even started to witness boldly for the Lord."*

Because Jesus handed them this eighth item for their briefcase, the Ephesian Christians were prepared for persecution. Jesus could write to them via John in Revelation 2:3 and say, *"You have persevered and have endured hardships for my name, and have not grown weary."*

The question, of course, is could Jesus write the same thing to us? Do we still live so much by this world's rules that those around us fail to see us as foreign citizens? Are we so inwardly backslidden that nobody hates us for the challenge that we bring?[6] Are we so used to keeping silent about King Jesus that the authorities see our faith as a threat which can simply be ignored? Paul tells us in 2 Timothy 3:12 that *"Everyone who wants to live a godly life in Christ Jesus will be persecuted."* That message hasn't changed.

So let's not shrink from using this eighth item in our briefcase and displaying courage under fire. To follow Jesus is a call to follow a new King. It means stepping up to serve on his Battery for People without Fear.

---

[6] Jesus' words in 16:1 are a stark warning that unless church leaders prepare Christians for the inevitability of persecution, they are bound to backslide – either inwardly to avoid it or outwardly when it comes.

Riding Fourth Together
(15:26–27)

*When the Advocate comes, whom I will send to you
from the Father... he will testify about me. And you
also must testify.*

(John 15:26–27)

Most Christians live as if God has sent them off to perform some great mission with their lives. All this talk about putting items in our briefcase might have made you think the same way. But God hasn't. He really hasn't. He has simply called you to be the fourth person working in *his* mission.

Make sure you don't rush over the final two verses of chapter 15. Jesus tells us something which is pure spiritual liberation. He tells us that the mission of calling the world to salvation is firstly *God's* mission, then secondly *Jesus'* mission since the Father sent him, and then thirdly the *Holy Spirit's* mission since the Father and Son have sent him.[1] Then and only then does it become our mission fourthly, since the Father, Son and Spirit have sent us. If you find the task of sharing Jesus with your neighbour tricky, let alone the task of world mission, then this should strike you as seriously good news. No wonder Jesus told us that *"my yoke is easy and my burden is light"*.[2]

John knew what it was like to work as the fourth person in a partnership. When we find him working as a fisherman in

---

[1] The Orthodox Church traditionally uses verse 26 and 14:16 to argue that the Holy Spirit proceeds from the Father but not from the Son. However, these verses need to be set alongside 1:33, 7:37 and 20:22.

[2] Matthew 11:30. A *yoke* is a pulling collar for two, or in this case four.

Luke 5, he and his brother James are described as Peter and Andrew's *koinōnoi*, or fishing *partners*, which is the sister word of *koinōnia* which Paul uses to describe us enjoying *fellowship* or *partnership* with the Holy Spirit in 2 Corinthians 13:14. Let's bear that in mind and reconsider what happens as Jesus gives the four fishing partners a miraculous catch of fish in Luke 5.

The fish have been prepared by *God the Father*. They haven't been magicked into Lake Galilee out of nowhere for the miracle. God has been working in their fishy lives to prepare them for this moment. The catch is provided by *Jesus the Son*, who tells Simon Peter where to let down his net successfully.[3] The fish are caught by a *third person* – in the story it is Peter, but in our own lives Jesus told Nicodemus in 3:5–8 that it is the Holy Spirit. Now and only now does John get a role in the story, as Peter calls him and his brother to come and partner with him so that they can help him land the catch which he and the Father and Son have just made. First the Father, second Jesus, third the Holy Spirit, fourth ourselves. Jesus wants to ensure that we realize that going on mission means us riding fourth together.

John is telling us to let God take care of our *strategy*. In the book of Acts it is the Lord who tells Philip to go to a desert road where he will meet a receptive African and open up a new continent for Jesus, and the Holy Spirit who shows him the chariot to choose before whisking him away as soon as his job is complete. It is the Lord who connects Peter to Cornelius and his Gentile household, and the Holy Spirit who both confirms that he should go and then demonstrates that God wants to save these Gentiles too. It is the Holy Spirit who decides that the time has come for the Gospel to be taken to Cyprus and Galatia, and who pinpoints Paul and Barnabas as the two men for the job. It is the Holy Spirit who tells Paul that now is not the time to preach the Gospel in Asia and Bithynia, and the Lord

---

[3] Jesus promises to do the same for us in Mark 1:17 – *"Follow me and I will make you fishers of men"*.

who tells him in a dream to go to Macedonia instead.[4] What we read about in those pages is simply the outworking of these two verses in John. The apostles remembered that they rode fourth in someone else's mission, and as they did so, they found the Father, Son and Spirit led them to places where they saw breakthroughs they could not have imagined if they had been planning on their own.

John is telling us to let God take care of our *team*. The one who took Philip away from Samaria in the midst of revival, who let one of Jesus' inner circle of Three be executed in the very early days of Church history, who plucked the church at Antioch's two best elders away to pioneer a new stage of his mission, who kept Paul in Judea when he planned to go to Rome, and kept him in chains in Rome when he wanted to walk free,[5] is more than able to manage your church team too. If you panic when key individuals leave your church or baulk at the thought of giving leaders away, you need to read what Jesus is telling us in these verses again. God wants you to have the same perspective as Paul, who wrote from prison in Philippians 1:12 that *"what has happened to me has actually served to advance the gospel"*.

John is telling us to let God take care of our *fruitfulness*. Since the Lord enabled the apostles to define the Gospel message in a way which *"seemed good to the Holy Spirit and to us"*, we can also trust him to do as Jesus promises in 16:7–14 – to tell us what we should be saying and convict people of what we say.[6] Since the Lord enabled them to live such godly lives and perform so many miracles that Peter exclaimed *"we are witnesses... and so is the Holy Spirit"*, and since Paul and Barnabas told their friends *"all that God had done through them"*, we can trust him to do as Jesus promises in 14:12 and perform such miracles through us too.[7]

---

[4] Acts 8:26, 29, 39; 10:3–6, 14–15, 19–20, 44–48; 13:2–4; 16:6–10.

[5] Acts 8:8, 26; 12:2; 13:2–4; 24:27; 28:16, 30–31; Romans 15:23–25; Philippians 1:12–14.

[6] Acts 15:28.

[7] Acts 5:32; 14:27; 15:4, 12.

The nineteenth-century evangelist D.L. Moody writes about an exhausted minister who was on the brink of breakdown when he heard Moody explaining how to ride fourth in God's mission. The man was reinvigorated and began to see conversions through the Father, Son and Spirit every day. Moody writes: *"I don't believe that man broke down at first due to hard work, so much as using the machinery without oil, without lubrication. It is not the hard work that breaks down ministers, but it is the toil of working without power. Oh, that God may anoint His people!"*[8]

If you are tired of trying to share the Gospel without seeing much fruit; if you are daunted by the size of the mission which lies ahead; if you don't know how to begin, or what to say or what to do; if you feel your calling is too great for you, then you are in the very place where Jesus wants you to be.

Because it isn't your mission. It's the Father's mission. Then the Son's mission. Then the Spirit's mission. Then only fourthly yours. Let's remember that this mission is God's, not our own, and then let's happily ride fourth together.

---

[8] D.L. Moody shares this observation in his book *Secret Power* (1881).

Thank God Jesus Has Gone Away (16:4–33)

Very truly I tell you, it is for your good that I am going away.

(John 16:7)

When I first became a Christian, I used to think how wonderful it must have been to live in Galilee when Jesus walked the earth. To be there when he turned water into wine, when he fed the five thousand, or when he healed the blind. To be there to hear his teaching and witness his miracles. It used to make me feel a bit jealous of the disciples and the other people mentioned in the gospels. Then I read John 16. Jesus tells us not to think as foolishly as I did. Things on earth have got far better since he went away.

205

Think about it. Although it sounds like a nice idea to live in Galilee with Jesus, getting an audience with him was actually pretty hard. Often he would hide from the crowds to be alone with his twelve disciples and their entourage.[1] Often he would hide from the entourage to focus solely on the Twelve. Sometimes he would leave the nine to pursue some more intense discipling of the Three. And of course every day he would leave them all behind to spend time fellowshipping alone with his Father. Being in Galilee when Jesus walked the earth was problematic. He could only be in one place at a time, and the chances were that it wasn't going to be with you.

---

[1] Acts 1:21–22 tells us that the Twelve had hangers-on. Luke 8:1–3 tells us that some of these were women.

That's why chapter 16 is such good news for us. Having hinted in 14:28 that his disciples should be glad he was going away, he now says explicitly in 16:7, *"It is for your good that I am going away."* How could it be good? Because when he ascended to heaven he would pour out the gift of the Holy Spirit on all God's People. *"Unless I go away, the Advocate will not come to you; but if I go, I will send him to you."* Instead of granting his followers an audience based on his limited availability, he would be present for each one of them 24 hours a day and 365 days of the year.

Jesus explains in verses 8–11 that this is fantastic news for *unbelievers*. Until his death and resurrection, he might have had time to counsel the odd Pharisee, Samaritan, tax collector or rich young ruler, but after his ascension he would be able to work in the heart of every unbeliever all the time. He would convict them in verse 8 through his Spirit that they must not deny their sin or God's offer of righteousness or that they would be judged if they refused it. The Devil might call himself the "prince of this world" and imagine that the cross was his final victory, but it would actually unleash his own condemnation. He simply wouldn't be able to defend himself on all sides against a Jesus who was able to be everywhere all the time.

This should encourage you in the mission God has called you to. Quite a lot, in fact. It is one of the reasons we can't reduce the scope of our mission to simply "friendship evangelism", since Jesus is at work in the lives of people all around us, whether or not they are our friends. It means that we will never meet a person in whose life Jesus isn't working, nor anyone he has not prepared for whatever snatched conversation we may have with them. Mark Dever encourages us:

> *You and I aren't called to use our extensive powers to convict and change the sinner while God stands back as a gentleman, quietly waiting for the spiritual corpse,*

his declared spiritual enemy, to invite God into his heart. Rather, we should resolve to preach the Gospel like gentlemen, persuading while knowing we can't regenerate anyone, and then stand back while God uses all his extensive powers to convict and change the sinner. Then we'll see clearly who it is that can really call the dead to life, and although he'll use us in the doing of it, it's not you and I who are actually doing it.[2]

Jesus adds in verses 12–15 that this is also fantastic news for *believers.* It means we aren't like Peter – hoping Jesus isn't sleeping or praying or reading Scripture or preaching or healing or ministering to the poor, so that we can talk to him. He has made his home inside us through the Holy Spirit, such that Paul says we should always be able to hear what Jesus is thinking since *"we have the mind of Christ"*.[3] Jesus reassures us that we can expect to hear him guiding and teaching us enough to be able to say "this seems right to the Holy Spirit and to me". We don't need to cajole him into speaking to us, since it glorifies the Father to reveal things to the Son, who reveals it to the Spirit, who reveals it to us, displaying his gracious willingness to use people like us as the fourth member of his team. It is a matter of God's glory that you know what the Trinity is thinking. Whatever good conversations Jesus may have had with the Twelve in Galilee, nowadays he promises that *"he will guide you into **all** the truth"*.[4]

Jesus closes in verses 16–33 by telling us that this is also fantastic news for *what goes on in heaven.* It felt so painful for the disciples to watch him ascend to heaven that a pair of angels

---

[2] Mark Dever in *The Gospel and Personal Evangelism* (2007).

[3] 1 Corinthians 2:16. Similarly, 1 Kings 3:9 describes true wisdom literally as having a *hearing heart*.

[4] By my calculations, if Jesus were still on the earth as one man today, you might reasonably expect him to be a visiting speaker at your church once every 27,000 years.

had to tell them to stop looking up and to start looking forward, but when they started to experience his presence with them after Pentecost, they no more grieved his departure than a new mother cuddling her baby grieves her labour pains.[5] They grasped that not only was Jesus with them on earth, but he was also interceding for them with the Father uninterruptedly in heaven, which is probably why three of the seven promises that God will answer our prayers in Jesus' name come here in verses 23–26. Paul writes in Romans 8:34–37 that *"Christ Jesus who died – more than that, who was raised to life – is at the right hand of God and is also interceding for us. Who shall separate us from the love of Christ? Shall trouble or hardship or persecution or famine or nakedness or danger or sword?... No, in all these things we are more than conquerors through him who loved us."*

Therefore Jesus ends chapter 16 in exactly the same way, warning us that troubles lie ahead but reassuring us that he has conquered and made us more than conquerors with him.

Of course he has, if he is now at work non-stop in every believer and unbeliever on the earth, and if he is also busy pleading our cause non-stop with his Father in heaven. That's why it's such a blessing that we weren't born to live in first-century Galilee. Let's be grateful that we live in the now, and thank God Jesus has gone away!

---

[5] Acts 1:11. Verses 20–22 certainly describes the rollercoaster of emotions they would feel over the next three days when Jesus died and rose again, but the primary meaning in the context of verses 23–28 has to be the emotions they would feel between Jesus going away at his ascension and coming back at Pentecost.

The Real Lord's Prayer
(17:1–26)

*After Jesus said this, he looked towards heaven
and prayed.*

(John 17:1)

Most people call Jesus' prayer in Matthew 6 *the Lord's Prayer*.
But it isn't really. It's what he gave the disciples as a model of
how they should pray: *the Disciples' Prayer*.

Many people assume that the prayer in John 17 is an
expanded version of the agonized prayer that Jesus prays in the
Garden of Gethsemane in Matthew 26. That's not right either.
John tells us that Jesus prayed this prayer while still en route to
the garden, and that he only reached it in 18:1.

No. What we have here is the real Lord's Prayer, the longest
recorded prayer of Jesus in the Bible, and a prayer which flows
out of the context which goes before. Jesus prays this prayer out
loud for the benefit of his disciples,[1] in order to show them the
kind of prayers he will be praying for them in heaven after his
ascension. Known for centuries as *Jesus' High-Priestly Prayer*,
the prayer in chapter 17 is an example of the intercession Jesus
makes right now for his Church before the Father.[2]

Jesus starts in verses 1–5 by praying for *himself*, and by
modelling his desire for us to *look and see the Living God*. Jesus is

---

[1] Remember, 11:42 taught us that it is not always a bad thing to think about
the people who are listening when we pray out loud!

[2] This name goes back at least as far as Cyril of Alexandria in the fifth century,
and it links this chapter to Romans 8:34–39, Hebrews 7:21–28 and 1 John
2:1.

only hours away from torture and crucifixion, yet he is doing all that John told us to do in the first section of his gospel. His eyes are not fixed on himself or on his tragedy or on his disciples.[3] They are fixed on the fact that God is his Father, that God's timing is perfect and that what really matters is completing the Father's plan. His prayer focuses on *eternal life*, a phrase which John has used fourteen times so far in his gospel but which Jesus only defines for us now: eternal life is knowing the Father and the Son, both in this life and the next. Eternal life – the phrase can equally be translated the *Life of the Age to Come* – has already begun for us if we have fixed our eyes on Jesus as the way to see the Living God.[4]

As he prays this way, Jesus wants us to see his complete fixation with the Father's glory. His prayer for himself is that he be glorified, but only so that the Father may be ultimately glorified. His prayer prepares him for being glorified through his death and resurrection, but only so that the Father may be ultimately glorified. Jesus wants to teach us that his prayers are always Father-centred, not self-centred or us-centred, so that we learn to keep our own prayers focused on the glory of the Living God.[5] By taking our eyes off ourselves and onto the Father's glory, he provides reassurance that God will not let our mission fail, and at the same time teaches us what the grand objective of that mission is.

He continues in verses 6–14 by praying for *his disciples* concerning his goal for them to *look and see who Jesus really is*. They have believed what he said in verse 5, that he is the glorious

---

[3] Jesus' heart was troubled like the stormy sea in 13:21 – the Greek word is *tarassō*, which is also used in 5:7, 11:33 and 12:27 – but he was more focused on the Father's plan than he was on his own pain.

[4] John also tells us we can experience eternal life today in 3:16, 3:36, 5:24 and 10:10.

[5] Note how God expects his glory to be the chief end of our own prayers in 1 Samuel 12:22, Psalm 79:9 and 115:1, Isaiah 48:9–11, Jeremiah 14:7 and Ezekiel 36:21–23. This is what *"hallowed be your name"* actually means.

Son of God who existed before the creation of the world.[6] They have believed he is the Messiah, have accepted his teaching in the second section of John's gospel, and have trusted in his name as he described it in his seven *"I AM"* sayings. Jesus tells the Father in verse 14 that he has taken his disciples out of this dark world like the rescuer in Plato's Allegory of the Cave, and he prays that they will experience the full joy which comes from living life in the sunshine beyond Satan's gloomy prison.[7]

Note the progression here. Jesus was fully focused on the Father when he prayed for himself in verses 1–5. Now as he prays for the disciples, he wants them to focus on him because it's by looking at who Jesus really is that we truly come to see the Living God. The world may hate them for it, but as they live their lives for Jesus' glory, they ultimately glorify the Father who sent him and fulfil the very purpose for which he created the world.

He moves on in verses 15–19 by praying for *his disciples to look and see what Jesus has given them*. He prays that his Father will protect them as they set out on his mission, and as they go to rescue many more of the prisoners in Plato's cave. He says in verse 18 that he has handed this mission on to them, just as the Father had handed the mission on to him. They need to be sanctified – fully set apart for mission[8] – and Jesus prays for them as they go into the world with the ten items he has given them in their briefcase.

Finally, he ends in verses 20–26 by praying for *future generations of believers*, that they will also *look and see what Jesus has given them*. Remember, Jesus is showing the disciples

---

[6] Jesus claims to be God extremely clearly in verses 5 and 24. To miss this is to be blinder than a Pharisee.

[7] There is nothing dreary about living for God's glory. Jesus stresses that it brings real *joy* in 3:29, 4:36, 10:10, 15:11, 16:20–24 and 17:13. A miserable Christian does not glorify God!

[8] Since Jesus also talks about himself being *sanctified* in verse 19, he cannot primarily be talking about us being set apart *from* sin, but about us being set apart *for* God's mission. Holiness means both.

what he will be praying as he sits next to the Father in heaven for the remainder of world history. He therefore prays that his Church will always be united together and united with the Trinity as described in part three of John. *"Father, I want those you have given me to be with me where I am,"* he prays in verse 24, referring to us being seated with him in heavenly realms. *"I have made you known to them, and will continue to make you known in order that... I myself may be in them,"* he continues in verse 26 as he describes his plan to make his home inside us on the earth. Jesus tells the disciples that these are things he will be praying for you and me in heaven, asking the Father that we will respond to the first three parts of John's gospel. Again the refrain is *"glory... glory... glory"*. It's what Jesus is praying for you to the Father right now.

The eighteenth-century preacher Jonathan Edwards writes:

> *It is manifest... that the glory of the Father, and his own glory, are what Christ exulted in, in the prospect of his approaching sufferings... as the end his heart was mainly set upon, and supremely delighted in... For it appears that all that is ever spoken of in the Scripture as an ultimate end of God's works is included in that one phrase, **the glory of God**.*[9]

So let's draw comfort from Jesus showing us that his prayers for us in heaven right now are always focused on God's glory. Let's follow the direction of his gaze by fixing our eyes on who Jesus is as the perfect revelation of the Living God. Then let's look at what he has given us to equip us to proclaim this message to the world. Let's do it all for the ultimate glory of the Living God.

---

[9] Jonathan Edwards wrote this in his dissertation *The End for Which God Created the World* (1765).

Item Nine: Body Armour (17:11-12)

Holy Father, protect them by the power of your name... While I was with them, I protected them and kept them safe by that name you gave me.

(John 17:11–12)

Jesus' disciples knew the importance of soldiers wearing body armour. There was no police force in Jerusalem, just Roman soldiers in the streets and the chief priest's guards at the Temple. Every day, the disciples walked past soldiers wearing breastplates and cuirasses. So when Jesus told them that the ninth item they needed on their mission was body armour, they can't have been surprised.

What was surprising was what the Christian's body armour was made of. Jesus prayed in verses 11–12 that his Father would protect his followers through his *name*, just as Jesus had protected them through God's name too. He was simply repeating what Proverbs 18:10 had always taught: *"The name of the Lord is a fortified tower; the righteous run to it and are safe."* But with one of the Twelve about to get picked off and destroyed by Satan, Jesus warned them that this body armour wasn't an optional item in their briefcase.[1]

When Jesus promised seven times in chapters 14–16 that God will answer the prayers we offer in his name, he was using *name* to refer primarily to authority. When he speaks about

213

---

[1] The implication in verse 12 is that Judas Iscariot was about to go to hell because he was never truly saved. He had never truly stepped into God's name as a fortified tower.

our being protected by his name in chapter 17, however, he is referring primarily to his identity.[2] Since Jesus has already warned us that if we follow him we will find ourselves under heavy enemy fire, let's consider briefly what Jesus is telling us to do, just using his seven *"I AM"* sayings.

Jesus told us in 10:11 that *"I am the Good Shepherd."* It links back to the name of Yahweh in the famous Psalm 23. The Lord told Israel in verse 1 of that psalm that he would protect them because he was their shepherd, and now Jesus promises the same to us. He did not abandon us even in the face of death, so when we come under attack we can cry out for him to shepherd us safely because we take refuge in his name.[3]

Jesus told us in 6:35 that *"I am the Bread of Life"*, which links to verses 1–2 of the psalm and the promise that we will lack nothing from the shepherd who feeds his sheep on green pastures and still water. Following Jesus on mission will mean losing family, friends, honour, respect, money and advancement, so we need to take refuge in his name as the one who is our all-sufficiency. Satan has used discontent to shipwreck countless Christians over money, sex or power. If we keep inside the fortress of the Lord's name, we are protected by walls of contentedness in him.[4]

Jesus told us in 14:6 that *"I am the Way, the Truth and the Life"*, which links to verse 3 of the psalm and the promise that God will lead us *"in paths of righteousness for his name's sake"*. When we look at Jesus, we see the truth, and he comes to live inside us and make us righteous. No wonder Paul describes the Christian's armour in Ephesians 6 as *"the belt of truth"* and *"the*

---

[2] Many translations mask how big a theme this is in chapter 17. Verses 6 and 26 say literally *"I have revealed your name"* and *"I have made your name known to them, and will continue to make it known"*.

[3] See also 1 Samuel 17:34–35. Jesus refers to his followers as *sheep* again in 21:15–17.

[4] John 17:11–12 can also be translated as a prayer to *"keep them in your name"*.

breastplate of righteousness". If we strap on John 14:6 as our daily body armour, the Devil cannot pierce us with his weapons.

Jesus told us in 8:12 that *"I am the Light of the World"*, the one who leads us out of Plato's cave into the sunshine. Verse 4 of the psalm rejoices that our God is enough light for us even when the circumstances of our lives feel very dark. Jesus' shepherd-rod and staff bring comfort even when we cannot see the way ahead. The disciples were about to need this when Jesus died and darkness reigned.[5] They were about to need what Paul described in Ephesians 6 as *"the shield of faith"*.

Jesus told us in 10:7 that *"I am the Gate"*, which links to verses 5–6 of the psalm. David talked about God admitting him into his banqueting hall and feasting him on the finest foods from his royal table. It sounds too good to be true in light of David's sinful adultery and murder, but John the Baptist has reminded us in 1:29 that Jesus is more than just our shepherd; he is also our atoning sacrificial lamb. When the Devil tries to tempt us into thinking that we are not seated with Christ in the heavenly realms or that paupers like us are not worthy of reigning as princes, we can run into the fortified tower of Jesus' name. It's what Paul described in Ephesians 6 as *"the helmet of salvation"*.

Jesus told us in 15:1 that *"I am the true Vine"*, as a symbol of our union together through the Holy Spirit. Verse 5 of the psalm uses a different metaphor to tell us that God anoints our head with the oil of his Spirit and makes our wine goblet overflow. You wouldn't want to come anywhere near me when I'm operating my electrical circular saw, and the Devil is scared to come near us too when we are connected to God's power supply.

Jesus told us in 11:25 that *"I am the Resurrection and the Life"*, and the psalm ends exactly the same way. David is not just convinced that God's name has ensured that *"your goodness and love will follow me all the days of my life"*, but also that this will

---

[5] Luke 22:53; 23:44–45.

be the case *"forever"*. When John's fellow disciples faced threats of execution and death, their biggest danger was not dying but preserving their lives through denying the one who could raise them from the dead. Ultimately, Jesus doesn't promise that we won't die. It's probable that some who read this chapter will receive a martyr's death themselves. But we can still be protected if we love Jesus more than death, and if at our martyrdom we run into the fortified tower of his name.

I have only had time to examine Jesus' seven *"I AM"* sayings. There is no time to examine the names Yahweh (*The One Who Really Is*), Messiah (*Anointed One*) or Jesus (*The Lord Saves* or *The Lord Heals*). If there were, we would discover that the Bible is a book of one precious name for God after another. These are all bricks in the great tower which forms our body armour. They are all part of why the ancient believers learned to say:

> *May the name of the God of Jacob protect you... Some trust in chariots and some in horses, but we trust in the name of the Lord our God.*

They are also why the Lord has always replied:

> *I will rescue him; I will protect him, for he acknowledges my name.*[6]

---

[6] Psalms 20:1, 7 and 91:14.

Jesus' Big Request
(17:15–19)

My prayer is not that you take them out of the world.
(John 17:15)

The last recorded outbreak of the smallpox virus in Europe was in 1972. A Muslim cleric got back to his home in Kosovo from a pilgrimage to Mecca and started displaying some very troubling symptoms from an illness he had picked up on his travels. When 150 of his neighbours started displaying those same symptoms too, one of them was taken north to a hospital in the capital Belgrade. When forty people at the hospital also started showing the same symptoms, the Yugoslavian government knew it had an epidemic on its hands.

The government's reaction was radical and decisive. It declared martial law and placed a perimeter around the infected villages in Kosovo and the hospital in Belgrade. No one was allowed in and no one was allowed out. Borders were closed. All non-essential travel and public meetings were banned. The government ruthlessly isolated those infected with the virus. It was a textbook response and within two months smallpox had once again been completely eradicated from Europe.

What happened in Kosovo and Belgrade in 1972 makes it easy for us to understand the big request in Jesus' High-Priestly Prayer. He had told his disciples in chapters 14–16 that, after his ascension and the Day of Pentecost, they would dwell with him in heaven and he would dwell with them on earth. The Gospel message which began with Jesus "tabernacling" on earth in one body in 1:14 would continue with his "tabernacling" in us all over the world. That's why Jesus makes his big request to his Father in verses 15–19: *"My prayer is not that you take them out of the world."* It is for them to be *in* the world but not *of* the world.[1] The Devil must not be allowed to quarantine their message and to insulate their power.

The early Christians understood this. The disciples' own experience in chapter 1 had been that Andrew invited his brother Peter, Philip invited his friend Nathanael, and probably John invited his brother James to come to Jesus.[2] The Early Church simply carried on this method so determinedly that Acts 8:4 tells us that even persecution strengthened their resolve to scatter and spread their contagion everywhere.

Tertullian described their strategy in a message delivered to Roman leaders in 197 AD:

> *We are but of yesterday, but we have filled every place among you – cities, islands, fortresses, towns, market-places, even the camps, tribes, companies, palace, senate, forum – we have left nothing to you but the temples of your gods... We are not Indian Brahmins or fakirs living in woods and exiling themselves from ordinary life... We go to your forum, your market, your baths, your shops, your workshops, your inns, your fairs, and the other places of trade.*[3]

It was a strategy which worked. As the Christians formed friendships with work colleagues, traders and neighbours in the crowded streets of their cities, and gave themselves to personal evangelism day in and day out, they succeeded

---

[1] Jesus uses the exact same phrase – *ek tou kosmou* – in both verse 15 and verse 16. Jesus doesn't want us physically *out of the world* because we are already spiritually *out of the world*.

[2] John also stresses this theme in 4:28–30 and 39–42, 4:53, 11:19 and 12:2.

[3] Tertullian in his *Apology* (37). He wasn't ashamed of this plan to spread the Christian "virus".

in winning the Roman Empire to Christ one precious life at a time. Church historian Kenneth Latourette concludes from all the evidence that

> *The chief agents in the expansion of Christianity appear not to have been those who made it a profession or made it a major part of their occupation, but men and women who carried on their livelihood in some purely secular manner and spoke of their faith to those they met in this natural fashion.*[4]

This hasn't always been the case in Church history, however. Jesus made this big request for a reason. Many periods have been more characterized by the opinion of Matthew Henry in his famous commentary on 2 Corinthians 6:11–18:

> *We should not join in friendship and acquaintance with wicked men and unbelievers. Though we cannot wholly avoid seeing and hearing, and being with such, yet we should never choose them for friends. We must not defile ourselves by converse with those who defile themselves with sin.*

Recently, I conducted a survey of British church leaders and their congregations. It made me realize we are a lot more like Matthew Henry than Tertullian. Less than a quarter of respondents had five or more significant relationships with a non-Christian, and a fifth confessed that they didn't even have one. Those are exactly the kind of statistics which delight the Devil, and which prompted Jesus to pray about how much he wants us in the world.

So, what does Jesus tell us to do in these verses if our own lifestyle is of the Matthew Henry rather than the Tertullian kind?

---

[4] Kenneth Latourette in his *History of the Expansion of Christianity, Volume I* (1945).

First, he tells us to remember that the Devil is defeated and that we are on the winning side. He prays for the Father to protect us in verse 15, because the body armour he has just described enables us to scatter through society without fear. The primary danger isn't ours, being polluted by the world, but the world's – that it will be infected by us![5]

Second, he tells us to remember that when we surrendered our lives to him we automatically signed up for his mission. He tells us we need to be *sanctified* – a word with two meanings. It refers both to being *set apart from* sin and to being *set apart for* service. Since he says in verse 19 and in 10:36 that he himself needed to be sanctified, it follows that it is the second of these two meanings that he has in mind. That's the irony when believers huddle together with diaries full of church meetings and Christian friends, in the hope that somehow this isolationism will make them more sanctified. Jesus tells us that the best way to be sanctified is to say yes to God's mission. We are never holier than when we roll up our sleeves and get our nice clean hands deep in the muck of the world.

Third, he tells us that sanctification comes by reading the Word of God and exposing ourselves to his truth.[6] The reason we neglect our mission is that Satan is a master at keeping Christian thinking quarantined and at making sure that people who are filled with God's power are insulated from the world. He is good at it because he knows his disintegrating hold on the cities and nations of the world depends on his desperate blockade of us inside a Christian world.

God's mission means spreading the Gospel from person to person. Take a look at your own lifestyle and let Jesus' big request reshape it.

---

[5] Where Matthew Henry is right is that 2 Corinthians 6:11–18 *does* warn, however, against marrying, working for or making political alliances with non-Christians when the price is compromising our love for Christ.

[6] 2 Thessalonians 2:13 and Ephesians 5:26 also teach that in order to be sanctified we need to expose ourselves to God's truth through his Word.

Item Ten: Unity (17:20–26)

I pray… that they may be one as we are one…
that they may be brought to complete unity.

(John 17:20–23)

The disciples were used to the idea of a general leading his troops out against a much larger army. The Roman generals did it for a living. Julius Caesar had invaded Britain in 55 BC with only 10,000 men. He had defeated the Gallic tribes of France at the Battle of Alesia in 52 BC despite being outnumbered four to one. Everyone in the Roman Empire knew that it wasn't an army's size that mattered but its discipline. It wasn't surprising, therefore, when Jesus told them that the tenth and final item in their briefcase must be *unity*.

While the barbarians tended to rely on numbers and mob tactics, the Roman generals drilled their legionaries to form a disciplined "triple line". If it was attacked by cavalry, it could adopt a square formation. If it was subjected to a hail of arrows, it could adopt the "tortoise" formation behind a united wall of shields. If it saw the opportunity to rush an objective, it could reorder into a "wedge" formation which channelled the soldiers' combined strength to punch through enemy lines. As the subject peoples of the Empire knew only too well, a united army doesn't need to be large to win the day.

That's why these last seven verses of Jesus' High-Priestly Prayer, and the last seven verses of part three of John's gospel, are an impassioned plea for Christian unity. Jesus knows he is about to leave only about 120 faithful followers behind, but he also knows that if his Father unites them then they will overcome the mob tactics of the enemy. He therefore prays for all the believers to be as united as the Trinity – all of them different and distinct and with differing roles, yet at the same time all entirely united as one.[1]

It had happened fairly recently, so the disciples must have known about the disastrous Roman defeat at the Battle of the Teutoburg Forest in 9 AD. Despite outnumbering the German barbarians by two or three to one, they had lost their disciplined order and unity while passing through the dense and narrow forest trails. Three mighty Roman legions had been strung out over ten long miles in disunited clumps, so when the Germans pounced the superior Roman numbers were powerless to save them. Those three legions had been slaughtered in the forest almost to a man. That's why this tenth item is more than just a late addition to our briefcase. It is of paramount importance, and it is the natural fruit of our using the other nine items properly.

Jesus explains that unity is a simple function of our laying hold of the *humility* and *loving obedience* he has already described. The disciples had still been bickering over dinner about which of them was the greatest, but those first two items in their briefcase demanded an end to their competitive rivalry.[2] Jesus promises in verses 21 and 23 that as the Holy Spirit produces these things in us, the world will see our selfless love and recognize that Jesus truly is the Messiah and that we truly are the People of God.

Jesus also explains that unity is a simple function of our receiving *the Holy Spirit*. He says to the Father in verse 22 that he has given us God's glory – probably referring to his having prepared the ground for us to receive the Holy Spirit – and that

[1] Jesus does not use *heis* as the normal masculine word for *one*, as might have been expected, to describe the oneness of the Trinity and of the Church in 10:30 and 17:11 and 21–23. He uses the neuter word *hen* as a way in Greek of expressing oneness in diversity.

[2] Luke 22:24–30. Jesus prayed so hard for Christian unity because he knew it would require a miracle.

one of the reasons he wants to baptize us with the Spirit is that this always leads to increased Christian unity. Paul picks up on this in 1 Corinthians 12:13, when he encourages us to be united on the basis that *"we were all baptized by one Spirit so as to form one body... and we were all given the one Spirit to drink"*. People who are full of God's Spirit are too focused on Jesus living inside them to risk grieving him away.

Jesus explains that unity is a simple function of our believing the same *Gospel*. It's true that the Gospel forces us to separate from those who are not true Christians at all – such as the one described in verse 12 – but it also convinces us that every believer has the same Saviour, the same righteousness, the same eternal life and the same glorious future. It is nonsensical to think that people who sit together with Christ in heavenly realms should be unable to share a room together on earth because of differences in emphasis and style. Jesus tells us that the Gospel has united us *already*, because each time he prays he asks the Father for us to *be* one, not *become* one.[3]

Jesus explains that unity is a simple function of our *partnership* in a mission fuelled by *miracles* and *prayer*. When troops are left idle in camp for too long they begin infighting, but when they are led out to war their petty differences are quickly set aside. Jesus expects us to be so much on the front foot for his mission that we are too busy praying together, casting out demons together, pressing forward in signs and miracles together, preaching the Gospel together and baptizing together to have any time for petty squabbles in the barracks.

Finally, Jesus explains that unity is a simple function of our putting on *body armour* and needing *courage under fire*. Not many arguments take place between people who are

---

[3] He uses the verb *eimi*, which means *to be*, not *ginomai*, which means *to become*. Similarly Paul tells us in Ephesians 4:3 to *keep* the unity of the Spirit, not *achieve* it. What is translated *"brought to complete unity"* in verse 23 is better translated *"perfected into one"* – that we may express more perfectly the fact we are one.

crouching behind a barricade or grovelling in the dust under a ricochet of enemy fire. In the same way, as our mission provokes persecution and angry reaction, we grow more and more united as we bear hardship together. Jesus tells us in verse 11 that it is while we are running for protection into the fortified tower of his name that we will find ourselves behaving as one, even as the Trinity is one.

As the Trinity is one. That's the nub of what Jesus is saying. Because if his army of missionaries fight one another, how will the world not think that their Triune God is the same? If his followers bring shame on themselves through their competition and pride, how will the world be able to look at them and see God's glory? If we forget this tenth item in our briefcase, then our plans and projects are as likely to succeed against the enemy as the disunited legionaries who died in Germany.

But if we do use those first nine items in our briefcase – humility, loving obedience, the Holy Spirit, the Gospel, miracles, prayer, partnership, courage under fire and body armour – we will find that they also lead us to use this tenth item, so that we behave as unitedly as the 120 on the Day of Pentecost. Divided we fall, but together we can march as a united force to reach the world, and to succeed as one for the Father's glory.

Part Four:

Look at Jesus and Win

(Chapters 18–21)

Man on Trial (18:1–19:16)

When Jesus came out wearing the crown of thorns and the purple robe, Pilate said to them, "Here is the man!"

(John 19:5)

Part four of John's gospel is a celebration of Jesus' victory, but you never would have guessed it from its opening verses. It starts with Jesus being betrayed by one of his disciples, with his being arrested by his enemies and with his being put on trial.[1] The hour has come for us to hear the world pass its final verdict over Jesus. As it does so, the hour has also come for us to recognize his total victory.

The first verdict is passed by the *high priest* of Israel. Technically that was Caiaphas, but John focuses on his father-in-law Annas because most devout Jews viewed him as the true high priest, despite the fact that the Romans had deposed him a few years earlier.[2] Unlike the synoptic gospel writers, John was actually there to witness Jesus' trial,[3] so he focuses on Annas as the real power behind the priesthood. Caiaphas had prophesied unwittingly in 11:49–50 that Jesus must be sacrificed to save God's sinful People, but it was Annas who engineered the final

---

[1] John doesn't name the *Garden of Gethsemane* in 18:1 – literally the *Garden of the [Olive] Oil Press* – because he expects us to know Matthew and Mark's gospels well enough to recognize the garden instantly.

[2] We can see this in Luke 3:2 and Acts 4:6. The Jews still considered Annas to be high priest for life, and defied the Roman governor by letting him rule through five puppet sons and a puppet son-in-law.

[3] Taken together, the gospels recount six trials of Jesus: before Annas, before Caiaphas, before the Sanhedrin, before Pilate, before Herod and before Pilate again. 18:15–16 suggests that John witnessed the first three.

decision that they would do so. As the high priest who officiated at Passover that year, he would unwittingly sacrifice Jesus as God's once-and-for-all Passover Lamb.[4]

Jesus' trial before Annas might have looked like a defeat, but it actually marked his victory. It exposed Israel's high priests as a failure and the world's need for a better, blameless High Priest instead of them. John tells us that they flouted Roman law by trying Jesus at night and in secret, and Moses' Law by beating him before he was even found guilty.[5] He describes their lack of interest in justice or in finding God's Messiah, and their desperate search for a legal fig leaf to cover up their naked crime. In contrast, he describes Jesus fulfilling his prophecy in 6:39 by sacrificing his life to save his followers,[6] and proving his authority by telling the soldiers *"I AM"* in such a way that they literally fell to the ground in fear.[7] Unlike Adam in another garden, he submitted meekly to his Father's will and uniquely qualified himself to act as High Priest for God's sinful People. It doesn't matter that Annas and Caiaphas can't see it. Their verdict sounds the victory of the man who stands on trial.

The second verdict is passed by *Israel* as a whole. The Lord had chosen them as a nation to be his missionaries to the world, but the Jewish crowd despise that calling and birthright as much as Esau did. Theirs was the promise of a better King who would save God's People and outlast Caesar, as they themselves had sung a few days earlier in 12:12–19. Now they deny that Gospel to the Roman governor when they tell him to release a murderer instead of their Messiah because *"We have no king but*

---

[4] John stresses that Jesus died at *Passover* in 11:55, 12:1, 13:1, 18:28, 18:39 and 19:14, just as he stressed in 1:29 and 36 that Jesus is *"the Lamb of God, who takes away the sin of the world"*. See also 1 Corinthians 5:7.

[5] See Acts 23:3.The Greek word *derō* means *to thrash* or *to flay*, which suggests that this beating drew blood.

[6] Note the way John treats his gospel like the Old Testament Scriptures. He expects us to do the same.

[7] This is what Jesus said literally in 18:5, 6 and 8. Even as he was arrested, he made it clear that he was Yahweh.

Caesar."[8] For all their trappings of religion – refusing to enter a pagan palace in 18:28 in order to be ceremonially clean to eat the Passover[9] – their hearts are in bitter rebellion against God's rule. They confess that Jesus is the true and better Missionary when their best attempt to justify his death is the charge in 18:30 that *"If he were not a criminal we would not have handed him over to you."* Their verdict marks the failure of Israel, not of Jesus, and admits that the only hope for God's mission to the world lies with the man who stands on trial.

The third verdict is passed by the *earthly government of Rome*. Great power requires great character, and here the Roman Empire failed. Pontius Pilate, governor of Judea, despised the Jews he was called to govern in 18:35, the truth he was called to discover in 18:38,[10] and the justice he was called to deliver in general. He knows full well that Jesus' Kingdom is of a different world from that of Rome and that the Jews are only claiming that *"anyone who claims to be a king opposes Caesar"* as a smokescreen for their sin,[11] declaring three times in 18:38, 19:4 and 19:6 that *"I find no basis for a charge against him"*. Yet in spite of this, he demonstrates the corruption and cowardice of Rome by flogging him, torturing him and crucifying him in order to protect his own career.[12] His verdict announces that

---

[8] See Mark 15:7; Luke 23:19; Acts 3:14. *Barabbas* meant *Son of the Father* in Aramaic, so he is a false Christ who demonstrates the willingness of Jesus to exchange his life to save the guilty and undeserving.

[9] They demonstrate the same religious hypocrisy in 19:31.

[10] Jesus replies literally *"You said it!"* to Pilate in 18:37, inviting him to respond to the truth on his own lips. Pilate, however, prefers lazy cynicism to genuine searching.

[11] The Sanhedrin used to stone prisoners to death but had been forced to ask Rome to execute its prisoners instead. John 18:32 explains that this was to fulfil the prophecies in Deuteronomy 21:22–23, Psalm 22:16, Zechariah 12:10 and John 3:14 and 12:32–33 that Jesus would be crucified according to Roman custom.

[12] Ironically, Josephus tells us that Pilate was sacked as governor anyway in 36 AD (*Antiquities of the Jews*, 18.4.2). Eusebius claims that he then committed suicide (*Church History*, 2.7.1).

the Roman Empire has failed to live up to its propaganda and that the world needs a far better King. That's why John tells us poignantly that at one point Pilate pointed at Jesus in 19:14 and announced, *"Here is your king!"*[13] His verdict proclaimed that the world's only hope lay in the Kingdom of the prisoner who wore a crown of thorns as he stood on trial.

The fourth and final verdict is passed by the *disciples*. After three years of intensive training, one sold his Master for a bag of silver and nine abandoned him in order to save themselves.[14] As for the two who followed Jesus, John confesses that he used his friendship with the high priests to gain entrance as a spectator, not to intervene,[15] and that even brave, sword-wielding Peter had his boasting exposed as bluster when he denied Jesus to three lowly servants huddled round the fire.[16] The soldiers let them go because they saw no threat in such an unimpressive bunch of nobodies without their Master, but don't mistake the failure of the disciples for the failure of the one who trained them. They merely demonstrate that the best of men are only men at best. Their failure proves that all of us desperately need God's sinless Saviour, and that we must find him by fixing our eyes on the triumphant man who stands on trial.

So don't be fooled by these opening verses into thinking that these chapters speak of anything less than total victory.

---

[13] John makes much of Pilate's two statements *"Here is the man!"* and *"Here is your king!"* in 19:5 and 14. Paul uses the same word for Jesus' *judgment seat* in Romans 14:10 and 2 Corinthians 5:10 as John does for the Roman one in 19:13.

[14] John doesn't mention Judas' kiss or his receipt of silver coins from the Jewish leaders, nor does he mention that Jesus healed Malchus' ear. He expects us to know all this already from the other gospels.

[15] We do not know how a common Galilean fisherman such as John had a relationship with the high priests. Some have speculated that they may have purchased some of his finest fish for their banqueting table. John also became the only disciple to stand as a spectator at the foot of the cross in 19:25–27.

[16] John shows his credentials as an eyewitness by being the only gospel writer to name Malchus and to know that one of the servants who terrified Peter was Malchus' relative.

Understand what John is telling us as Pilate points to a bruised and bloodied and defeated Jesus with the victory cry: *"Here is the man!"* He is telling us that Jesus is the true High Priest, the true Israel, the true King and the true Saviour of the world. He is telling us to fix our eyes on the one who plucked victory from the gaping jaws of seeming defeat. He is inviting us to grasp the message of the fourth and final section of his gospel. He is telling us to join the victory celebration of the man who stands on trial.

Coronation Day (19:1–24)

Pilate had a notice prepared and fastened to the cross. It read: JESUS OF NAZARETH, THE KING OF THE JEWS.

(John 19:19)

Napoleon Bonaparte was not a humble man. In December 1804, he was determined to make his coronation as emperor of the French such a lavish event that its noise would echo across the world. It would be everything that Jesus' coronation day was not.

Napoleon received a golden laurel wreath which linked him back to the Roman Caesars, and an ornate golden crown which linked him back to the Emperor Charlemagne. Jesus received a crown of thorns which linked him back to the curse on Adam's sin in Genesis 3:17–19 and to the ram caught by its horns in the thicket in Genesis 22. God had provided the ram to save the life of Isaac on Mount Moriah, and now he decreed that Jesus must die on that same mountain to save the world.[1]

Napoleon set out for his coronation from the Tuileries Palace, home of the former kings of France, in a magnificent carriage pulled by eight perfectly groomed horses. Jesus left the palace of the Roman governor on foot like a beast of burden on his coronation day, as he buckled under the crushing weight of his wooden cross.[2]

---

[1] See Genesis 22:2; 2 Chronicles 3:1; John 8:56. Calvary was an outcrop of Mount Moriah, which is why Abraham prophesied in Genesis 22:14 that a better sacrifice *would be provided* there in the future.

[2] John expects us to know from the synoptic gospels that Jesus eventually collapsed and needed help from Simon of Cyrene to carry his cross. He leaves out this detail in order to emphasize Jesus' sense of isolation.

Napoleon wore a cloak of purple velvet which was decorated with the finest ermine. Jesus also wore a cloak of purple, but it was an old soldier's cape and its only decoration came from the flow of blood from his back as the result of a brutal Roman flogging. Napoleon was given his cloak as a badge of honour from some of his adoring courtiers. Jesus was given his cloak as part of the mocking pantomime which was performed by the soldiers, complete with punches and sarcastic cries of *"Hail, king of the Jews!"*

Napoleon was loved by the crowds who lined the streets of Paris to shout *"Hail, Napoleon!"* and *"Long live the Emperor!"* Jesus was hated by the crowds who filled Jerusalem with cries of *"Crucify! Crucify!"* and *"Take him away! Crucify him!"*

When Napoleon reached Notre-Dame Cathedral, he was given such a lavish mantle to wear that it required four attendants to support its weight for him. When Jesus reached Calvary, he was stripped of his clothing and four greedy soldiers drew lots to divide it.[3]

Napoleon's crown bore a shiny gold cross, as he rested his feet on a velvet cushion and held an antique royal sword in his hand. Jesus' cross was wooden and spattered with his blood as he was pinned to it by the executioner's nails which were riven through his feet and hands.

Napoleon sat for three hours on his golden throne in Notre-Dame, surrounded by courtiers and wealthy friends who sang about his many victories. Jesus hung for six hours on his wooden cross at Calvary,[4] flanked by two thieves and surrounded by enemies who crowed over his defeat.[5]

---

[3] We can assume that there were four soldiers from the fact that they divided the clothes into four piles. *Calvary* comes from the Latin word for *Skull*, whereas *Golgotha* comes from the same word in Aramaic.

[4] The synoptic gospels tell us that Jesus was crucified from 9 a.m. to 3 p.m. (see Mark 15:25, 33), so when John tells us that Pilate tried Jesus at the sixth hour he must be using the same Roman clock which he used in 1:39 and 4:6, and therefore mean 6 a.m. See the footnote on 1:39.

[5] In 19:18, John describes the two criminals as *heteroi*, or *others unlike him*, not as *alloi*, or *others like him*. He does not tell us that one of them was converted

Napoleon's coronation took many months of planning and cost almost 10 million francs. Jesus' coronation took place hurriedly and on a budget, as his enemies rushed to murder him before the Sabbath began at nightfall.[6]

Napoleon insisted that reports of his coronation should proclaim his greatness and describe him as *"His Imperial and Royal Majesty, Emperor of the French, King of Italy, Protector of the Confederation of the Rhine and the Grand Duchy of Frankfurt, Mediator of the Helvetic Confederation."* Jesus received nothing but a simple, trilingual placard which Pilate dictated to read: *"Jesus of Nazareth, the King of the Jews."*[7]

Napoleon refused to be crowned by the Pope and seized his own crown rather than accept it as the gift of another. Jesus seized nothing, but submissively told Pilate that his coronation service had been decreed by his Father's authority. Paul explains in Philippians 2 that *"Though he was in the form of God, he did not count equality with God a thing to be grasped... He humbled himself by becoming obedient to the point of death, even death on a cross."* It was so unlike Napoleon's magnificent coronation that my five-year-old son asked me earlier this year why its anniversary had been misnamed "Good" Friday.

What my son didn't know was that less than ten years after Napoleon's noisy coronation amidst shouts of *"May the Emperor live forever!"*, he was toppled, imprisoned, exiled, and seven years later was dead. What he didn't know was that the paint was barely dry on Jacques-Louis David's magnificent painting

233

---

since he knew that Luke had already done so.

[6] Since Jesus was crucified on the day before the Sabbath, most people assume that this means Friday. However, 19:31 suggests that it may refer to the additional midweek Sabbath which occurred the day after the Passover (Leviticus 23:6–7). If so, then it fits better with Matthew 12:40 and means that Jesus ate the Passover meal a day early with his disciples before actually being crucified on the Wednesday or Thursday.

[7] Pilate put up this sign as revenge for the way the Jewish leaders had manipulated him. It was in Aramaic (the local language), Greek (the international language) and Latin (the language of government).

of Napoleon's coronation, in which every eye is turned towards the Emperor, when the fickle eyes of the world turned to his defeat instead. What he didn't know is that the brief and noisy pomp of this world's rulers is nothing like the eternal victory which accompanied Jesus' painful coronation. Paul continues: *"Therefore God has highly exalted him and bestowed on him the name that is above every name, so that at the name of Jesus every knee should bow, in heaven and on earth and under the earth, and every tongue confess that Jesus Christ is Lord to the glory of God the Father."*[8] No one is looking at Napoleon now, but every eye must look to Jesus as God's everlasting King.

Shortly before he died in exile on the island of St Helena, Napoleon turned to his friend, General Montholon, and confessed:

> *I know men, and I tell you that Jesus Christ is not a man... I die before my time, and my body will be given back to earth, to become food for worms. Such is the fate of him who has been called the Great Napoleon. What an abyss between my deep misery and the eternal kingdom of Christ, which is proclaimed, loved, and adored, and which is extended over the whole earth! Call you this dying? Is it not living, rather?*[9]

Let's learn from a toppled emperor, and let's worship the crucified-yet-victorious King.

---

[8] English Standard Version. Paul's statement that Jesus became King in a new way at Calvary is consistent with verses such as Psalm 2:6–7, Isaiah 53:12, Acts 2:36 and Hebrews 2:9.

[9] Quoted by John Abbott in his biography *The Life of Napoleon Bonaparte* (1860).

Satan's Worst and God's Best (19:25–42)

When he had received the drink, Jesus said,
"It is finished."

(John 19:30)

Prime Minister Winston Churchill addressed a group of London councillors on 14th July 1941, as German bombs were falling on the city:

We ask no favours of the enemy. We seek from them no compunction... We will have no truce or parley with you, or the grisly gang who work your wicked will. You do your worst – and we will do our best. We shall never turn from our purpose, however sombre the road, however grievous the cost, because we know that out of this time of trial and tribulation will be born a new freedom and glory for all mankind.[1]

The end of John 19 sees Satan at his worst. Hell's undiluted hatred is poured out on Jesus' crucified body. But John also peppers his description of Satan working his worst with vivid clues that God was busy working his best behind the scenes. As Churchill put it as he tried to rally London in the darkest moments of World War, God was using this trial and tribulation to birth new freedom for all humankind.

---

[1] Robert Rhodes James in *Winston S. Churchill: His Complete Speeches, Volume VI* (1974).

The Devil thought he had outflanked Jesus by enlisting one of the Twelve as a turncoat to lead the Jewish leaders to him.[2] He hadn't realized, as John hints in 18:1, that King David had also crossed the Kidron Valley to the Mount of Olives when he was betrayed by his own close friend Ahithophel. At the moment when Satan thought he had gained the upper hand over Jesus, he was merely fulfilling the prophecy in Psalm 41 that the Messiah would be betrayed by one of his closest friends.[3]

The Devil thought he had outwitted Jesus at his trial by using strong and wilful Jewish leaders alongside a weak and fearful Roman governor. He hadn't realized, as John hints in 19:9, that these trials would simply fulfil the prophecy in Isaiah 53:7 that the Messiah would keep silent before his judges. Nor did he understand it would fulfil the prophecy in Luke 19:14 that the Jewish nation would refuse the rule of its Messiah.[4]

The Devil delighted at Jesus' torture, not imagining that even these anguished scenes would be a vehicle to glorify the Lord. He forgot that spices smell strongest when they are crushed in a person's hand, and that godly character shines brightest when circumstances are dark all around. When Jesus was subjected to the kind of flogging which could kill a man and when he was subjected to such an emotional torment that it may even have ruptured the walls of his heart in 19:34, that was the moment when his deepest character was revealed to all the world. Even in extremity, he continued to obey his Father and to spend his dying breaths caring for the needs of his grieving mother.[5] When

---

[2] Finding Jesus during the day was easy, but Mark 12:12 tells us the leaders were too scared of the crowds to arrest him in public. Judas' role was vital because he led them to him at night, away from the crowds.

[3] Compare John 13:18 and 18:1 with 2 Samuel 15:12 and 23.

[4] John expects us to know already from Matthew 27:30 that it also fulfilled the prophecy in Micah 5:1.

[5] It is not clear why Jesus entrusted his widowed mother to John when he had several half-brothers to take care of her. Perhaps he knew that none of them would be able to house and look after her like John. Some readers put

Jesus' body was torn apart by his executioners, it simply showed that he was full of love right down to his very core.[6]

The Devil thought he had pulled off a remarkable victory when he finally saw Jesus being executed on a cross. He missed what John sees and hints at in verse 17, that it fulfilled the requirement in the Jewish Law that sacrifices for sin must be taken outside the city.[7] He missed the Old Testament prophecy which John quotes in verses 23–24, that Jesus' nakedness fulfilled the prophecies about the Messiah in Psalm 22:18.[8] He forgot that Deuteronomy 21:22–23 predicted that the Messiah would be hanged from a piece of wood, while Psalm 22:16 and Zechariah 12:10 added that he would be pierced through his hands and feet.[9] John hints in verses 28–29 that it fulfilled Psalm 69:3 and 21 when he grew thirsty and was tormented by his enemies, who gave him vinegar to make his parched throat even worse.[10] Satan couldn't see that the priests were smearing the blood of God's Passover Lamb over a vertical and horizontal piece of wood like a Hebrew door frame, or that the Father was fulfilling the Passover festival right down to the tiny detail of Exodus 12:46 in verse 36. Satan thought he was doing his worst, but John assures us that in the background God was doing his very best.

Now John goes on the offensive himself and tells us something of the victory which Jesus won that day. He calls the

19:25 together with Matthew 27:56 to argue that John was Mary's nephew and Jesus' cousin, but there was no tradition of this in the Early Church.

[6] He also displayed this same love in Luke 23:34, when he asked his Father to forgive his executioners.

[7] Hebrews 13:11–12 explains that his going out of the city fulfilled Leviticus 4:21 and Numbers 19:3.

[8] Jesus would also fulfil Psalm 22:1, 8, 15 and 31 in Matthew 27:43 and 46 and John 19:28 and 30.

[9] Paul explains the importance of the Deuteronomy prophecy in Galatians 3:13.

[10] Psalm 69:21 and Luke 23:36 make it clear that this drink was not offered in mercy for pain relief, but in cruelty. Jesus also fulfilled Psalm 69:4, 9, 22–23 and 25 in John 2:17 and 15:25, Acts 1:20 and Romans 11:9–10 and 15:3.

crown of thorns a *stephanos* in verse 2, which was the Greek word used for the *victory crown* awarded at the athletic games. He tells us in verse 30 that Jesus died when he *"gave up his Spirit"*, not when his enemy managed to wrest it from him, since he had prophesied in 10:17–18 that *"I lay down my life – only to take it up again. No one takes it from me, but I lay it down of my own accord."* The crucifixion was not something that Jesus simply *endured*; it was something he *embraced* as the price of final victory.[11]

Jesus dies with a cry of victory on his lips: *"Tetelestai! It is finished!"*[12] He meant that every one of those Old Testament prophecies had been completed, so he could finish with the one which ends Psalm 22: *"He has done it!"* He meant that everything which Adam had lost through his sin in the Garden of Eden had been completely restored through the one who passed wherever Adam failed. *"The Son of Man came to seek and to save what was lost"* he had taught in Luke 19:10 – save *what* was lost, not just *who* was lost[13] – and through his death in place of Adam's children he had managed to achieve his goal. Jesus rejoiced as he died that he had undone sin's curse on humankind and had ushered in a new era of victory and grace.

So let's rejoice with Jesus like the soldier who stabbed his corpse in verse 35 and was converted by what he saw.[14] Let's rejoice like Joseph of Arimathea and Nicodemus, both Sanhedrin members who broke ranks with their former friends in order

---

[11] Hebrews 12:2 describes this as *"the joy set before him"*. John 17:20–26 suggests this joy was primarily about *God being glorified*.

[12] This was actually the sixth of Jesus' seven recorded sayings from the cross. In order they are: Luke 23:34, Luke 23:43, John 19:27, Matthew 27:46, John 19:28, John 19:30 and Luke 23:46.

[13] When the verse is simply translated *"to save the lost"*, it misses the true depth of what Luke literally says.

[14] Matthew 27:54 tells us that not only the centurion, but also his men were converted. Luke 23:39–43 tells us that one of the two criminals crucified with him was also converted.

to join Jesus on the winning team instead.[15] Let's rejoice like the debtors across the Roman Empire when they saw the word *tetelestai* stamped across their debts and recognized that finally those debts had been paid off in full.[16]

This isn't to minimize the pain of Satan's worst on Jesus' body, any more than Winston Churchill tried to fool himself that German bombs didn't hurt his city. It is simply to understand the background John gives to the story. It is to grasp that *"out of these trials and tribulations has been born a new freedom and glory for all mankind"*.

---

[15] See Mark 15:43; Luke 23:50; John 3:1. Since 35 kilograms of myrrh and aloes was very expensive, once they blew their cover these two Jewish leaders worshipped Jesus very lavishly.

[16] Jesus presumably said *"It is finished!"* in Aramaic, so we must see a significance in John's decision to translate it with the Greek word which was commonly stamped across the record of a debt once it had been repaid.

Risen (20:1–18)

Mary Magdalene went to the disciples with the news: "I have seen the Lord!"

(John 20:18)

If Jesus' victory was easy to miss when he was crucified and buried, then that all changed on the morning of his resurrection. When Paul proclaimed Christ's victory in Athens by saying that God *"has given proof of this to everyone by raising him from the dead"*, he really meant what he was saying.[1] The resurrection of Jesus convinced the first believers that their crucified Messiah was in fact the almighty conqueror of the world.

It convinced Mary Magdalene when she went to Jesus' tomb at the start of chapter 20. She understood so little about the prophecies that the Messiah would rise from the dead that she took him for a gardener and asked him what he had done with Jesus' body. When she recognized him as her Lord and Rabbi, her life and outlook were transformed, as were those of Peter and John when her news brought them running despite the fact that verse 9 tells us they didn't understand those prophecies any more than she did. They simply took the resurrection as living proof that Jesus had just won a mighty victory.

Given how important John tells us the events described in this chapter are, we might expect them still to be the talking-point of our time. Sadly, our culture is often as lazy and cynical as Pontius Pilate in 18:38.

---

[1] Acts 17:31. We find similar statements in Matthew 12:38–42 and John 2:18–21.

Some people *deny the basic facts* behind the resurrection. After the American Civil War, when men like Mark Twain and Robert Ingersoll led the way in doing so, a retired Union general named Lew Wallace was so challenged by one of them that he set out to study the life of Jesus for himself. He intended to write a novel set in New Testament times which would explain why the resurrection wasn't true, but the more he studied the gospels and the ancient evidence the more he found himself convinced of Jesus' victory. He found that no serious historian denied that Jesus had been crucified and buried, since none of the early enemies of Christianity felt it credible to do so. He also found that the charge described in Matthew 28:12–15 – that the disciples stole the body – was quietly dropped when the crowds clearly saw that such a story simply couldn't be true.[2] Since the tomb was dug into a rock face and had no back door,[3] Jesus could not have swooned and then managed to revive and escape the guards, and nor could tomb robbers have slipped in while their backs were turned.[4] When Lew Wallace eventually published his book *Ben-Hur: A Tale of the Christ* in 1880, he had renounced the claims of Ingersoll for the solid proof of the resurrection. He told his readers that *"Long before I was through with my book, I became a believer in God and Christ."*[5]

Other people *argue that there are too many contradictions* in the four gospel accounts and use them as a reason to reject

---

[2] Roman guards who had truly lost a corpse in that way would have been executed (as in Acts 12:19), but these were not. Disciples who had truly stolen the corpse would not have been willing to die for what they knew was a lie. It was such a ridiculous claim that the opponents of Christianity quickly dropped it.

[3] Matthew 27:60, which also tells us that the tomb belonged to Joseph of Arimathea. There was no question of Jesus' followers getting confused and going to the wrong tomb.

[4] Besides, grave-robbers stole the precious grave clothes and left the corpse – not the other way around!

[5] He wrote this in the second volume of *Lew Wallace: An Autobiography* (1906).

the resurrection. The eighteenth-century English poet Gilbert West vowed to write a book which would list them and pluck the heart out of Christianity once and for all. He researched so diligently that in 1747 when he published his book *Observations on the History and Evidence of the Resurrection of Jesus Christ*, it earned him an honorary doctorate from Oxford University. But, like Lew Wallace, the book he published was not the one he set out to write. *"I am not ignorant how little reputation is to be gained by writing on the side of Christianity, which by many people is regarded as a superstitious fable, not worth the thoughts of a wise man,"* he admits in his introduction, but then he goes on to explain the facts he found.

Most of his so-called contradictions had been based on superficial misunderstandings, such as which women went to the tomb and at what time in the morning.[6] Even his most serious difficulties had been resolved by grasping that each account added complementary, not contradictory detail to the others.[7] Faced with the historical triumph of the eleven down-and-out disciples, Gilbert West was forced to argue in his conclusion that only through the resurrection *"were the first preachers of the gospel – weak, ignorant and contemptible as they were – furnished with strength sufficient to overthrow the... superstitions, prejudices, and vices of mankind".* Christianity conquered the Roman Empire because it was based on *"an argument whose conclusiveness was visible to the dullest capacity".*

Other people *dismiss these events as if they were mere mythology.* An English businessman named Albert Ross tried to

---

[6] For example, John doesn't say that Mary was the only woman at the tomb, and he suggests she wasn't when she says in 20:2 that *"**We** don't know where they have put him."* Similarly, Matthew 28:1, Mark 16:2, Luke 24:1 and John 20:1 are all simply different ways of telling us that the women went to the tomb at break of dawn.

[7] For example, when Matthew says an angel sat on the stone, Mark says an angel sat inside the tomb, Luke says two angels stood outside the tomb and John says two angels sat inside the tomb, they are simply describing different moments on that same eventful morning.

do so in the 1920s, when Christianity was increasingly viewed as a fairy tale and a bygone relic from a superstitious age. However, when he finally published *Who Moved the Stone?* under the pen-name Frank Morrison in 1930, he began with a chapter entitled "The Book that Refused to Be Written" and confessed what he had found. There was no reason for the gospel writers to say that women were the first witnesses to the resurrection, when they knew that female evidence was not taken as seriously in first-century law courts as that of men like themselves – unless, of course, they did so because they were simply telling events as they happened. John wrote as an eyewitness about events as they happened in order to take us on the same journey that he travelled in verses 5–8 from *seeing* to *considering* to *perceiving* and to *believing*.[8] Frank Morrison writes in his introduction that such reflection *"effected a revolution in my thought... The conviction grew that the drama of those unforgettable weeks of human history was stranger and deeper than it seemed... The irresistible logic of their meaning came into view."*

Most of all, people *simply ignore the evidence altogether.* I got into conversation recently with a well-educated businesswoman who could speak eloquently about issues of finance and politics but had never given any serious thought to the resurrection. *"Jesus?"* she asked, as if surprised by the very question. *"I don't think he ever existed. And even if he did, we all know people don't come back from the dead, do they?"* John knows that too, but it's precisely why he won't let us sidestep the facts behind the resurrection. *"The man who saw it has given testimony, and his testimony is true,"* he tells us from the foot of Jesus' cross in 19:35. *"He knows that he tells the truth and he testifies so that you also may believe."* Now he stands outside the empty tomb and warns us in 20:31 not to ignore this proof that Jesus is who he says he is and that he has won a resounding victory.

---

[8] These verbs in Greek are *blepō*, *theōreō*, *eidō* and *pisteuō* respectively. The stone had not been rolled away to let Jesus out (20:19), but so that the world could look inside.

"These are written that you may believe that Jesus is the Messiah," John implores us, *"and that by believing you may have life in his name."* Gilbert West in the eighteenth century; Lew Wallace in the nineteenth; Frank Morrison in the twentieth: and now you in the twenty-first century. John invites you to tread the same road as they did and to reach the same life-changing conclusion that Jesus has risen from the grave.

Therefore Look Up
(20:19-23)

The disciples were overjoyed when they saw the Lord.

(John 20:20)

The resurrection of Jesus transformed the disciples. Most Christians know that, but not to the degree that John wants to teach us in these five verses. We tend to look at the exploits of the disciples in the book of Acts and put it all down to the Day of Pentecost, but John warns that this was only half the story. Unless we understand that Pentecost was preceded by Easter Sunday, he warns, we will not experience the same successes as the disciples.

In verses 19-20, John tells us that it was the resurrection which made them do as he taught us in part one and *look at Jesus alone*. Until Jesus appeared in their room on Easter Sunday evening,[1] their eyes looked down in disappointment and at the outside world in fear. When he appeared, their eyes began to look up, and it radically altered the trajectory of their lives. Putting more fuel in a rocket will not make it fly any higher if it is pointed towards the ground. In the same way, the power of Pentecost first needs the facts of Easter Sunday to shift the direction of our gaze.

---

[1] Although John only records four of Jesus' ten resurrection appearances, the full list is: (1) Mark 16:9-11 and John 20:11-18; (2) Matthew 28:9-10; (3) Mark 16:12-13 and Luke 24:13-32; (4) Luke 24:33-35; (5) Luke 24:36-49 and John 20:19-25; (6) Mark 16:14 and John 20:26-31; (7) John 21:1-25; (8) Matthew 28:16-20 and Mark 16:15-18; (9) 1 Corinthians 15:7; (10) Mark 16:19-20, Luke 24:50-53 and Acts 1:9-12.

My wife and I have a family tradition of watching the annual Oxford and Cambridge University Boat Race with our children. Both crews generally row as hard as one another and the result is normally quite close, but there is always a remarkable difference in the two crews' faces after they have crossed the finish line. The losing crew always look exhausted as they hunch over their oars, like men who have been rowing flat out for several days, but the winning crew always look up with eyes full of energy, as if they haven't just rowed the gruelling four-mile race at all. It's amazing the difference it makes to a group of people when they realize that they are on the winning team.

Until Jesus appeared in the room on Easter Sunday, the disciples looked just like a losing boat race crew in Luke 24:17.[2] Their eyes looked down and out towards the angry Jewish leaders, or down and in towards each other and their need to pool their strength behind locked doors if they were to survive. They fixed their eyes on the failure of their one-time friend Judas Iscariot[3] and on the seeming failure of their beloved-yet-crucified Messiah. When Jesus appeared, however, they were overjoyed and their eyes flashed with energy like a winning boat race crew.

In verse 20, John tells us that it was also the resurrection which made them do as he taught us in part two and *look at who Jesus really is*. They didn't merely look at Jesus; they looked at his nail-pierced hands and his spear-struck side. They finally understood his seven *"I AM"* sayings and rejoiced that he was Yahweh. They grasped, like Paul in Romans 1:4, that the resurrection had proved once and for all that he was the Son of God and that nothing could stand in the way of his victory. Luke 24:36–49 describes this encounter in much more detail and tells us that they watched Jesus eating broiled fish and then

---

[2] There are plenty of gloomy Spirit-filled churches because John 20:20 tells us that the Day of Pentecost alone is no substitute for the joy of Easter Sunday.

[3] John doesn't mention Judas' suicide. He expects us to know about it already from Matthew 27:1–10.

listened while *"he opened their minds so they could understand the Scriptures."* It wasn't just the power of Pentecost which turned depressed disciples into Christ's conquerors. It was looking at who Jesus really was and finally grasping that in him they were able to see the Living God.

In verses 21–23, John also tells us that it was the resurrection which made them do as he taught in part three and *look at what Jesus had given them.* John tells us that Jesus greeted them twice with what must have been the Hebrew word *shalom*, which meant *peace* or *safety* or *contentment* or *healing* or *salvation.* It meant that they were part of Jesus' winning team, and it paved the way for the greatest handover verse in the whole of John's gospel: *"As the Father has sent me, I am sending you."*[4] Luke describes this same commission as Jesus telling them that *"repentance for the forgiveness of sins will be preached in his name to all nations, beginning at Jerusalem. You are witnesses of these things"*, but John chooses to focus instead on two of the items we have in our mission briefcase.[5] We must combine the power of the Spirit in verse 22 with the authority which is ours through the Gospel in verse 23.[6] It was this combination which caused the disciples to unite in loving unity and prayer in Acts 1 before the Day of Pentecost and to appoint a replacement for Judas who could be a *"witness with us of his resurrection".*[7] Easter Sunday positioned the Church

---

[4] Jesus uses a Greek "perfect tense" to stress that this handover does not mean he has retired. He says *"the Father **has sent** me"* because his sending still stands. We simply get to ride fourth with the Trinity to victory.

[5] Jesus cannot have filled the disciples with the Spirit in verse 22 or else he would not have told them to *wait* in Luke 24:49. He does, however, use an "aorist imperative" which implies that he expected them to receive something of the Spirit then and there, perhaps resulting in the fruit of Luke 24:45.

[6] Verse 23 is not telling a few clergymen to absolve their congregations, but every Christian to go out and preach the Gospel to the world.

[7] Peter keeps emphasizing that they are witnesses to the resurrection in Acts 2:32, 3:15, 4:20 and 10:39–41.

properly on its launch pad, so that the Day of Pentecost could catapult it to the world.

Without this grasp of the resurrection, we will not do as John teaches in part four and *look at Jesus and win*. Experiences of the Holy Spirit will turn us inward for a self-indulgent pamper party and draw the same rebuke as Jesus gave Mary Magdalene in 20:17: *"Do not hold on to me... Go instead to my brothers and tell them."* Jesus calls his followers "brothers" here for the first time in John's gospel because the resurrection has changed who we are. Jesus' God and Father is now our God and Father too. He wants to shift our gaze, prepare our engines and make us ready to steward the power of Pentecost when it comes.

Is your own Christian life or your own church like a losing boat race crew, with tired eyes looking inwards or merely looking out in fear? Have you experienced the revolution in your thinking which lifted the disciples' eyes in a moment on the evening of Easter Sunday? If not, the solution is not just to ask God for more power, for even the disciples' enemies could tell that the Day of Pentecost had not been enough to change Christ's defeated army into determined warriors. The book of Acts tells us that *"They saw the courage of Peter and John and... took note that these men had been with Jesus."*[8]

Spend some time focusing on the risen Lord Jesus today. Let him lift your downcast eyes and make you ready to receive God's mighty power. Let him remind you that you are on the winning team.

2 LOOK AT JESUS AND WIN

248

[8] Acts 4:13. Luke links this fresh courage specifically to the resurrection in verses 2 and 10.

Therefore Believe
(20:24–31)

Blessed are those who have not seen and yet have believed.

(John 20:29)

That's all very well for you to say, John. You were actually there to see the risen Jesus. Most of us haven't had the privilege of examining his resurrected body to see that we are on the winning team. If that is your objection, then John has seen it coming and he responds by telling you about his friend Thomas.[1]

Thomas wasn't there on Easter Sunday. Although history remembers him as "doubting Thomas", he was actually the only disciple who had the courage to step outside. For a whole week he was forced to trust the word of John and the other disciples that he was on the winning team. He refused, insisting that *"Unless I see the nail marks in his hands and put my finger where the nails were, and put my hand into his side, I will not believe."*[2]

For 300 years after Easter Sunday and Pentecost, the Christian message spread like wildfire across the entire

---

[1] Each time John mentions Thomas, he points out to his readers that his name was Aramaic for the Greek *Didymus* or *Twin* (11:16, 20:24 and 21:2). Since Peter and John's brothers were both disciples but Thomas' twin wasn't, some readers speculate that his gloominess stemmed from his twin dying young or rejecting Jesus. This may be true, but it is equally possible that his twin was a sister.

[2] Thomas' doubts sound reasonable but they actually come from his pessimistic disposition (11:16) and his refusal to fix his eyes on Jesus instead of on the disappointment of the past few days.

ancient world. Miracles were commonplace and pagan cities fell like dominoes to the Gospel. Things began to change after the conversion of Emperor Constantine in 312 AD, however, when Christian eyes shifted their hope from the power of the resurrection to the power of Rome. *"Silver or gold I do not have, but what I do have I give you,"* Peter had said in Acts 3:6, yet by the time Augustine of Hippo was converted in 386 AD the Church had plenty of silver and gold but very little of what Peter had.

Augustine was a man of faith. He tried to return the corrupt and backslidden Church to the message of Jesus' death and resurrection. His commentary on John is one of the finest works ever written on the gospel. However, when he came to Jesus' promise in John 14:12 that his followers would perform greater miracles than he did, Augustine responded like Thomas. It simply didn't tie in with the Christian reality which he saw:

> *Let not the servant exalt himself above his Lord, or the disciple above his Master... What works was He referring to, but the words that He was speaking?... There is no need for us to suppose that all of Christ's works are to be understood. For perhaps He was speaking only of these works He was currently doing, and the work He was currently doing was speaking words of faith.*

God was very gracious towards Thomas, and he was gracious towards Augustine too. On Easter Sunday in 424 AD, only five years after he had completed his commentary on John, Augustine finally saw a miracle. A brother and sister named Paulus and Palladia were well-known in Hippo for what Augustine describes as *"a hideous shaking in all their limbs"*. While a large congregation waited for Augustine to arrive to begin the Easter service in Hippo Cathedral, Paulus was in the congregation praying that God would heal his affliction.

Suddenly he fell down and lay as if he were asleep, but not trembling as he tended to do even in his sleep... Behold! He rose up and trembled no more, for he was healed and stood quite well, staring back at those who were staring at him. Who then could stop himself from praising God? The whole church was filled with the sound of people shouting.[3]

Augustine was now faced with a dilemma. He had preached that miracles were in the briefcase of the apostles, but not in ours, yet he felt that this was his own equivalent of Jesus appearing to Thomas and saying *shalōm*. He felt that Jesus had invited him to *"Put your finger here; see my hands. Reach out your hand and put it into my side. Stop doubting and believe."* He felt that Easter Sunday in 424 AD had been his own encounter with the risen Jesus, like the one the disciples had on the first Easter Sunday. He decided to believe.

He invited Paulus to dinner and helped him write down his testimony of healing. He gathered the whole church together on the Wednesday and made the brother and sister stand before them while he read out the testimony. As he shared his own conviction that *"blessed are those who have not seen and yet have believed"*,[4] the congregation suddenly started shouting. The man's sister, Palladia, had been shaking convulsively, but she had also been healed while Augustine was speaking! *"Such a shout of wonder arose from the men and women together that the exclamations and the tears seemed like they would never come to an end... They shouted God's praises without words, but with such a noise that our ears could scarcely bear it."*

---

[3] Augustine tells this story at the end of *The City of God* (22.8), which he completed in 426 AD. Like many of us, Augustine needed to graduate from believing that God *could* perform miracles in theory to believing that he *would* perform them in his own town.

[4] Jesus' words to Thomas in 20:29 link back to the chapter "How Faith Happens" and the promise of 7:17.

We live in an age like Augustine's. We are so unused to fixing our eyes on the risen Jesus that we can doubt the promise of the Holy Spirit, the power of the Gospel, our continued need for miracles, our authority in prayer, our partnership with the Trinity, and that we are truly on the winning team at all. From time to time, God breaks in with "Thomas moments" when he grants us a glimpse of what the disciples saw and urges us to worship the risen Jesus as *"My Lord and my God!"*, as Thomas did.[5] He urges us to believe that Jesus is risen, Jesus is Yahweh, Jesus is captain of the winning team, and Jesus will not take away any of the ten items he has given us in our briefcase.

Augustine records this Easter Sunday breakthrough at the end of his book *The City of God*. Writing two years later, he tells his readers that great fruit awaits anyone who responds to such "Thomas moments" with faith. *"What am I to do? I am so pressed by the promise of finishing this work that I cannot record all the miracles I know... I have seen frequent signs of the presence of God's power in our own time in similar fashion to that in which he gave it in the past."* In just two years in Hippo since that Easter Sunday, Augustine personally knew of *"almost seventy miracles at my time of writing"*.

That's what John has in mind when he ends chapter 20 with a call for us to trust in what he says the disciples saw and to look out for the risen Jesus ourselves. It's what Jesus had in mind when he promised doubters in 11:40: *"Did I not tell you that if you believe, you will see the glory of God?"*

---

[5] Yet again, Jesus makes it clear to us that he is the Living God. To miss this is to be blinder than a Pharisee.

Therefore Expect Success
(21:1–14)

They were unable to haul the net in because of the large number of fish.

(John 21:6)

We have talked about seven miraculous signs in John's gospel, but technically there are eight. Bishop Westcott considered this eighth sign to be the most important of them all:

> *It is not, I believe, fanciful to see a significance even in the number of these miracles. Seven are included in the record of Christ's ministry, and an eighth completes the typical representation of His work after the Resurrection. Seven, according to the early belief, was the figure of a completed creation; eight, the figure of the Resurrection, or new birth.*[1]

253

John gives this eighth sign to teach a lesson about the victory which is ours through the resurrection. He wants us to see what he and Peter saw in their fishing boat, and to convince us that we should expect great success on Jesus' mission.

Peter and John had been fishing partners before they met Jesus. Several months after they met him, Jesus had come to their workplace and performed a fishing miracle in Luke 5. They had fished all night and caught nothing, but when the carpenter told them to go back into deep water and let down their nets once more, they obeyed. When they did so, they *"caught such*

---

[1] Brooke Foss Westcott in his *Introduction to the Study of the Gospels* (1860).

a large number of fish that their nets began to break... and filled both boats so full that they began to sink". It was the catch of a lifetime, but they left it all behind to follow Jesus and fish for people for the rest of their lives.[2]

An awful lot had happened since then, and Peter wasn't sure how much that calling still applied. He had denied Jesus three times and felt disqualified from Christian leadership. When Jesus told him on Easter Sunday to go to Galilee to meet him there,[3] he returned to the comfort of a boat and fishing nets – back on old familiar ground to escape his thoughts. He was no more successful at night fishing this time around than he had been two years earlier, but he was equally obedient when a stranger called from the shore and told him to throw his net out on the other side of the boat.[4] Suddenly, Peter sees a miracle which is just like the one which made him leave his fishing nets the first time, and John gasps, *"It is the Lord!"* Peter isn't interested in his massive catch of fish now any more than he had been two years earlier, and he immediately jumps overboard to get to Jesus. He dares to hope that Jesus may be promising him a continuing role in his mission and that he can still expect great successes as he goes.

Note the similarities between this miracle and the one in Luke 5. Both times God lets Peter fish unsuccessfully all night in order to teach him the lesson of 15:5, that *"apart from me you can do nothing"*. Both times Peter has to express his faith with concrete action, by going back into deep water or by drawing in his net to throw it out again on the other side of the boat. Both times Jesus calls him to leave his catch of fish behind in order to

---

[2] The miracle described in Luke 5:1–11, Matthew 4:18–22 and Mark 1:16–20 took place in summer 28 AD. They had met Jesus in autumn 27 AD in John 1, and this new miracle took place in spring 30 AD.

[3] Matthew 28:7, 10, 16.

[4] There was evidently something different about Jesus' resurrection body, since it could walk through walls in 20:19 and was not instantly recognized by his followers in John 20:15 and 21:4 and Luke 24:16.

start fishing for an altogether better catch of precious souls of men and women.[5]

Note also the deliberate differences, though. For a start, Jesus is already cooking fish on the fire for breakfast by the time they reach him. It's as if he is telling them that he doesn't really need their help in his mission at all, but that he and the Father want to include them as *little children* in the family business.[6] John tells us in verse 11 that the fish they caught were large, but Jesus calls them literally *little fish* in verse 10, because they are small fry compared to what they can expect as they follow him on mission. Another difference is that Peter grasps the Gospel far better now and rushes to lay hold of Jesus instead of begging him to leave. Most significant of all, while the nets began to break and the boats began to sink in Luke, this time the nets hold firm because the disciples are not the same men who set out to follow Jesus two years before.[7] Peter had denied Jesus, Thomas had doubted him and Nathanael had deserted him, but the resurrection meant that they had been changed enough to handle whatever great successes Jesus was about to give them as they went out on God's mission.

Peter understands this and is overcome with excitement that Jesus still wants him on his team. The boat is not far from land but Peter demonstrates his willingness to take a lead in Jesus' mission by leaping fully clothed into the water.[8] He is

---

[5] To emphasize this, John uses the same Greek word for the disciples *dragging* in their net in verses 6 and 11 as he did for Jesus *drawing* the world to salvation in 6:44 and 12:32.

[6] Although some translations render the word *paidia* in verse 5 as *friends*, its literal meaning is *little children*. Only Jesus would address a bunch of burly fishermen that way!

[7] There does not appear to be any great significance in the number 153 other than that there were more fish this time than before. Four partners were able haul in that catch, but seven of them could only tow it this time.

[8] It was unusual for Peter to put his coat on instead of taking it off to jump into the water. Either he hoped to be able to walk on water, or he wanted to demonstrate his willingness to jump back into Jesus' mission.

willing to leave his safe surroundings and jump into the water of the world to fish for people.[9] Jesus promised in 15:16 that *"I chose you and appointed you so that **you might go** and bear fruit"*, so we cannot complain about our lack of fruitfulness if we haven't learned to go. We need to swim among the fish who need catching, the lost who need saving, the sick who need healing, and the world which needs redeeming. We need to embrace Jesus' teaching in 17:4 that true worship means far more than singing songs – it also means partnering with Jesus in world mission.

Jesus deals gently with Peter's three denials and recommissions him for service. He deals gently with our own past failures too, but he commands us to trust in his resurrection victory and expect great successes as we go. No more huddling together in our fishing boats, and no more playing at fishing as in former days gone by. The risen Lord Jesus is calling us to go. It is time for us to leap overboard and play our part in his great victory.

That's precisely what Eusebius says happened during the first 300 years of Church history:

> *They did the work of evangelists, filled with an ambition to preach Christ to those who had not yet heard the message of faith, and to deliver the holy gospels to them. They simply laid the foundations of the faith in foreign lands, and when they had done so they appointed others as shepherds and trusted them to care for the new growth, while they themselves went on again to other countries and nations with the grace and cooperation of God. A great many miracles were done through them by the power of God's Spirit, so that great crowds eagerly*

---

[9] Paul may be hinting at this too when he uses the same Greek word in Ephesians 4:11 to describe the apostles *preparing* people for God's mission as Matthew 4:21 uses for them *preparing* their nets for fishing.

embraced the religion of the Creator of the universe at only their first hearing.[10]

This is also how we need to write the final pages of Church history. John gives us this eighth and final miraculous sign as a promise that Jesus' resurrection victory means that we are included in his mission, and that we can expect great successes as we go.

---

[10] Eusebius of Caesarea, writing in the early fourth century in his *Church History* (3.37.2–3).

Therefore Love the Church
(21:15–17)

Jesus said, "Simon son of John, do you love me?"
He answered, "Yes, Lord, you know that I love you."
Jesus said, "Take care of my sheep."

(John 21:16)

John had spent too long as a fisherman on Lake Galilee to think that catching fish was all that really mattered. Jesus had found him mending his nets in Matthew 4:21 because John had learned the hard way that a fisherman's job was to get his catch all the way back to shore. That's why he doesn't end his account of Jesus' eighth miracle with a promise that we will win many souls to Jesus. He ends it with some clear instruction about how we must steward those souls after we have caught them.

Think about it. It's very fashionable today for Christians to despise the local church and a commitment to structured fellowship and meetings. Some Christians even speak the word "church" as if it were a dirty word. Contrast this with Peter, who poured his life into local churches in Jerusalem, Judea, Achaia and elsewhere. Contrast it with John, who didn't just address the book of Revelation to Christians in general but *"to the seven churches in the province of Asia"*.[1] When Jesus told the disciples to go and make disciples of all nations, they responded by planting and caring for a series of local churches.

That's the theme of verses 15–17, even though the talk is of sheep and lambs and flocks rather than of churches. It's easy

---

[1] Revelation 1:4. In case we miss this, he repeats it in 1:11, 2:7, 2:11, 2:17, 2:29, 3:6, 3:13, 3:22 and 22:16.

for us to forget that the normal Greek word for a church leader in John's day was *poimēn*, which means *pastor* or *shepherd*.[2] It's easy for us to forget that Peter wrote a letter in which he told church leaders to *"be shepherds of God's flock that is under your care, watching over them – not because you must, but because you are willing... And when the Chief Shepherd appears, you will receive the crown of glory that will never fade away."*[3] What we read in these three verses is some of the clearest teaching on how true believers will feel about the local church, and how the church is God's net to preserve the souls we catch for Jesus. They go alongside Jesus' explanation of his victory plan to Peter in Matthew 16:18: *"I will build my church, and the gates of Hades will not overcome it."*

In verses 15–17, Jesus tells us that *God grows us through the local church*. Three times Jesus asks if Peter loves him – one time for each of his three denials[4] – and three times he asks him to prove it by the way he loves the body of believers.[5] Telling Jesus we love him is easy, but we can prove it by the way in which we pour out our lives for those he has chosen. *"Do you love me more than these?"* Jesus asks Peter with deliberate ambiguity. If he means *more than these nets and fishing boats*, then he is telling him to sacrifice his own agenda and plans to serve God's People. If he means *more than these other disciples*, then he is telling him to stop boasting as he did in Matthew 26:33, and to

---

[2] This word is used interchangeably with *presbuteros* or *elder*, and *episkopos* or *overseer*. See Acts 20:17 and 28.

[3] 1 Peter 5:1–4. Peter never forgot the words which Jesus spoke to him on this occasion.

[4] John makes a deliberate link between Jesus' three questions and Peter's three denials, since this Greek word for *fire of burning coals* is only used in the New Testament in John 18:18 and 21:9.

[5] Jesus' first two questions are about *agapē* love, but his third question and Peter's three replies are about *philos* love. We probably need not read too much into this, however, since the conversation took place in Aramaic and John uses the two words interchangeably in 19:26 and 20:2, 3:35 and 5:20, and 11:5 and 36.

stop acting like the proud believer in 1 Corinthians 12:21 who tells his fellow Christians: *"I don't need you!"* Christian maturity isn't measured by our talk but by our willingness to serve the needs of others.

Jesus tells us in verse 15 that *God grows new believers through the local church*. That's why it's so ironic when Christians give up on church in the hope of being more fruitful through other means. Jesus tells Peter that new believers are *little lambs* and that we do not truly love him as our shepherd unless we care for them.[6] A few days after he said this, Jesus would commission the Eleven in Matthew 28 to go and make *disciples* (not just *converts*), which was the word used by rabbis to refer to those they gathered in community to learn together. A few days after that, Peter would see 3,000 converted through his first evangelistic sermon and react instinctively in Acts 2:42–47 by gathering them daily in the Temple courts to listen to preaching, to pray, to share the Lord's Supper, to scatter into one another's homes for deeper fellowship, and to share one another's lives. The result was that he not only preserved his catch but also found that *"the Lord added to their number daily those who were being saved"*. If we aspire to fish with similar success, then we dare not abandon the net which Peter used.

The early-twentieth-century British missionary Roland Allen despaired of the way that so many would-be evangelists neglect the local church:

> *Men have wandered over the world, "preaching the Word", laying no solid foundations, establishing nothing permanent, leaving no really instructed society behind them, and have claimed St Paul's authority for their absurdities... Many missionaries in later days have received a larger number of converts than St Paul; many*

---

[6] The Greek word translated *lambs* means literally *little lambs* and must refer to newborn Christians.

have preached over a wider area than he; but none have so established churches. We have long forgotten that such things could be.[7]

Jesus tells us in verses 16–17 that *God grows existing believers through the local church.* Wolves love to pick off weak and isolated sheep, so it shouldn't surprise us that the great wolf Satan works hard to disconnect Christians from one another – either from commitment to church altogether, or at the very least to a watered-down version of it.[8] He doesn't want us to experience what Jesus describes as *taking care of* and *feeding* his sheep. He doesn't want us to realize that Peter and his friends founded the practice of Christians gathering on Sundays for structured worship, and that abandoning such meetings isn't progress but spiritual suicide.[9] Just listen to Justin Martyr's description of the way that Christians grew in their faith as early as 150 AD:

On the day called Sunday, all who live in the cities or in the country gather together to one place, and the memoirs of the apostles or the writings of the prophets are read, as long as time permits; then, when the reader has ceased, the leader gives verbal instruction, and exhorts people to imitate such good things. Then we all rise together and pray, and when our prayer is ended – as I have already said – bread and wine and water are brought... Sunday is the day on which we all hold our common assembly.[10]

So if you love Jesus, learn from these two fishing partners. Give yourself to a local church in the same way that Peter and John

---

[7] Roland Allen in his classic book *Missionary Methods: St Paul's or Ours?* (1912).

[8] Thomas provides a great example in chapter 20 of how *absence* leads to *isolation* and then to *doubt*.

[9] See Acts 20:7; 1 Corinthians 16:2; Revelation 1:10.

[10] Justin Martyr in his *First Apology* (chapter 67). Sunday gatherings have always been vital to Christianity. We neglect them at our peril.

did, as the most effective way of building up new converts and existing believers in the Lord. If you want to catch fish and bring them safely back to shore, use the net God has provided. *"Zeal for your house will consume me,"* the Psalmist prophesied about Jesus back in John 2:17. You will know you love him if a similar zeal for God's house consumes you too.

Therefore Expect Setbacks (21:15–25)

Jesus said this to indicate the kind of death by which Peter would glorify God. Then he said to him, "Follow me!"

(John 21:19)

For anyone, being captured by the communists in Vietnam was a nightmare. For Commander James Stockdale, it became a living hell. As the highest-ranking US naval officer captured during the Vietnam War, he was subjected to excruciating torture.

Stockdale was held for seven and a half years in a prison which the Vietnamese referred to as "the hell hole". While men subjected to far less torture gave up the will to live and were buried in the prison courtyard, he stubbornly refused to die. After his repatriation at the end of the war, with his back and limbs so badly broken that he never fully recovered, he explained what had kept him alive: *"I never lost faith in the end of the story. I never doubted not only that I would get out, but also that I would prevail in the end and turn the experience into the defining event of my life, which, in retrospect, I would not trade."*[1] John has used this final section of his gospel to convince us that we will also succeed in Jesus' mission if we do the same.

But James Stockdale didn't stop there. When he was asked what kind of prisoners gave up and died, he shot back,

> *Oh, that's easy. The optimists... The ones who said, "We're going to be out by Christmas." And Christmas would*

---

[1] Interviewed by Jim Collins in his management book *Good to Great* (2001).

*come, and Easter would go. Then they'd say, "We're going
to be out by Easter." And Easter would come, and Easter
would go. And then Thanksgiving, and then it would be
Christmas again. And they died of a broken heart.*

James Stockdale discovered the reason why John ends this final
section with a warning that we had better expect plenty of
setbacks in Jesus' mission along the way.

In verses 15–17, John reminds us that even Peter failed. If
the man who could preach and see 3,000 saved, who could heal
people through contact with his shadow and who could even
raise the dead to life failed three times on the night of Jesus' trial
by disowning his Master, then we can be pretty sure that we will
fail at times too.[2]

In my very earliest weeks as a Christian, I denied Jesus
like Peter. I was still a teenager and very afraid of one particular
bully. He backed me into a corner at a party and told me, *"I
hate Christians and I've heard you've become one. Is that true?"* I
thought fast but I thought like Peter, and assured him I hadn't.
I sold my new Master to save my skin, and a cock must have
been crowing somewhere. If you've ever been a failure for Jesus
like Peter or me, then John has some good news for you. Jesus
wasn't surprised; he knew you would fail him all along. He
didn't save you out of naïve optimism about your character, and
he sits with you each time you fail, full of confidence for your
future. Failures like you and me are just the kind of people he
can use. John warns us not to let our past disappointments rob
us of victory in the future. God has great successes for humbled
losers like Peter, you and me.

In verses 18–19, John warns us that even Peter suffered.
He was flogged and forced to rely on the body armour in his
briefcase, reminding himself to rejoice that he had been *"counted
worthy of suffering disgrace for the Name"*. He was thrown into

---

[2] Acts 2:41; 5:15–16; 9:32–42.

jail twice and only rescued from death when angels came to free him in response to prayer in Jesus' name.[3] Nevertheless, John reminds us that Jesus warned that one day he would be chained and dressed in prison clothes before being led, unrescued, to a to a martyr's death. By the time John wrote his gospel, the day had already come, and Eusebius fills in the missing detail: *"Peter appears to have preached in Pontus, Galatia, Bithynia, Cappadocia and Asia to the Jews of the dispersion. And at last, having come to Rome, he was crucified head-downwards."*[4] Jesus warned his followers that trouble and hardship await anyone who follows him, explaining in 16:1 that *"All this I have told you so that you will not fall away."* John does not seek to raise your spirits with empty promises about Thanksgiving. Instead, he strengthens your resolve with the gritty reality of Easter.

In verses 20–22, John reminds us that Peter was forced to endure what felt like injustice. John's brother James died within thirteen years of Jesus' ascension,[5] and Peter died within thirty-five years. John outlived the rest of the Eleven to die at the ripe old age of about a hundred, but he warns us not to complain that this is unfair.[6]

Jesus told Peter to stop looking round at others and asked him, *"What is that to you? You must follow me."* Don't look at others and complain that your own Christian life is a disappointment. God has a unique path marked out for each of us, and we only fail if we let jealousy distract our feet from it. Peter triumphed by dying as much as John triumphed by surviving. They both looked at Jesus alone and trusted in the perfect plan of the Living God.

---

[3] Acts 5:18–20; 5:40–41; 12:1–11.

[4] Eusebius of Caesarea in *Church History* (3.1.2).

[5] John refers to Jesus' ascension in 20:17 and to his Second Coming in 21:23, but he does not recount the ascension itself since it had already been covered in some detail in Luke and Acts.

[6] Acts 12:2. Irenaeus tells us in *Against Heresies* (3.3.4) that John died some time after 98 AD.

In verses 23–25, John warns that we will sometimes misinterpret God's Word and be disappointed when we discover we were wrong. John's readers at Ephesus mistook Jesus' conversation with Peter to mean that their apostle John would never die, so he ends his gospel with a warning they are heading for disappointment. It may sound stupid that they thought that way, but they were no more stupid than I was when I went abroad as a missionary at the age of twenty-one and limped home a year later in confusion and spiritual despair when my optimistic hopes for instant success were confronted by the brick wall of mission-field reality. Commander James Stockdale continues:

> *This is a very important lesson. You must never confuse faith that you will prevail in the end – which you can never afford to lose – with the discipline to confront the most brutal facts of your current reality, whatever they might be.*

That's why John ends this fourth and final section of his gospel with a warning for us to expect setbacks on our road to victory. It's why he ends with Jesus recommissioning Peter by repeating the same command twice which he gave him and his fishing partners at the start of their Christian journey: *"Follow me!"*

Follow me to victory. Follow me to success. Follow me to complete God's mission through partnership with me in the power of my Spirit. But get ready to partner with me in that mission on a road which passes through Calvary on its way to resurrection victory. Be ready to follow me as I warned you in 16:33:

> *I have told you these things, so that in me you may have peace. In this world you will have trouble. But take heart! I have overcome the world.*

Conclusion: Look and See the Living God

Anyone who has seen me has seen the Father.

(John 14:9)

Robert Sanchez didn't see it coming. It felt like just another normal day driving his packed commuter train across Los Angeles. His morning shift was so dull and predictable that he exchanged forty-five text messages with friends in the three hours it took him to criss-cross the city. His afternoon shift was so uneventful that he read seven more text messages and sent five back in return. Twenty seconds after sending the last of them at 4:22 p.m., he wished he hadn't. He suddenly saw a freight train hurtling towards him on the same piece of track. He hadn't noticed the red light telling him to stop at the previous signals because he had been busy checking a message on his phone. At 4:22 p.m. on 12th September 2008, Robert Sanchez learned too late the danger of fixing our eyes in the wrong place. He didn't even have time to reach the brakes before colliding with the freight train at eighty miles per hour. The horrifying vision of his shattering windscreen was the last thing he ever saw.[1]

John has finished his gospel and he doesn't want you to make the same mistake as Robert Sanchez. That's why he shouts a warning in each of its twenty-one chapters for you to fix your eyes on Jesus and see the Living God. As one of Jesus' closest

---

[1] This was the National Transportation Safety Board's conclusion in 2011 at the end of their investigation into the Chatsworth train collision. I am not judging Robert Sanchez for his mistake. We can all be like him.

companions and an eyewitness to his ministry, he turns to you in his closing verses and urges you to live very differently as a result of what you have learned.

John trusts you will remember the message of chapters 1–4, and his plea for you to *look at Jesus alone*. He has seen too many of his friends in Jerusalem and Ephesus make a train wreck of their lives by looking at religious teachers or prophets or so-called Christian heroes like himself, instead of at the one he describes in these pages as *"the Lamb of God, who takes away the sin of the world"*. He doesn't want you throw away Christ's offer of salvation because your eyes are blinkered by your culture or blinded by the thinking of this world. *"The man who saw it has given testimony, and his testimony is true,"* he told you when a Roman soldier was converted at the foot of the cross in 19:35. *"He knows that he tells the truth, and he testifies so that you also may believe."* Your response to God's offer of salvation in these pages is as much a matter of life or death as Robert Sanchez's decision to look at the messages on his phone. John reminds you in 20:31 that he has *"written that you may believe that Jesus is the Messiah, the Son of God, and that by believing you may have life in his name"*.

John trusts you will remember the message of chapters 5–12 and *look at who Jesus really is*. He doesn't want you to grow overfamiliar with Jesus, as Robert Sanchez grew fatally overfamiliar with his railway line. He doesn't want you to major on minors and miss the significance of Jesus' seven *"I AM"* sayings, his seven miracles and his promise to lead you out of Satan's cave into the sunshine. He doesn't want you to be like the lame man healed in chapter 5, who failed to turn what he saw into saving faith and had to be warned by Jesus to *"stop sinning or something worse may happen to you"*. He doesn't want you to be satisfied with paddling in the shallows of Christianity, when Jesus calls you to dive ever deeper. Those who are saved through Jesus can still make a train wreck of their discipleship if they fail to fix their eyes on Jesus to discover more and more about who their Saviour truly is. John's words in 20:31 can just as easily be translated as encouragement that he has *"written that you may **go on believing** that Jesus is the Messiah, the Son of God, and that by **going on believing** you may **go on having** life in his name."*[2]

John trusts you will remember the message of chapters 13–17, and his call to *look at what Jesus has given you*. He wants you to realize that it isn't just your own life at stake here, just as Robert Sanchez's distraction also killed 25 of his passengers and injured 135 more. John doesn't want you to neglect any of the ten items which Jesus has given you in your briefcase for his mission, which is why his gospel is jam-packed with miracles, with answers to prayer, with teaching about the Holy Spirit, with handover verses and with instruction on how we can each carry on Jesus' mission. The enemy wants to distract you, but John has deliberately cherry-picked material from Jesus' ministry to help you keep your eyes fixed on the task in hand, for the sake of the millions who have yet to be saved. *"Jesus did many other things as well,"* he explains in his final verse. *"If every one of them were written down, I suppose that even the whole world would not have room for the books that would be written."*

Finally, John trusts you will remember the message of chapters 18–21, and the reasons why you can *look at Jesus and win*. You will need this message on days when it seems all hope is lost and you are tempted to give up on Jesus' mission. You will need to remember that God's best outwitted Satan's worst, and that even a crucifixion can become a coronation in God's hands. You will need to remember what was accomplished through the resurrection and what Jesus promises his followers if they go with his Gospel and build local churches all across the world. There will be setbacks, but there will also be mighty victories if

---

[2] We saw in the introduction to this book that John's present tense in this verse can be translated either way.

you refuse to let your eyes get distracted from the fact that you are on the winning team.

As John ends his gospel, other witnesses join him in 21:24, agreeing that *"We know that his testimony is true."* They are probably the church elders at Ephesus,[3] but they might as well include the great army of believers who have read this gospel before you and who have learned to fix their eyes on Jesus and see the Living God.

As you end this book, they join with John in urging you not to be a Robert Sanchez in making a train wreck of your life and the lives of others by fixing your eyes anywhere other than on Jesus. He is fully God and fully man. He is the Lamb of God. He is the great I AM. He is the Saviour of the world. He is your partner in world mission. He is the one who says to you what he said outside the tomb in Bethany: *"Take away the stone... Did I not tell you that if you believe, you will see the glory of God?"*[4]

The men of Bethany ran forward in faith to roll away the stone. They fixed their eyes on Jesus and saw the Living God. Heaven watches in excited anticipation to see what you will do with the message of John's gospel today.

---

[3] We saw earlier that the *Codex Toletanus* claims that John wrote this gospel at the request of the wider church leadership in Asia. John also appears to call his fellow elders to testify with him in 3 John 12.

[4] John 11:38–41. Martha used a "perfect tense" in 11:27 to tell Jesus literally *"I have believed"*, but she needed to put her faith into practice afresh every day.

TITLES TO DATE IN THE **STRAIGHT TO THE HEART** SERIES:

OLD TESTAMENT

ISBN 978 0 85721 001 2

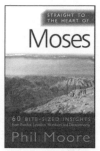
ISBN 978 0 85721 056 2

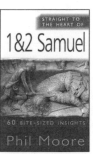
ISBN 978 0 85721 252 8

NEW TESTAMENT

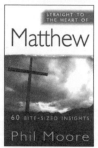
ISBN 978 0 85721 988 3

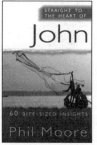
ISBN 978 0 85721 253 5

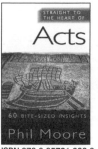
ISBN 978 0 85721 989 0

ISBN 978 0 85721

ISBN 978 0 85721 002 9

ISBN 978 1 85424 990 6

For more information please go to **www.philmoorebooks.com** o
www.lionhudson.com.